"The insights of the authors combined remind us of how far we have come and how far we have yet to go."

Donna E. Shalala, PhD
FORMER SECRETARY OF HHS

"This is an amazing book of stories by pioneering women in medicine. Not only does it serve as a record, but as a resource for future generations, as an inspirational and motivational textbook for the next generation of women to finally shatter the glass ceiling on the shoulders of these giants."

Carolyn D. Runowicz, MD

"I recognized many of the stories, emotions, and quotations in this book and felt I had found many friends who had experiences similar to mine. The honest reflections of these amazing women about their careers is powerful. There are many learning moments in each and every chapter. It is a must read and, more important, a must have to refer back to when one is struggling with one's own management issues during a tough day . . . week . . . or year!"

Julie Freischlag, MD

"Everyone knows that "girls are smarter than boys" and this wonderful book just proves the rule! I should know. Member of the second co-educational class at Vassar (Class of 1977), co-founder of Dual Doctor Families (1982), successfully married to another physician for 32 years (and counting), and proud parent of fraternal twin daughters in medicine and health policy. I am confident that all aspiring physician leaders of both genders will greatly benefit from reading this delightful book!"

David B. Nash, MD, MBA

"While women have made enormous progress in breaching the glass ceiling in medicine, there are still many obstacles in the way toward achieving true gender equality. This book will go a long way toward giving women the tools they need to navigate those obstacles for themselves and be in positions to eliminate them entirely for other women."

Linda Babcock, PhD

"*Lessons Learned* provides very human, genuine, and useful answers to the questions: Should I pursue a career in medical management, how do I go about doing so, what price will I pay (as a physician and wife, mother, etc.) for leaving clinical practice and what are the rewards?... This thoughtful book is extremely helpful to anyone, male or female, considering the transition from medical practice to medical management."

"This book is astonishing, sad, and, as far as I can tell, one-of-a-kind."

"The book offers the personal stories of women in positions of leadership in hospitals, academia, pharmaceutical companies, and biotech. Many of them are inspiring. All of them are informative."

"As a person with a career in medicine, I regret that I didn't have the insights packed into these chapters. I recommend this book to anyone interested in fairness and the health of our nation."

"*Lessons Learned: Stories from Women in Medical Management* is a collection of compellingly honest reflections of 24 women who know what it is like to live in the real world of medicine."

"We can all learn lessons from the women who tell their stories in this book."

"... Dr. Deborah Shlian profiles 24 individuals — including herself — who have maneuvered the gauntlet of modern medicine. What emerges is a fascinating and moving portrait of their journey — one that digs deep and unearths the tears and heartbreaks, as well as the joys and triumphs. No two stories are the same, and indeed, no two careers are the same. There are practical life lessons to be found here, as well as encouragement and inspiration for other women in the field."

"A big part of the solution, perhaps, will come from attaining a greater understanding of the individual challenges involved in this journey. It is in that spirit that Dr. Shlian has put together this wonderful book. It's concise, relevant, and very readable. If you have even a passing interest in medicine or management, then this is the one to pick up."

"I recommend this book to both women and men, physicians and non-physicians. All of us can benefit from the "lessons learned" -- both in the workplace and in life."

LESSONS LEARNED

Stories from Women Physician Leaders

EDITED BY

Deborah M. Shlian, MD, MBA

American Association for PHYSICIAN LEADERSHIP

PUBLISHER
Nancy Collins

EDITORIAL ASSISTANT
Jennifer Weiss

DESIGN & LAYOUT
Carter Publishing Studio

COPYEDITOR
Pat George

ACKNOWLEDGMENTS

This was truly a labor of love for me: the opportunity to highlight the career paths of so many talented women who are such wonderful role models for future physicians. I want to thank all of them for their willingness to take their valuable time to share their personal stories – for many, the Covid pandemic only added to their already-busy responsibilities.

Thanks to the American Association for Physician Leadership for sponsoring this project — specifically Nancy Collins and Jennifer Weiss for their expertise. Thanks to Patricia George for her excellent copy editing and to Laura Carter for the beautiful cover design.

Thanks to my husband Joel for his unfailing love and constant encouragement.

DEBORAH M. SHLIAN, MD, MBA

You can't be what you can't see.

— MARIAN WRIGHT EDELMAN

TABLE OF CONTENTS

PROFESSIONAL ORGANIZATIONS: AMWA AND JOINT COMMISSION

FUTURE LEADERS

ABOUT THE EDITOR

 Deborah M. Shlian, MD, MBA, is a board-certified Family Practitioner with more than three decades of clinical and management experience. Dr. Shlian has been able to balance work life with writing, producing several nonfiction articles, chapters, and books on medical management issues. She also writes fiction. All have won literary awards, including the Florida Book Award's Gold Medal. For her personal story, check out chapter 26.

Contact Dr. Shlian at shlianbooks@gmail.com

Physicians in Leadership

By Theresa Rohr-Kirchgraber, MD, FACP, FAMWA

 IN 1995, the American College of Physician Executives (now renamed the American Association for Physician Leadership) published the first monograph dealing with women physician executives titled *Women in Medicine and Management: A Mentoring Guide.* At that time, most of the 17 contributors were primary care physicians in middle management or just beginning to transition from clinical medicine to leadership.

Seventeen years later, in 2013, 24 women physicians, most of whom had reached more senior positions, shared their stories in *Lessons Learned: Stories from Women in Medical Management*: how they chose medicine, why and how they moved into leadership, the value of formal management degrees, and how they balanced work and personal life. The hope was that their experiences could serve as guides for younger women physicians aspiring to executive roles within medicine.

This latest version, *Lessons Learned: Stories from Women Physician Leaders*, updates the stories of these women and adds nine more, including two young residents who share their hopes for future roles as leaders within medicine. The group is diverse demographically, geographically, and specialty-wise. The women represent virtual every area of healthcare: government, academia, hospitals, provider groups, managed care, professional organizations, the pharmaceutical industry, research, and consulting. A few are entrepreneurs, having started and run their own companies.

The contributors in this update not only share the usual barriers they face as they strive for leadership roles in medicine, but the unique challenges the COVID-19 pandemic created.

In the Foreword of the 2013 publication, the question was asked "Are we there yet?" The Overview of this book explores some of the reasons the answer unfortunately is "not yet." Almost three decades since the first monograph, woman physicians continue to represent a relatively small group of senior physician leaders.

Since 1915, when the American Medical Women's Association (AMWA) became the first national women physicians' organization, AMWA has recognized the unique abilities that women physicians contribute to medicine. Committed to the advancement of women in medicine, AMWA has consistently advocated for policy reform that would create equitable opportunities for women physicians. Though the number of women in medicine has grown significantly since 1915, there has not been a concomitant increase in senior leadership positions.

Not only is there not one single path to leadership, but there are often hidden roadblocks along the way. The early founders of the AMWA recognized the unique perspective women bring to the healthcare field. From the beginning of the organization, they wanted to empower women physicians, to advocate for collective health practices, and to conduct research directed at the impact of sex and gender in health and disease.

Over the years, the AMWA has created new opportunities for those passionate about medicine. As president-elect of AMWA, I plan to continue this mission, feeling strongly that talented women physicians should occupy as many positions of power as possible within the healthcare system.

The stories collected here by Dr. Deborah Shlian can serve as wonderful guides for younger women physicians. They include those who have attained leadership positions in a more traditional manner as well as those who attained their positions after much trial and error. In their stories, we travel with them as defeat becomes success and a few steps back leads to a different direction.

From these women, we can all learn that that if there is not a path, we can create one. If the path is not well trodden, we must walk it and make it passable for the next generation. If the path is narrow, we must walk with others as we widen it. None of us is on this journey alone. We stand on the shoulders of those who have gone before us, beside those who are with us, and for those who come after us.

In deep appreciation for those who have agreed to share their wisdom and their journey.

THERESA ROHR-KIRCHGRABER, MD, FACP, FAMWA
President, AMWA 2015-2016, 2022-2023
Professor of Medicine, Augusta University/University of Georgia Medical Partnership
Theresa.RohrKirchgraber@uga.edu

"With each opportunity came a choice and a certain risk. But in the end, it has been those forks in the road that have made all the difference."

DEBORAH M. SHLIAN

CHAPTER ONE

An Overview

By Deborah M. Shlian, MD, MBA

"HOW DID YOU BECOME A HEALTHCARE LEADER?" is a question that unfortunately even in 2021 sometimes carries the same implications as "What's a nice girl like you doing in a place like this?"

The sense that the role of leader within the healthcare system is not an appropriate career goal for a woman physician was just beginning to change with the publication of a 1995 monograph titled *Women in Medicine and Management: A Mentoring Guide.* At that time, women represented about 19% of all American physicians, a jump from just under 8% in 1970. By 2012, with the publication of the update of the original monograph, titled *Lessons Learned: Stories from Women in Medical Management*, 30.4% of practicing physicians in the United States were women.[1] A decade later, with this latest update, women make up 36.3% of all practicing physicians in the country.[2]

The rise in the number of female physicians is the direct result of a steady increase in the number of female medical students. According to the Association of American Medical Colleges' annual report on medical school enrollment,[3] 2019 marked the first time that the majority of U.S. medical school students (50.5%) were women (Figure 1). At the same time, while medical school classes continued to include more racially and ethnically diverse students, those groups remain significantly underrepresented in the overall physician workforce when compared with the general population and the patients they serve.

In terms of specialties, there have been significant shifts. Only seven specialties had more than 1,000 female physicians in 1970, whereas 25 specialties had more than 1,000 female physicians by 2006[3] and 35 by 2019[4] (Figure 2).

Although a majority of women physicians are still more prominent in primary care specialties such as family medicine, internal

1

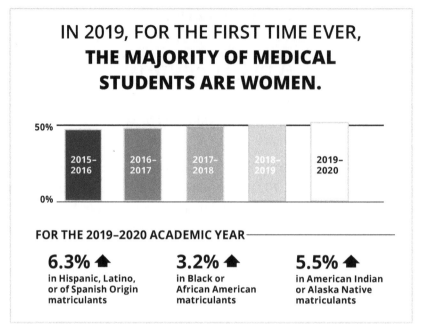

Figure 1. From the American Medical Association

medicine, pediatrics, and obstetrics/gynecology as well as psychiatry and anesthesiology, younger graduates today are choosing residencies in virtually every specialty, including cardiothoracic and neurosurgery (Table 1).

While the progress of women doctors has sometimes been a slow, albeit continuing journey, it may not be long before women dominate medicine, especially as the number of male applicants and matriculants has been declining — especially with regard to Black men.[5]

These trends are creating a quiet gender revolution — one that brings new opportunities and tensions. Within the broader context of the evolving role of women in American society, women physicians continue to explore new career paths — paths that include both clinical medicine and medical leadership.

Power and Promotion

The good news is that women have been entering medicine in increasing numbers for more than three decades. The not-so-good

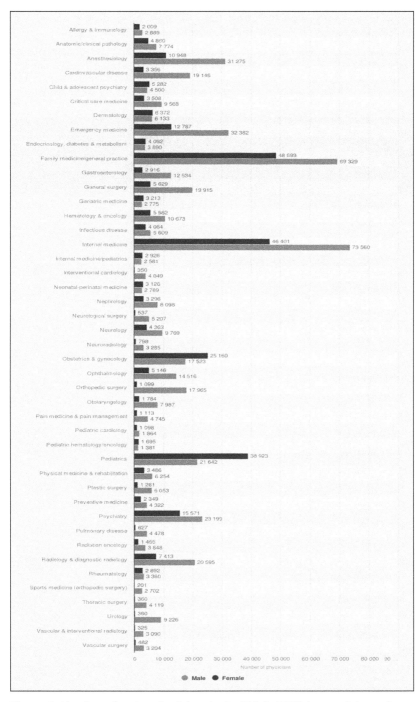

Figure 2. Number of active physicians in the U.S. in 2019, by specialty and gender. From the American Medical Association; AAMC. © Statista 2021

Table 1. Residency Applicants from U.S. MD-Granting Medical Schools to ACGME-Accredited Programs by Specialty and Sex, 2020–2021

This table displays the number of U.S. MD-granting medical school graduate residency applicants to ACGME-accredited residency programs by sex, and the average number of applications individuals of that sex supplied to ACGME-accredited residency programs of the corresponding specialty. The academic year refers to residency training that begins in 2020–2021.

ERAS Applicants from U.S. M.D.-Granting Medical Schools by Specialty and Sex	Men		Women	
	Applicants	Average Number of Applications	Applicants	Average Number of Applications
Anesthesiology	1,264	43.1	651	42.2
Child Neurology	83	18.7	116	23.1
Dermatology	368	55.3	428	75.4
Diagnostic Radiology/Nuclear Medicine/Nuclear Radiology	25	1.4	6	2.3
Emergency Medicine	1,400	51.6	901	52.2
Emergency Medicine/Anesthesiology	9	1.0	4	1.0
Emergency Medicine/Family Medicine	31	2.4	22	2.2
Family Medicine	1,404	35.6	1,525	33.4
Family Medicine/Osteopathic Neuromusculo-skeletal Medicine	3	1.0	0	0.0
Family Medicine/Preventive Medicine	31	1.4	26	1.3
Internal Medicine	5,072	32.2	3,731	32.0
Internal Medicine/Anesthesiology	32	2.1	14	1.9
Internal Medicine/Dermatology	74	2.6	74	2.0
Internal Medicine/Emergency Medicine	52	6.9	32	8.3
Internal Medicine/Medical Genetics	18	1.8	8	2.1
Internal Medicine/Pediatrics	212	21.4	295	25.5
Internal Medicine/Preventive Medicine	30	1.7	26	1.5
Internal Medicine/Psychiatry	50	7.2	35	7.7
Interventional Radiology-Integrated	353	19.6	99	18.9
Neurodevelopmental Disabilities	8	3.9	13	3.4
Neurological Surgery	245	70.6	93	70.9
Neurology	361	27.3	324	32.1
Nuclear Medicine	10	3.4	2	5.0
Obstetrics and Gynecology	227	54.9	1,253	61.7
Orthopaedic Surgery	919	79.5	235	73.8
Osteopathic Neuromusculoskeletal Medicine	5	4.0	1	1.0
Otolaryngology	372	60.1	193	63.1

ERAS Applicants from U.S. M.D.-Granting Medical Schools by Specialty and Sex	Men		Women	
	Applicants	Average Number of Applications	Applicants	Average Number of Applications
Pathology-Anatomic and Clinical	222	24.4	149	23.3
Pediatrics	740	28.7	1,645	30.0
Pediatrics/Anesthesiology	12	3.8	13	3.6
Pediatrics/Emergency Medicine	20	3.2	20	3.2
Pediatrics/Medical Genetics	23	6.0	27	5.7
Pediatrics/Physical Medicine and Rehabilitation	10	2.6	5	2.2
Pediatrics/Psychiatry/Child and Adolescent Psychiatry	29	7.0	51	6.8
Physical Medicine and Rehabilitation	294	34.4	126	33.1
Plastic Surgery	17	1.1	11	1.3
Plastic Surgery-Integrated	140	63.5	129	66.6
Preventive Medicine	56	10.6	61	8.2
Psychiatry	831	47.2	837	48.3
Psychiatry/Family Practice	38	4.4	54	4.1
Psychiatry/Neurology	15	2.5	12	2.5
Radiation Oncology	236	25.0	109	26.9
Radiology-Diagnostic	945	46.5	360	46.4
Surgery-General	1,913	42.8	1,317	52.9
Thoracic Surgery-Integrated	66	20.5	29	22.4
Transitional Year	2,166	12.9	1,387	11.2
Urology	265	71.7	127	76.0
Vascular Surgery-Integrated	175	16.4	74	16.3

Note: Applicants who declined to report sex are not reflected.

news is that women are still underrepresented and underutilized in positions of power — especially at the most senior levels. Unfortunately, 60 years after the so-called "sexual revolution," even as the percentages are rising, there is a relative paucity of women in positions of power in every single sector across this nation.

In 2012, Barnard College President Debora Spar described a 16% ghetto in which women in leadership positions maxed out across politics, aerospace, engineering, Hollywood films, higher education, and Fortune 500 companies.[6] A similar situation existed for women in medicine.

A decade later, the percentage of women physicians attaining senior roles has improved, but only slightly. Men still dominate leadership positions in every area within the healthcare system. A 2020 survey of over 3,000 women physicians revealed that only 28% were currently in any kind of leadership position.[7]

Moreover, the gender pay gap that still plagues women in the United States remains evident within the healthcare industry. Several studies have shown that female physicians earn 8% to 29% less than male physicians. A report published in 2020 by the physician network Doximity[8] found after analyzing 44,000 physician salaries that the wage gap between male and female physicians is 28% this year, with male doctors earning over $116,000 more annually than their female counterparts.

The gaps varied by specialty, where the widest pay gaps were for orthopedic surgery (an average pay gap of $122,677) and otolaryngology (an average pay gap of $108,905). There were no specialties in which women and men were paid the same, or women earned more than men. The smallest pay gaps were for nuclear medicine (an average pay gap of $9,255) and hematology (an average pay gap of $35,673).

The recent research article, which was published by the New England Journal of Medicine,[9] is based on an analysis of 24.4 million primary care office visits in 2017. The analysis of the office visits compared female and male clinicians in the same physician practices.

Academia

In academia, the glass ceiling has long been the metaphor for the systemic barriers that have prevented women from obtaining senior-level positions. Twenty-six years ago, leaders at the academic medical center (AMC) that arose from the first women's medical college in the United States initiated what is now known as The Hedwig van Ameringen Executive Leadership in Academic Medicine (ELAM) Program for Women to promote the careers of senior female leaders in academic healthcare. The hope was that graduates of ELAM would ultimately transform the existing patriarchal culture and promote gender equity.

At the time of its founding in 1995, just over two decades had passed since the enactment of Title IX, the key policy intervention responsible for the rapid increase in women's enrollment in U.S. medical schools.[10] Women's enrollment exceeded 40% of the medical student body,[11] and the time seemed ideal to implement a leadership development program focused on women who would soon enter the senior-most positions in the field, but had few female role models before them.

Unfortunately, despite the ELAM program and the number of female graduates available for leadership positions in 2021, women still do not hold professor or full professor positions at the same rate as their male peers. The data show that women are not ascending to leadership roles, holding a greater share of the entry-level, service, and teaching only positions than their male counterparts.

This is true for both tenured and non-tenured tracks even after adjustment for the department (see Faculty Roster: U.S. Medical School Faculty table at www.aamc.org/data-reports/faculty-insti-tutions/interactive-data/2020-us-medical-school-faculty). Instead, women continue to cluster in characteristically untenured faculty positions, largely in traditionally "nurturing" specialties, and pri-marily in administrative posts dealing exclusively with student and minority affairs. For example, out of 148 deans, only 28 are women physicians (Table 2). In US medical schools, only 22% of all full pro-fessors and only 16% of department chairs are women physicians.

While female physicians today are significantly more likely to pursue careers in academic medicine than their male counter-parts, according to a study published in 2000 by researchers at the University of Kansas Medical Center in the *New England Journal of Medicine*,[12] they are still less likely to be promoted to senior faculty and leadership positions.

In 2020, Kimber Richter, PhD, PMH, professor of population health at KU Medical Center, updated that landmark paper.[12] Richter analyzed data from the years of the original study (1979–1997) and from 1998 to 2018. She and her colleagues found that across all

Table 2. Number of US Allopathic Deans in 2017 Stratified by Gender and Terminal Degree

	Total	MD (%)	Other doctorate (%)	Bachelor's or master's (%)
Dean				0
Total	148	146 (98.6)	2 (1.4)	(0)
Men	120	118 (98.3)	2 (1.7)	(0)
Women	28	28 (100)	0 (0)	0 (0)
p-Value*		1.0		
Vice dean				17 (10.0)
Total	170	115 (67.6)	38 (22.4)	10 (9.6)
Men	104	71 (68.3)	23 (22.1)	7 (10.6)
Women	66	44 (66.7)	15 (22.7)	1.0
p-Value9		0.96	1.0	
Senior Associate Dean				
Total	312	206 (66.0)	72 (23.1)	34 (10.9)
Men	193	133 (68.9)	45 (23.3)	15 (7.8)
Women	119	73 (61.3)	27 (22.7)	19 (16.0)
p-Value*		0.21	1.0	0.039
Associate Dean				
Total	1185	763 (64.4)	292 (24.6)	130 (11.0)
Men	658	456 (69.3)	150 (22.8)	52 (7.9)
Women	527	307 (58.3)	142 (26.9)	78 (14.8)
p-Value*		0.00010	0.11	0.00023
Assistant Dean				
Total	744	419 (56.3)	222 (29.8)	103 (13.9)
Men	379	237 (62.5)	115 (30.4)	27 (7.1)
Women	365	182 (49.9)	107 (29.3)	76 (20.8)
p-Value*		0.00065	0.82	<0.00001
All Deans				
Total	2559	1649 (64.4)	626 (24.5)	284 (11.1)
Men	1454	1015 (69.8)	335 (23.0)	104 (7.2)
Women	1105	634 (57.4)	291 (26.3)	180 (16.3)
p-Value*		<0.00001	0.061	<0.00001

p-Values compare the proportion of women deans with a particular degree to the proportion of male deans with the same degree.

*p <0.0026.

years, women were 12% more likely than men to choose a career in academic medicine; however, after they were hired, academic medical centers promoted those female junior faculty at consistently lower rates than men in the same positions.

Over the three decades, on the whole, women assistant professors were:

- 24% less likely than men to be promoted to associate professor, even after the data were adjusted for department type, graduation year, and race (female physicians are more diverse than males).
- 23% less likely than men to be promoted to full professor.
- 54% less likely than men to become chair of a department.

Richter and her colleagues found that the gender gap has actually widened for promotions to full professor. Women in the first study, who graduated between 1979 and 1997, were 21% less likely to be promoted from associate professor to full professor than men. Women in the later study, who graduated after 1997, were 38% less likely to be promoted to full professor than men – a decrease of 17 percentage points in rates of promotion.

These findings were true not only across levels of promotion, but also within departments for basic science as well as clinical departments that were predominantly female-oriented such as pediatrics and OB-GYN.

The results of the study likewise challenged the perception that women have been gaining ground in academic medicine. Women constituted 21% of full professors in 2014, according to AAMC data, an increase over the 10% of full professors they accounted for in 1979, according to the original *NEJM* study. But as the KU study found, more women entering academic medicine could account for this increase. What most studies have failed to evaluate is whether women have been promoted at the same pace as men.

Academic productivity has been cited as the primary reason for the gender gap. Darcy Reed and colleagues compared publication records, academic promotion, and leadership appointments of women and men academic physicians at the Mayo Clinic over the span of their entire careers using a longitudinal cohort design.[13]

While Mayo is admittedly an untenured system unlike the typical tenured academic model, the study revealed that although the academic productivity of women lagged behind men in the early and middle stages of careers, publication rates were similar between genders in the later stage of academic careers.

The authors concluded that academic productivity in mid-career may not be an appropriate measure of leadership skills for women, stating that "a paucity of qualified women in leadership positions both deprives organizations of the unique skills and perspectives women bring to such roles."

Richter, in her more recent study, concluded that the need to publish research in medical and science journals for advancement was negatively affected by the fact that women are underrepresented among editors and editorial boards.

"That can create publication gaps, due not only to how research is reviewed but also the kinds of research that are viewed as important," she said. "Service on editorial boards is a big factor in promotion, so if women are not getting those positions, they have less ammo for the promotion and tenure process." Lack of advancement of women in medical and professional societies can also factor into the promotion process.

Richter also cited a number of other potential reasons that may explain why women do not get promoted at the same rates as men, including an "old boys' club" mentality and climate; the tendency of leadership, which is mostly male, to promote people with whom they identify; the fact that nearly one in three women physicians and medical researchers report experiencing sexual harassment at work, as well as women continuing to bear a disproportionate share of family responsibilities, such as child and elder care, which can impact their productivity and career goals, a problem that the COVID-19 pandemic has likely exacerbated.

In terms of gender disparity in pay, a 2020 study published in *JAMA Network Open*[14] found that female department chairs at public medical schools earned on average $70,000 to $80,000 less per year than men. Women who have held their chair positions for more than a decade annually earned $127,411 less than their male peers.

So, where should academic medicine go from here? Since 1995, more than 1,000 women have graduated from the ELAM program. Its success is evidenced by the number among those graduates who are deans at U.S. medical schools (15) and U.S. public health schools (6). A total of 38 alumnae have served as past, interim, or permanent U.S. and Canadian medical school deans.

Nevertheless, individual programs like ELAM cannot possibly address the tremendous need that persists. Other institutions are developing internal programs such as FIU's 4th-year medical student elective Seminars in Physician Leadership. The University of Michigan's Rudi Ansbacher Women in Academic Medicine Leadership Scholars Program[15] offers programming similar to ELAM but reaches far more than the maximum of two nominees Michigan is allowed to send to ELAM each year.

These programs are essential for promoting greater participation of women in the leadership of academic healthcare and for developing other evidence-based interventions that target the root causes of gender inequity.

AAMC recently issued a call to action on gender equity, focusing on the need for leaders of academic health institutions to ensure that their structures and processes are equitable and to be accountable for progress on gender equity metrics.[16]

Hospitals

Women are likewise underrepresented at the highest levels of hospital administration, despite the fact that according to the U.S. Bureau of Labor Statistics,[17] women comprise at least 80% of the healthcare industry's workforce today and are the largest consumers of healthcare. Only 19% of key leadership roles in hospitals are held by women (physicians and non-physicians).

This gender inequality issue is compounded by the fact that few physicians in general are tapped for senior hospital management roles. According to a 2009 paper published by Gunderman and Kantor,[18] only 235 (fewer than 4%) of 6,050 hospitals in the United States at the time were headed by physicians of either gender. In 2014, only approximately 5% of hospitals leaders were physicians.[19]

Of 143 women leaders of hospitals and health systems in 2018, only 20 (13.9%) were physicians.[20]

A 2019 study by the executive search firm Korn Ferry found that more than 55% of nearly 200 hospitals admitted that women in their organizations had been overlooked due to gender. Sixty percent ranked their development programs for women as fair, poor, or non-existent while 76% did not have programs within their organizations to help women advance.[21]

A larger percentage of men report being given clear expectations for success in their roles than women. Men are 13% more likely to receive leadership skills training than women and are 22% more likely to be assigned a formal mentor, according to a recent leadership transition report by Development Dimensions International.[22]

Insurance Companies

The situation for women physicians is no better in insurance companies. Of the five top health insurance companies (Aetna/CVS, Cigna, Humana, United Healthcare, and Anthem), none are headed by physicians, male or female, in 2021.

Pharmaceutical and Biotech Companies

By 2020, the number of women graduating with a medical, biomedical, or biological degree at least equaled that of men. However, fewer than 10% of biopharma chief executive officers (CEOs) are women and even fewer are women physicians.[23] Of the 16 highest-paid women CEOs in the biopharma industry, only three are medical doctors.

A 2007 landmark Healthcare Business Association (HBA) E.D.G.E. paper titled "The Progress of Women Executives in Pharmaceuticals and Biotechnology: A Leadership Benchmarking Study" tracked the career progress of women in general.[24] The research was sponsored by Booz Allen Hamilton, Novartis, Sanofi-aventis, Wyeth, Abbott Laboratories, AstraZeneca, Celgene, Ernst & Young, Johnson & Johnson, and Merck & Co., and used insights from three study arms: 82 senior executives who gave in-depth interviews, 237 mid-level managers who responded to a comprehensive

Internet survey, and human resources data and questionnaires submitted by 12 of the top 50 life sciences companies.

Based on findings from E.D.G.E participants at that time, women held 17% of senior management positions in the life sciences industry. This number varied widely among firms, topping out at 57%. Several companies had no women in senior management at all. In middle management, female representation was higher, with women occupying roughly one-third of positions. This number was consistent between biotechnology and pharmaceutical companies and across companies in Europe and the United States. Within all life sciences companies, the greatest representation of women middle managers was in research and development (37%) and corporate functions (34%). The lowest representation was in information technology, where women held only 12% of middle management positions.

Why a Glass Ceiling for Physicians of Both Genders?

Several phenomena seem to account for the glass ceiling experienced by both male and female physicians.

First, physicians have had a poor public relations image in terms of their business acumen. Many physicians themselves feel they are bad at business; they have the perception that they cannot manage the financial management of a large organization and could never aspire to COO or CEO roles.

Second is the pervasive concern by non-physicians that doctors who have the power to influence patient decision-making will place their own financial self-interests ahead of the well-being of their patients and steer them toward expensive procedures that do not necessarily create better outcomes.[24]

A third reason for so few physician managers at the top is based on a historical perspective. Earlier in this century, there were far more physician CEOs in hospitals; in 1935, physicians were in charge of 35% of all hospitals.[25] However, World War II brought a transition point as a number of non-physicians entered the medical administration corps. At war's end, many of these men trained

13

in running hospitals during the war were eager to do the same in the civilian world. At the same time, the technology of healthcare had increased and most physicians were willing to relinquish their administrator roles, preferring to devote their time to the scientific and clinical side of medicine.

For years, physicians who remained in hospital administration tended to be retired military men, doctors who had encountered physical problems, and even some who couldn't succeed in private practice. When they became administrators, they were often shunted off into clinically focused areas such as education, medical staff credentialing and hiring, and quality assurance issues.

In 1970, a *Fortune* magazine cover story[26] warned the country that "much of US medical care, particularly the everyday business of preventing and treating routine illness is inferior in quality, wastefully dispensed and inequitably financed." That same year a *Fortune* editorial declared: "the time has come for radical change . . . the management of medical care is too important to leave to doctors who are, after all, not managers to begin with."

Paul Starr's "social transformation of American medicine" launched in 1982. In the final chapter of his Pulitzer Prize-winning book with the same title,[27] he expressed concerns about the coming of the corporation and the re-focus from the 1970s emphasis on "health care planning" to "health care marketing" just one decade later. He was obviously prescient. Indeed, healthcare in the United States since then increasingly has become perceived in terms of an economic service, organized and delivered through large, complex managed systems.

This new paradigm altered traditional positions of power and influence within healthcare as the power of large corporate providers and large purchasers grew, and the dominance of physicians and professional organizations diminished. Very quickly, non-physician business school graduates began displacing graduates of public health schools as well as doctors in top echelons of medical care organizations, taking on mainstream management roles, including financial, strategic planning, and policy-making responsibilities. This same trend (*i.e.*, physicians as traditional medical directors, non-physicians as operational managers) was seen not only in hospitals, but also in most insurance companies and managed care organizations.

Despite the fact that there has been lots of discussion about including physician leaders in more senior positions in all aspects of healthcare, those at the highest levels are still predominantly non-physicians and mostly male.

Regardless of how reform ultimately evolves, the 2010 passage of the Affordable Care Act set in motion disruption of the status quo that presented both challenges and opportunities for physicians interested in leveraging their expertise to influence healthcare delivery as medical leaders. A career in medical management became a positive choice for female as well as male physicians.

In addition to having excellent physicians at the core of the healthcare system clinically, a compelling case can be made for a physician-executive who possesses the skills and knowledge about the organization of medical care and can act as liaison among all those with an interest in medicine, including patients, healthcare providers, insurers, economists, and other administrators.

In a 2011 paper, Amanda Goodall[28] found that the highest rated hospitals according to the *US News and World Report*'s "Best Hospitals" ranking were led disproportionately by physicians. Goodall acknowledged that because there is no other hard evidence published about the relative merits of having physicians and non-physician managers in leadership positions, her discussion merely starts the empirical process.

As Tracy Duberman, PhD, wrote in *Physician Executive*,[29] physician leaders in 2012 and beyond will be measured by "the results they achieve, the value or efficiency with which they achieve good outcomes, and improvements in performance resulting from a focus on teamwork through superior coordination, information sharing, and teaming across disciplines."

With the healthcare delivery system evolving faster than ever, today's physician leaders not only need to have a broad base of skills and knowledge (*e.g.*, understanding the current requirements for physician reporting, health care financing, accountable care organizations, clinical process improvement, utilization management, clinical decision support systems, team based care and more), but must also be strategic thinkers and effective communicators.

What Makes a Good Manager?

Generally speaking, physicians and managers have different perspectives, goals, and objectives. Physicians are trained to focus on individual patients, their needs and problems. Physicians' decision-making tends to be methodical and highly rationalized, often requiring a great deal of autonomy. On the other hand, healthcare managers are trained to focus on the organization and its problems as well as on larger socioeconomic issues of the environment.

While managers' decision-making is careful and ideally rational, it generally requires collaboration, often without having all the information they would like and nearly always with budget issues in mind. Clearly, many of the skills required to be a good clinician (such as the ability to weigh factors involved in a decision, to put into perspective the relationship between cost and the impact of a decision on a patient's health, and to recognize when healthcare services can do no more for a patient) are transferable to the role of manager.

However, for the role of manager, some skills must be newly learned. As the professional leader, the manager becomes the activator of the organization's central nervous system. He or she must diagnose the organization as an environment and act in it as a leadership figure to whom and about whom subordinates have significant feelings. The leader must motivate, meaning getting things done through others, while simultaneously maintaining a balance among conflicting interests in the organization. He or she must manage change in an orderly fashion.

In practice, a difficult patient can be referred. Management generally does not have the same luxury. Problems keep coming no matter how many already exist. Rarely can managers refer a difficult issue to someone else. While delegation can help and in fact is a necessary skill for the manager, it does not relieve him or her of responsibility.

Most important, managers do not get daily strokes from patients. They must derive satisfaction from the knowledge that a particular decision or program has changed the care patients receive in a positive way.

Management Credentials: An Ongoing Controversy

As healthcare organizations are forced to balance complex quality and cost issues, talented physician executives are in increasing demand. Although there is general agreement that physician executives should have strong clinical credentials, a continuing question and controversy in medical management is the nature of the educational background that is best for a successful management career.

Certainly, the traditional hospital/clinic arrangement, with total separation of administrative and clinical matters, is rapidly becoming obsolete. The issue is particularly sensitive for physicians who have already spent a number of years in medical practice or even medical management. Will informal training suffice, or are physician executives faced with the necessity of obtaining formal degrees in management?

Some large physician groups like the Cleveland and Mayo Clinics have explicitly introduced leadership training for their doctors, generally affiliating with local business schools.[30] Likewise, management and leadership education has been incorporated into some medical degree programs.[31-34]

At the time of the original 1995 publication of *Women in Medicine and Management*, few physicians held MBAs. As recently as the late 1990s, there were only five or six joint MD/MBA programs in the United States. By 2011, there were 65.[35] Statistics about these joint programs are limited, but Dr. Maria Y. Chandler, a pediatrician with an MBA who is associate professor in the medical and business school at the University of California at Irvine and up until recently president of the Association of MD/MBA Programs, states that as of 2020 there were 61 confirmed active programs.

Despite these trends, we will probably continue to have two separate groups of physicians in management: those who are less interested in formal degrees and those who see their careers in a longitudinal sense and who want to go back to the university setting to get a "ticket" to go with their MDs.

Whether one goes the university route or learns only on the job, management, like medicine, is ever-changing, and skills and knowledge will need to be constantly supplemented by extensive reading of the pertinent management literature and attendance at appropriate seminars and courses. A new literature has emerged, focusing on key competencies required to be an effective physician leader.[35-36]

Are Women Better Managers Than Men?

In the 26 years since the publication of the first version of this book, women have made incredible strides in terms of the level of formal education achieved and numbers within the workforce. Yet relatively few have risen to the highest levels in politics, Fortune 500 companies, or healthcare organizations — public or private.

The commonly cited reason for their poor showing in leadership positions, apart from sexism, has been that women choose not to be leaders, that they lack interest and skill in leadership, and that they choose to devote their time to their families rather than concentrating their attention on professional advancement. While past studies justifying male physicians as administrators declared that men like wielding power more than women do, there is more agreement today that when women have an opportunity to be decision makers as medical managers, they enjoy the role.[37] A 2011 survey conducted by McKinsey[38] showed that women's interest in being leaders increases as they move from entry-level positions to middle management.

Not only do women enjoy management roles, they make excellent leaders. In fact, in a 2008 PEW survey,[39] the public rated women better than or equal to men in 7 of 8 leadership traits. Dr. Alice Eagly, one of the top scholars on gender and leadership, agrees. Her studies show that women are more likely than men to possess the leadership qualities associated with success. According to Eagly, women are more transformational than men — they care more about developing their followers, they listen to them and stimulate them to think "outside the box," they are more inspirational, and they are more ethical.[40]

When David Ross, assistant professor of management at Columbia's Business School, and Cristian Dezso, his colleague at the University of Maryland, studied the top 1,500 U.S. companies over 15 years ending in 2006, they found that the firms with women at the top performed significantly better. This was especially true for the firms that put high emphasis on innovation. Such firms often belong to creative industries and tend to spend disproportionately on research and development.[41]

The study provides evidence for the existence of the so-called "female management style," which holds that female executives tend to manage in a more democratic way, as opposed to the more autocratic approach associated with the stereotypical male boss. That democratic style fosters creativity, teamwork, and desire to solve problems.

The late Dr. Bernard Bass was the distinguished professor emeritus in the School of Management at Binghamton University where he was also the founding director of the Center for Leadership Studies. He developed the current theory of transformational leadership, predicting that in the future, women leaders would dominate simply because they are better suited to 21st century leadership/management than are men.[42]

2022 and Beyond

In spite of Bass' hopeful prediction, and evidence supporting the quality or even superiority of women as managers, men continue to dominate leadership positions. What is preventing highly qualified women from reaching the top?

According to Dr. Eagly and others, women have to overcome obstacles to attain leadership positions, while men are offered a "free pass." Eagly claims that as a society, our image of a leader is "male," so we more often select or promote men. Men still tend to control the hiring and favor men over women. We are simply reluctant to change the status quo. Unfortunately, when pollsters ask, "Is the United States ready for a woman president?" the majority still answer "No."

Lessons Learned: Stories from Women Physician Leaders sets out to document the career paths that some successful women physician leaders have taken. Ten (Drs. Cary, Hammond, Calmes, Batchlor, Petersen, LeTourneu, Yaremchuk, Ford, Gabow and Shlian) were contributors to the original 1995 monograph. In *Lessons Learned: Stories from Women in Medical Management* published in 2013, these 10 continued to share their experiences in the last 17 years. Fourteen (Drs. Pescovitz, Parker, Young, Komives, Roldan, Haseltine, Maglioto, Sennholz, Ferguson, Terrell, Asmar, McCormick, Strahlman, and Goonan) were new contributors. In this latest version, 22 have updated their experiences since 2013 and seven new extraordinary women physicians (Drs. McKee, Neuzil, Esserman, Chin, Hanna-Attisha, Garner, and Padmanabhan) tell their stories.

The women in this book have found success in many different areas of medical management. They include corporate medical directors, managed care executives, managers within government, the pharmaceutical industry, academic leaders, hospital executives, and entrepreneurs.

All of these women say they enjoy management, that they opted for their management positions as "part of their overall career enhancement." Most say that their desire to be managers grew out of a desire to be policy makers, to have a chance to provide top management support for medical practitioners, and to influence the larger picture (how groups of patients receive care and also the environment in which services are delivered).

In 1995, only one woman noted the emerging importance of professional roles in managing the technical complexity of cost containment. Today everyone agrees that this is a priority. As a result, we have included two physicians just beginning their careers (Drs. Gonzalez and Sosa) who discuss their aspirations for leadership roles in the future.

Whatever the reasons for choosing to transition from clinical medicine to medical leadership, all the stories are compelling.

Readers (both female and male) embarking on a management career, or even those already on a career path, may learn from the failures as well as the successes that each of the contributors to this book has found along the way.

REFERENCES

1. AAMC. *2012 Physician Specialty Data Book*. AAMC Center for Workforce Studies. Washington, DC: AAMC; November 2012.
2. Boyle, P. Nation's Physician Workplace Evolves: More Women, A Bit Older, and Toward Different Specialties. AAMC News. February 2, 2021.
3. AAMC. Annual Report on Medical Enrollment, 2019.
4. AAMC. Physician Specialty Data Reports from 2008-2020.
5. Morris, DB; Gruppuos, PA; McGee, HA; et al. "Diversity of the National Medical Student Body—Four Decades of Inequities. *NEJM*. 2021;384:1661-1668.
6. Bennett, L. Women and the Leadership Gap. *Newsweek*. March 5, 2012.
7. Medscape. Women Physicians Report 2020: The Issues They Care About. Medscape, July 15, 2020.
8. Cheney, C. Doximity: Physician Compensation Growth Stalls in 2020. HealthLeaders Media. October 30, 2020.
9. Ganguli, I; Sheridan, B; Gray J; et al. Physician Work Hours and Gender Pay Gap—Evidence from Primary Care. *NEJM*. 2020; 383(14):1349-1357.
10. Carnes, M. A Piece of My Mind. What Would Patsy Mink think? *JAMA*. 2012;307:571–572.
11. AAMC. Table 1: Medical students, selected years, 1965–2015. www.aamc. org/system/files/reports/1/2015table1.pdf.
12. Richter, K; Clark, L; Wick, J; *et al*. Women Physicians and Promotion in Academic Medicine." NEJM. 2020;383:2148-2157.
13. Reed, D; Enders, F; Lindor, R; McClees, M; Lindor, K. Gender Differences in Academic Productivity and Leadership Appointments of Physicians Throughout Academic Careers. *Academic Medicine*. 2011;86(1):43-47.
14. Mensah, M; Beeler, W; Rotenstein, L; et al. Sex Differences in Salaries of Department Chairs at Public Medical Schools. *JAMA Internal Medicine*. 2020;180(5):789-792.
15. University of Michigan Office of Faculty Affairs and Faculty Development. Rudi Ansbacher Advancing Women in Academic Medicine Leadership Scholars Program, June 17, 2020.
16. AAMC. Gender Equity in Academic Medicine, June 17, 2020.
17. U.S. Bureau of Labor Statistics. Labor Force Statistics from the Current Population Survey, January 22, 2021.
18. Gunderman, R and Kantor, S. Perspectives: Educating Physicians to Lead Hospitals. *Academic Medicine*. 2009;84(10):1348-1351.

19. Harvin, A; Griffith, N; Weber R. Physicians as Executives: Opportunities and Strategies for Health-System Pharmacy Leaders. *Hospital Pharmacy*. 2014; 49(10):985-991.

20. Becker's Hospital Review. 143 Women Leaders of Hospitals and Health Systems, 2019.

21. Kacik, A. Few Women Reach Healthcare Leadership Roles. *Modern Healthcare*. May 22, 2019.

22. Mitchel, H. "10 Numbers that Show Gender Pay Gap in Healthcare." Becker's Hospital Review. June 16, 2021

23. BioSpaces. Top 16 Highest-Paid Women CEOs in the Biopharma Industry. December 10, 2020.

24. Healthcare Businesswomen's Association. The Progress of Women Executives in Pharmaceuticals and Biotechnology: A Leadership Benchmarking Study. HBA E.D.G.E. in Leadership Study. Healthcare Businesswomen's Association 2007.

25. Maher, M. *Money-Driven Medicine: The Real Reason Health Care Costs So Much*. New York: HarperCollins; 2006.

26. Fortune Magazine. *Our Ailing Medical System: It's Time to Operate*. New York: Harper & Row; 1970.

27. Starr, P. *The Social Transformation of American Medicine: The rise of a Sovereign Profession and the Making of a Vast Industry*. New York: Basic Books; 1984.

28. Goodall, A. Physician-Leaders and Hospital Performance: Is There an Association? IZA Discussion Paper # 5830. July 2011.

29. Duberman, T. Developing Physician Leaders Today Using the 70/20/10 Rule. *Physician Executive*. 2011;37(5):66-68.

30. Stoller, JK, Berkowitz, E, and Bailin, PL. Physician Management and Leadership Education at the Cleveland Clinic Foundation: Program Impact and Experience Over 14 Years. *Journal of Medical Practice Management*. 2007;22:237-242.

31. Fairchild, DG; Benjamin, EM, Gifford DR, and Hout, SJ. Physician Leadership: Enhancing the Career Development of Academic Physician Administrators and Leaders. *Academic Medicine*.2004; 79; 214-218.

32. Stern, DT and Papadakis, M. The Developing Physician — Becoming a Professional. *NEJM*. 2006;355:1794-1799.

33. Baker, CJ and Hafferty, FW. Professionalism. NEJM. 2007;356:966.

34. Freudebhem, M. Adjusting, More MDs Add MBAs. *New York Times,* Sept. 5, 2011.

35. Chaudry, J; Jain, A; McKenzie, S; and Scwartz, RW. Physician Leadership: The Competency of Change. *Journal of Surgical Education*. 2008;65: 213-220.

36. Stoller, JK. Developing Physician-leaders: A Call to Action. Journal of General Internal Medicine. 2008;24: 876-878.

37. MacEachern, MT. *Hospital Organization and Management*. Chicago, IL: Physicians Record Co; 1935.
38. Barsh, J and Yee, L. Changing Companies' Minds About Women. *McKinsey Quarterly*. September 1, 2011. www.mckinsey.com/business-functions/people-and-organizational-performance/our-insights/changing-companies-minds-about-women.
39. Pew Research Center. A Paradox in Public Attitudes. Men or Women: Who's the Better Leader? Pew Research Center, August 25, 2008. www.pewresearch.org/wp-content/uploads/sites/3/2010/10/gender-leadership.pdf.
40. Eagly, A and Carli, L. Through the Labyrinth: The Truth About How Women Become Leaders. Boston: Harvard Business Review Press; 2007.
41. Dezso, CL. and Ross, DG. Does Female Representation in Top Management Improve Firm Performance? A Panel Data Investigation. *Strategic Management Journal*. 2012; 33(9): 1072-1089 https://onlinelibrary.wiley.com/doi/abs/10.1002/smj.1955.
42. Bass, BM and Riggio, RE. Transformational Leadership (2nd ed), New York: Psychological Press 2006.

Government

"I still want to know:
Why are there two sexes?"

– Florence Haseltine

CHAPTER TWO

Sex and Science Drove My Life

By Florence Haseltine, MD, PhD

FOR ME, A LIFETIME OF ACCOMPLISHMENT began decades ago with the simplest of scientific question: Why? The solution lay in the two driving forces of my life: sex and science.

A child blessed with deep curiosity about the origin of gender, I didn't expect easy answers. I wanted the entire scientific story, and determined then and there to unscramble the toughest mysteries myself.

As a biophysicist, obstetrician-gynecologist, reproductive endocrinologist, National Institutes of Health research head, professional journal editor, best-selling novelist, inventor, and advocate for women's health, I guess you could say that I have cut a wide swath through science, medicine, and government since my early years as an inquisitive youngster living on a scientific outpost.

My efforts to include women in clinical trials have forever changed medicine. Along the way, I have also penned a best-selling book, earned several patents, created award-winning computer applications, set up my own business, and raised two daughters who are already making significant contributions to their fields.

And it all began with an inquisitive moment in a desert town.

The Beginnings

In China Lake, California, a remote military outpost where my father was among the many research scientists, I was an intensely curious youngster, desperate to understand the mysteries that surrounded me. I peppered my physicist father with endless questions, demanding to know why there had to be both boys and girls. Even though he was an uncommunicative man, he made a few attempts

26

but then exasperated, answered with his own question: "When you grow up, why don't you figure it out?" The challenge set me on a lifelong quest that was unrelenting — and often difficult.

Struggling to come to terms with my inability to read, which I now attribute to dyslexia unknown at the time, as a youngster I gravitated to math and science. By the age of 12, I had decided that I would one day become a doctor. But first, I had to contend with the unremitting boredom of a closeted community that was removed by distance and geography from the rest of the world. A literal oasis in the middle of California's Mojave Desert, China Lake was rich in scientists, researchers, and natural beauty, but impoverished in things to do. I harnessed my own brainpower for entertainment and vowed to leave the desert behind as soon as possible.

Within a few days of my high school graduation, I took Greeley's words literally and boarded a bus headed West for the University of California at Davis. My summer studies in basic biology, conducted by the National Science Foundation, opened an entirely new world of scientific possibilities and a chance to begin addressing the queries that dogged me.

Education

From Davis, I went to the University of California at Berkeley, where I was the rare female majoring in biophysics. Studying among skeptical male classmates, I proved my doubters wrong for the first of many times. Not only did I earn my degree, but I moved across the country to continue my studies at the ultimate bastion of male scientific achievement, the Massachusetts Institute of Technology. There, I earned a PhD in biophysics in 1970 and married a class-mate. When I learned I'd have to remain at MIT while my husband finished his work on his PhD, I got a divorce and moved to New York, determined to deliver on my childhood pledge to become a physician. I studied at the Albert Einstein College of Medicine, happy to find accepting peers bound by a passion for "the art of medicine."

Several years later, I interned at the University of Pennsylvania, completed my residency at Boston Hospital for Women (Brigham and Women's Hospital), and was board certified in obstetrics and gynecology as well as in reproductive endocrinology. I became an assistant and associate professor in the Department of Ob/Gyn and Pediatrics at Yale University.

During my time in Boston, I met a fellow scientist-physics professor, Alan Chodos, who would become my second husband. With time and infertility treatments, we had two daughters. Anna, the oldest is a gerontologist at UCSF and Elizabeth is an associate director of the OxBow, an artist residency program.

During a sabbatical year at Yale, I decided that I lacked a proper understanding of business, a problem I remedied by studying strategic planning and business development at the Yale School of Organization and Management.

At Yale, I served on several academic committees, often as the sole woman member, distinguishing myself as a tireless, if outspoken, advocate for women's advancement and professional development. I also set down my experiences as a physician in a novel that went on to be a top seller. In *Woman Doctor*, I fictionalized the very real personal and professional challenges I had faced while becoming an MD.

Finally able to devote my full attention to the study of sex differences, I won research grants from the Center for Population Research at the National Institutes of Health, the same Center I would later lead. I focused on in vitro fertilization and later broadened my scope to explore the behavioral impact fertility treatments had on couples.

Revolutionizing Research

I quickly unearthed a serious oversight in the manner data for medical investigations was collected. Because clinical trials and biomedical research routinely included only male subjects, the ways women responded to illness and disease were virtually unknown. Deeply concerned about the implications for female patients, I vowed to change the system. Happily, my efforts have forever altered medical research.

In 1985, I was tapped to become the director of the Center for Population Research at the National Institutes of Child Health and Human Development at the National Institutes of Health. The commute from my New Haven home to my new Washington, DC, office created a personal challenge, but it was worth it. In my role, I successfully influenced the direction of national reproductive health policy.

During my tenure, the office's budget rose to more than $350 million annually, funding a wide variety of projects: clinical trials for novel contraceptives for men and women, research on early pregnancy and implantation mechanisms, support for under-appreciated yet critical health challenges facing women including pelvic organ prolapse, studies of population dynamics and impacts on health, as well as the relationship between maternal literacy and children's academic achievements in resource poor settings.

In 1990, I established the Society for Women's Health Research (SWHR), becoming its first president. The organization soon documented the clear sexual bias plaguing biomedical research. SWHR's findings prompted a Government Accounting Office (GAO) investigation into research methodology, highlighting the failure of most studies to comply with National Institutes of Health guidelines mandating diverse clinical trial populations. Determining that most such studies violated these NIH requirements, the government established new policies that set inviolable new rules for broad-based data. To coordinate the research and monitor compliance, NIH created the Office of Research on Women's Health (ORWH).

Throughout, I worked to expand my message beyond the research community. As editor-in-chief of the *Journal of Women's Health*, I reported on the state of scientific inquiry. I also edited the comprehensive report *Women's Health Research: A Medical and Policy Primer* published by the Society for Women's Health Research and led its follow-up studies. Additionally, I served as a founding member of the Organization for the Study of Sex Differences (OSSD), an international society that coordinates connections between basic and clinical scientists from multiple scientific disciplines with shared interests in sex difference-related topics.

My interest in the area of mentoring is not simply limited to the fact that one should be mentored. I am very interested in the many different ways people mentor as well as why people are willing to be mentors. My articles[1,2,3] span four decades, from 1977 to 2005.

29

Again, these articles demonstrate my keen interest in the advancement of young people.

I have been fortunate to have been honored for my contributions to reproductive medicine and women's health. A frequent speaker, I have won awards from professional societies, advocacy groups, and the federal government for my public service, and I was elected to the Institute of Medicine. I am proud of the fact that I have been credited for the GAO's success in building data on women and minorities into its clinical research, which was re-assessed favorably in 2000, and for the loan repayment program now funded by many NIH institutes which helps medical researchers pay off their debt.

New Projects

As Emerita Director at the Center for Population Research at the Eunice Kennedy Shriver National Institute for Child Health and Human Development (NICHD) of the National Institutes of Health (NIH), I continue to break new ground.

I helped architect the RAISE Project (Recognizing the Achievements of Women in Science, Medicine and Engineering), devoted to enhancing the status of professional women in science, technology, engineering, mathematics, and medicine. RAISE provides valuable information and analysis of national and international scientific awards and award recipients disaggregated by sex. RAISE is being considered as a Department of State "best practice" program to help inform other nations as part of a global agenda on advancement of women in science.

Ever curious, I tested entrepreneurship with the launch of Haseltine Systems Corporation in 1995 to design products for people with disabilities. I earned two patents for my Haseltine Flyer, a container that protects wheel chairs during air travel.

Two more patents on an internet application, granted in 2007, provides shoppers with a customized system that allows them to see and share photos of prospective clothing purchases with others. I recently released a smart phone application, Embryo, which allows users to manipulate 3D images and videos of human eggs, sperm, and fertilization from the famous Carnegie Embryo Collection.

I facilitated the collaboration among the National Library of Medicine, the National Museum of Health and Medicine, and NICHD that spawned application. Especially fun was that I not only conceptualized Embryo, but also acquired the programming skills needed to build it, ultimately earning a 2011 National Library of Medicine honor.

Out of Texas: Two Senior Ladies, Out of Retirement and Into the Pandemic

I retired in 2012. My friend, Anajane, retired in 2009. The two of us grew up together on that military base in the middle of the Mojave Desert. We arrived as four-year-olds in 1946 and by the age of six knew each other. We lived four houses away on the same street. We each wanted to pursue careers in science or medicine. Whereas I went straight to Berkeley, she went to Whittier College. But after a year she transferred and was my roommate. We signed up for Organic Chemistry together and she worked hard, forcing me to go along.

A year later she married, and I was her maid of honor. The year after that, she was mine.

But then we parted. She stayed on the West coast and I moved east. With no Facebook or LinkedIn, we were able to keep track of each other only intermittently. She became an expert in laboratory management related to transplantation, and I pushed to make women's health research a national issue.

After Anajane's retirement, she consulted in her field and after my retirement, I helped advocacy groups with databases and websites. But in the fall of 2018, an opportunity arose that would lead to the use of both our talents in the COVID pandemic. I was recruited to the University of Texas at Arlington to help with program development. Quickly realizing that the University needed to certify its Genomics Center so that clinical studies could be done, I recruited Anajane. She knew what had to be done and how to do it. Within six months of her arrival, UTA had the certification it needed. No one knew that a month later we would need that certification to jump into the pandemic whirlpool.

COVID struck and the university required a testing facility to monitor the students working and living in groups, the athletes, ROTC, the band, and others. Because, and only because, Anajane had lined up the necessary regulatory work, we moved ahead. My role was to make sure we got the support of the administration and to set up the database to track the tests.

Moving ahead was not always easy, as we had to get the materials to do the tests, but we did it and were operational within 3½ months, in time for the summer and fall semesters. We gathered help where we could, and with a fabulous laboratory scientist and a great technician, we now satisfy the testing requirements for our college athletes and other UTA community employees and students.

There were so many firsts for Anajane and me that some days we can't believe what we did. We are approaching our 80th birthdays, and know that without this opportunity we would have been sitting out the pandemic just hoping to survive. But now we are participants in college sports.

James Baker, the UTA Director of Intercollegiate Athletics said "Being able to have our athletes tested on campus and at the rate of testing that we require by NCAA and Sun Belt and the cost it would've been to us would have made it impossible for us to do. This was huge for our program as it allowed us to have a season this year."

My curiosity has taken me a long way from a desert town that has since all but vanished, but it has returned me – time and again – to the wonder of science. Questions, I insist, can still change the world. I still want to know: Why are there two sexes?

REFERENCES

1. Haseltine, FP. Why Be a Role Model When You Can Be a Mentor? Women's Leadership and Authority in the Health Professions Conference at Santa Cruz, June 19-21, 1977.
2. Shapiro, EC; Haseltine, FP; and Rowe MP. Moving up: Role Models, Mentors, and the "Patron System." *Sloan Management Review.* 1978; 19:51-58.
3. Haseltine, FP. Why Be a Mentor? In: DC Fort (ed). *A Hand Up — Women Mentoring Women in Science.* Washington, DC: Association for Women in Science (AWIS): 2005;.353-366.

CHAPTER THREE

Boundroid

By Margaret (Maggi) Cary, MD, MBA, MPH

BOUNDROID^{SM} IS NOT A WORD you will find in any standard dictionary. If you could, its definition would read Boundroid *(n): A person who works at the interface among people, groups, and/or cultures to intentionally create change; a particular form of change agent.* Boundroids possess innate and acquired abilities to effect change. They cross personal, social and organizational barriers that separate individuals or groups of people, preventing the free exchange of energy, ideas and opportunities. Boundroids are ubiquitous, but difficult to recognize if you are blind to their skills and unable to pick up their distinctive trail.

Over 26 years have passed since the first edition of *Women in Medicine and Management: A Mentoring Guide.* It has been almost a decade since the second edition. More women continue to enter medicine, dentistry, and veterinary medicine. Some graduating classes have more women than men.

As I wrote in the first edition, I wanted to be a physician since fourth grade. I loved science and wanted to help people. I took some side roads and eventually left direct patient care for management. I preferred working in groups rather than alone. I have been fortunate in being a lifelong learner, enjoying "knowledge transfers" with others and in having many, many people who believed in me and helped me.

After completing medical school and the Santa Rosa, California, residency in family medicine, I managed my own private practice and then co-directed an emergency department in a ski resort. Some of my other activities include turning around a money-losing occupational medicine clinic, earning a Master of Business Administration (MBA), and developing and co-anchoring a nationally aired Public Broadcasting System coproduction, "The Health Care Puzzle."

At the time of the publication of the previous edition of this book, I was a member of President Clinton's administration, as one of Secretary Donna Shalala's regional directors in health and human services. I intended to stay one term. The job was one of the most challenging and rewarding jobs I had ever had, so I stayed for the second term. As the second term was winding down, I started looking for another job.

Find a need and fill it, whatever it takes.

In 2000, the president of Acueity, a medical device start-up in the Bay Area, and I began discussing my joining the company. I had co-authored a seminal text on telehealth, *Telemedicine and Telehealth: Principles, Policies, Performance and Pitfalls*, and the president wanted me to bring my knowledge of medical technology, medicine, public policy, and communications skills to Acueity. I would stay in Denver and commute to San Francisco when I wasn't visiting clients. I had lived in the Bay Area for some of my high school and college years and returned to Sonoma County for my residency training.

I thought this new commute would be an opportunity to reconnect with my family and friends. Moreover, the product intrigued me. Acueity sold micro endoscopes with a diameter of less than a millimeter. The market edge was the patented optics, created by two cinematographers, that provided detailed resolution of the smallest details. The initial use was for ductoscopy to diagnose ductal carcinoma *in situ*. I thought of additional uses. I could use my skills and contacts to further the company's goals. The optimal job for a Boundroid – the intersection of medicine, federal government, business, and public policy.

Find a need and fill it, whatever it takes.

In late 2000, the tech bubble imploded and funding dried up. One of the partners in the healthcare communications company we had hired asked me to join as medical director, continuing to live in Denver, but now commuting to Philadelphia. Living in Denver and working in the Bay Area had not been as easy as I'd thought it would be. I was tired of being on the road. Connecting with my friends was difficult, given weekday traffic and the distances. The few family members in the Bay Area were nearly 100 miles away. Most evenings I returned to an empty hotel room after a walk in a nearby park.

Why, then, would I even *consider* a job with a longer commute between Denver and Philadelphia — a place where I knew no one and wasn't familiar with the culture? Because here was another opportunity to be a Boundroid. The new position would combine my expertise as clinician, federal government employee, writer, policy analyst, and public speaker. I could learn the details of marketing, advertising, and public relations, all of which measure their effectiveness with research, much as medicine does.

I enjoyed the people I worked with – the creativity and camaraderie — but had a hard time, in the end, promoting another "me too" drug when we had more than 40 million uninsured people in the United States. The friendliness of the staff and the extensive wine by the glass selection of the Penn's View Inn, where I stayed, did not compensate for eating dinner alone and returning to another empty hotel room. I wanted to sleep in my own bed. So when Donna Marshall, president of the Colorado Business Group on Health, began recruiting me as her chief medical officer, I listened. I liked Donna (and still do) and wanted to return to mission-driven work, where I fully believed in what I was doing. I decided to return to Colorado.

In 2003, I received an offer from the Veterans Health Administration (VHA) in Washington, DC, to develop and implement VA+Choice, a complicated program to allow Medicare-eligible veterans to use their Medicare benefits at VA facilities, purportedly developed on the back of a napkin by the (then) Secretaries of Health and Human Services and the Department of Veterans Affairs with their respective Under Secretaries. I had enjoyed working at Health and Human Services, the federal government's mission resonated with me, and I enjoyed working with my colleagues. The

VHA post required a physician with a background in health policy, public health, and business, who also had excellent communication skills — a small universe in 2003. This was another chance to build on the skills I had developed in my previous jobs.

I was committed to Denver and my 20-year history living there, to my family in Boulder, swearing I would only leave my house feet first in a box. The VHA post meant moving to Washington, DC. I looked at strengths and weaknesses, opportunities and threats for each choice and ultimately decided to move. The chance to be a Boundroid again was irresistible.

I hit the ground running, learning about VA's electronic health record (EHR), information technology (IT) system, coding and billing. I enjoy being on a vertical learning curve. Bob Perreault, the man who hired me, was an excellent boss. He gave me free rein to meet with whomever I wished at VA without going up through the chain of command. At the time I didn't realize how uncommon this is in bureaucracies. Bob introduced me to VA's leaders who could help. He was one of the best bosses I have ever had. We trusted each other, an essential piece of an effective and productive relationship.

As part of accountability I was evaluated by an external organizational development consultant, who wrote:

> "Maggi has done a phenomenal job of laying out the implementation strategy and the elements for the program. Most folks focus only on the process pieces of the program, i.e., how the system is to work, and they normally minimize or ignore the vision building, the involvement of stakeholders and partners, the development of staff and the marketing and PR work that will help guarantee success. Maggi has taken all of that into account. I think you will find her efforts very impressive."

My previous experiences and expertise meshed well in this post. I came in early and stayed late, working on weekends.

The Medicare Prescription Drug, Improvement, and Modernization Act of 2003 renamed +Choice plans to "Medicare Advantage" and I renamed VA+Choice to VAAdvantage, the first Medicare Advantage program in the United States. Then, for reasons relating to leadership changes at the top in 2004 (one of the risks in federal government positions), VAAdvantage was shelved.

In 2006, I moved from the business to the clinical side of the Veterans Health Administration to manage more than 20 Field Advisory Committees of medical specialties. The committees had languished for years. My job was to engage them with the Office of Specialty Care Services, their home office. I asked committee members what they would like from the Washington, DC, policy office. One item was management and leadership training.

Drawing on my private sector experience, I created and delivered one- to two-day physician leadership development workshops around the country, all with outstanding evaluations. VHA's standard evaluation takes six weeks and I wanted a quicker turnaround, so I developed my own assessment, collated the responses, then shared with all who wanted it. I enjoyed the work and wanted to include other faculty.

Find a need and fill it, whatever it takes.

In 2004, while I was at VHA, my youngest brother was driving supply trucks for the U.S. military in Iraq, the same trucks targeted for improvised explosive devices, or IEDs. During his first month overseas, his 11-year-old daughter found her mother, Kelly, comatose. The daughter awakened her 16-year-old sister and called 911. Kelly had experienced a brain bleed and lingered for a couple of weeks. During most of her hospital stay, her open brain was swathed in bandages, following the craniotomy to decrease her intracranial pressure (the pressure inside her skull). She never awakened. After she died, my other brothers, my stepmother, her husband, and I stepped in to care for my nieces while their father completed his contract.

I was now one of a group responsible for the health and wellbeing of two young girls while their father had a risky job far away. My summer's month with them was one of the high points in my life. We made pies from the apples in our yard, saw films, and held a birthday party for my younger niece's twelfth. I thought about their needs over my own. I remember having something – I don't remember what it was – that one of them wanted. Without thought and without weighing the pros and cons, wondering if whatever it was could be replaced, I gave it to her.

Find a need and fill it, whatever it takes.

The repeated theme in my career has been to find a need and fill it, whatever it takes — often a unique need or a unique way to fill it. My first Boundroid experience was in 1983 when I turned around a Denver clinic. I had moved from California to Colorado. I needed a job and chose the one that was most appealing to me. Rose Hospital was in the vanguard of buying medical practices. My preference was the clinic in downtown Denver in a new building with designer furniture, but another physician was hired for that position. I was stuck with the occupational and general medicine clinic in a run-down house in industrial Denver. Depending upon which way the wind blew, I smelled cat food, lamb, or fertilizer.

Rather than just accepting the situation, I began thinking larger, thinking tactically and strategically. Industrial injuries were our cash cow. Local drop-ins were not as profitable. Caring for them was good for community support and I enjoyed my patients. Without knowing exactly what I was doing at the time, I visited the foremen at the factories who referred those hurt on the job for medical care. I gave classes at the factories on preventing back injuries and industrial safety. This led to more business. I created occupational and physician therapy offices in the clinic basement so that our patients spent less time off work to have their therapies. They did not have to travel to the main hospital located several miles south and on the other side of the freeway. The hospital still captured the revenue.

Find a need and fill it, whatever it takes.

Keep in mind that filling these needs may have unexpected consequences, positive and negative. In the 1980s turning around an occupational medicine clinic offered a wide-open future, and my work was in the industrial part of Denver, a perfect location. After transforming a clinic that was in the red for three years into a profit-winning operation within 90 days, I negotiated a contract with a lower base, but with bonuses based on billed charges, not collected charges. My yearly salary rose.

I was transferred to another location in a working-class residential Denver area, with lots of close-by private doctor offices as competition. Unfortunately, I couldn't build another successful medical clinic here. Most of the neighborhood residents worked during the day and went to clinics closer to their jobs or to free clinics. The hospital was reluctant to open on weekends or evenings and, truthfully, so was I. Management changed at the hospital and the new manager had different ideas that I wasn't sure would work in the environment. I finally left and the clinic closed.

Because of my turnaround success with the occupational medicine clinic, the chief executive officers (CEOs) of Denver's competing clinics pursued me to join their businesses. I chose the more financially successful, thinking I would again have both management and patient care roles. Instead, I was put into a line job, which meant I was simply another physician seeing patients and completing the appropriate on-the-job injury forms. I had no input into building the business or in client outreach. Worse yet, I had to punch in and out on a timecard and was paid an hourly rate. This was not the job I signed up for. I completed my contract and resigned.

I wanted to reinvent myself and so I returned to university to earn an MBA. I founded a consulting company. I read about the Miles Institute for Physician Patient Communication (now the Institute for Healthcare Communication) in the *Wall Street Journal*, and joined the first train-the-trainer course, delivering workshops in Colorado.

When I wrote for the second edition of this book, I had envisioned and created the Community of Champions, national leadership development workshops for physicians in the Veterans Health Administration. In October 2013, I left VA to coach and teach in my own business. I continue to teach the Personal Essay/Narrative Medicine course at Georgetown University School of Medicine, as well as a course called Hacking Happiness.

In 2016, I began coaching a medical student at Georgetown University School of Medicine. I worked with Jack one-on-one with his writing and as a leadership coach. We quickly realized the benefits of a coach for medical students and co-founded A Whole New Doctor, an all-volunteer coaching and leadership development program for medical students, based at Georgetown. We have students from several medical schools and are implementing our next A Whole New Doctor program at the Kirk Kerkorian School of Medicine at the University of Nevada, Las Vegas.

After I completed my residency training, I'd had enough of academic medicine. I wasn't interested in being pimped or shamed. The irony is, I find myself back in academic medicine, under my own terms. I love facilitating others' learning and seeing their eyes light up.

Who knows what my next reinvention will be?

Find a need and fill it, whatever it takes.

One key to success at any job is to listen to the folks who are already there. Ask what they like, what could be improved, and what they'd like to see happen. Relationships are the foundation for all we do. Life is a balancing act — the balance of risk and security. As a lifelong learner, I look for new ideas, for new ways of being and doing. I'm fortunate to have a life where one experience leads to the next.

My three requirements for employment are
1. Do meaningful work with people you respect and value;
2. Make enough to live on; and
3. Don't work with assholes.

In the first edition of *Women in Medicine and Management*, I offered the following, which still holds.
- Have purpose and meaning in your life. Your goals may change.
- Be authentic.
- Speak the truth.
- Join a community.
- Make friends and acquaintances and maintain the relationships you develop. Be interested in the person, not the position.
- Listen, listen, listen – especially in a new job. Develop exemplary listening skills.
- Figure out who your boss is and what your boss wants, and do it. Do a quality job on time.

- Let folks (especially your boss) know what you're doing while maintaining humility.
- Share power.
- Develop and continue improving your communication skills – writing, speaking. Take classes and ask for critiques. Join Toastmasters. Join your local chapter of the National Speakers Association.
- Be positive. It's good for your health, for that of your colleagues, and for the organization.
- Be a lifelong learner. Think about interconnectedness and complexity. How can you connect your learning? How can you share what you've learned to add value?
- Be flexible and adaptable, ready to reestablish priorities in a changing environment.
- Don't take life – or yourself – too seriously. Have fun along the way.

For this third edition I've added the following:

- Be vulnerable and open with your colleagues. Share your feelings. Listen to Brené Brown's TED talks.
- Exercise, eat healthy food, and take walks in the woods.
- Journal your thoughts, feelings, and experiences, even if only five minutes each day.
- Do things for others. You, as the giver, will get more out of the giving than the receiver.
- Practice mindfulness.

The journey *is* the destination.

Academia

*"Shoot for the Stars — when you miss,
you might land on the Moon.... Pursue
the Moon Landings with zeal!"*

– Ora Hirsch Pescovitz

CHAPTER FOUR

Trying to Make the World a Better Place

By Ora Hirsch Pescovitz, MD

As EARLY AS I CAN REMEMBER, my parents taught me to make choices that leave the world in a better place. This philosophy drove me to become a physician and researcher. This is the philosophy by which my husband Mark and I raised our children. And this is the philosophy I follow – and share – as a leader. Making this world a better place in big and small ways is at the core of everything I try to do.

My love of research began in high school. When I was in ninth grade, I took a class called Research and Development. I was the only girl in the class, which I saw as a great advantage. During the first week of school, the teacher had us design a study using the scientific method. I decided to evaluate whether plants would grow better under the influence of classical music, the music of the Beatles, or no music at all. Sadly, all of the plants died, which made it clear that I wasn't destined for a career in botany.

However, the experience of investigation and the process of discovery — the fact that you could ask a question that hadn't been answered and design an experiment to investigate the question — ignited my passion for science and made me realize I wanted to dedicate my life to investigating questions that would result in ways to make sick people better. Although I didn't know the term at the time, that was the moment I decided to become a physician-scientist.

When I entered a six-year medical program at Northwestern in 1974, I was one of 12 women in a class of 60. Notably, today, women make up half of incoming medical students at most schools.

At the time, I never saw being a woman as a disadvantage. It was during my time in medical school that I met my future husband, Mark Pescovitz.

When I was in medical school, everyone said to me "of course you'll be a pediatrician, because you're a girl and girls like children." Of course, this sexist assumption got right under my skin and caused me to vow that I would be anything BUT a pediatrician. And so I set out to become a surgeon.

Throughout my training, I fought every inclination toward pediatrics. I even went so far as to put off my required pediatrics rotation until the middle of my senior year. When I finally started that rotation, however, something unexpected and transformative happened: I found that I loved the specialty of pediatrics and that I identified with the values, ideals, and personalities of other pediatricians.

I knew I had found my calling and pursued the subspecialty of pediatric endocrinology. I was drawn to academia and knew that I would likely spend my career in the pursuit of discovering new knowledge and educating a future generation of students.

Upon completing medical school in 1979, Mark and I headed to the University of Minnesota where I completed my residency in pediatrics while Mark completed his residency in general surgery. From there, we moved to Maryland, where I completed my pediatrics residency at Children's Hospital National Medical Center in Washington, DC, as well as a fellowship in endocrinology at the National Institutes of Health's Institute of Child Health and Human Development, while Mark did research in immunology at the National Cancer Institute.

During these four amazing and productive years, we welcomed our first two children – Aliza and Ari – who were born 16 months apart. At the end of my fellowship, I had 27 publications and had presented numerous papers at national meetings about my research. It had been a time of explosive research discoveries and I was fortunate to have been at the center of many of the exciting advances in numerous areas, especially in growth and puberty.

Unfortunately, when it was time for Mark to return to Minnesota to complete his surgical residency and a fellowship in transplantation,

I was not offered a position. It was a period of enormous turmoil for me, especially since I had received excellent offers from higher-ranked institutions. Eventually, I was offered a low-level instructor-level position and a salary that was less than I had been paid as a fellow at the NIH.

But shortly after my arrival, when I got an NIH grant funded, I was promoted to an assistant professor in the University of Minnesota's Department of Pediatrics. And, two years later, in 1987, we rounded out our family with the addition of our daughter, Naomi.

When Mark completed his fellowship, we were ready to move again. Mark and I received a number of offers for positions at various – but different – universities. Mark was very excited about a position he was offered at Indiana University School of Medicine, but I was not offered a position there and also couldn't imagine living in Indianapolis! After much debate and discussion, we decided to let his career guide our next step, and the five of us were off to Indy.

The next 21 years that we spent in Indiana turned out to be ones that I treasure deeply, both personally and professionally. I watched my three children evolve into wonderful adults, had the honor of treating many inspiring young patients at Riley Hospital for Children, continued to pursue a productive research career, and bolstered Indiana University's position as a focal point for biomedical research and a catalyst for Indiana's life sciences initiative.

Upon arriving in Indiana, I accepted an appointment as an associate professor of pediatrics, and physiology and biophysics. Over the next several years, I began to establish myself within the IU community, becoming director of IU's section of pediatric endocrinology/diabetology in 1990, the Edwin Letzter Professor of Pediatrics in 1998, executive associate dean for research affairs at IU School of Medicine from 2000 to 2009, president and CEO of Riley Hospital for Children from 2004 to 2009, and interim vice president for research administration from 2007 to 2009.

I spent 30 years of my career conducting basic and translational research in molecular endocrinology and treating children with growth and pubertal disorders. Pediatric endocrinology is a wonderful subspecialty because you have the opportunity to break down very complex issues and identify simplified solutions, as well as help children and families. I have myriad examples of small and large contributions that I can reflect on in both discovery and training that were exceedingly gratifying.

In 2007, I experienced a serious career disappointment when I was one of two finalists for the presidency for Indiana University. I have great admiration for President McRobbie who was selected for the position, but I was personally devastated. After it became public that I had been a finalist for the position, numerous search firms contacted me about other positions and it led to my next big career move.

It also led me to begin to think about a philosophy that I realized had actually been guiding me before:

Shoot for the Stars — when you miss, you might land on the Moon.... Pursue the Moon Landings with zeal!

In 2009, my Moon Landing was the position of health system CEO and executive vice president for medical affairs at the University of Michigan. It was a wonderful opportunity, and also one of the most difficult decisions of my career. But, just like we did two decades before, Mark and I discussed the options and decided it was an opportunity I couldn't and shouldn't pass up. Our kids were grown and Mark's career as a transplant surgeon was thriving. We decided that, like many dual-career couples, we would make it work.

The opportunity to run one of the top integrated academic health systems in the nation was exceptional. The University of Michigan Health System (today known as Michigan Medicine) was then a $3.3B system with more than 120 health centers and clinics, $490M in research funding, and 27,000 employees. I led the system's wide-ranging strategic planning efforts, advanced diversity, equity and inclusion across the health system, raised $450M in philanthropic funds, and expanded the system's advancement efforts, among other initiatives.

On Life and Loss

On December 12, 2010, my life changed forever when my beloved husband, Mark, was killed in a tragic car accident. Until Mark's death, I thought my life was nearly perfect.

47

Mark was a committed volunteer and leader in the medical, Jewish, arts and music communities; a surgeon who always put patients first; a researcher determined to find new ways to save and improve lives; an artist who absorbed and reflected the world around him; and a dedicated father, husband, brother, and son who embraced the true beauty and meaning of family. He was my soul mate, and navigating the world without his love, companionship, and friendship seemed unbearable at first.

Moving On

But, the world does not stand still, even when tragedy strikes. I realized that no matter how difficult my circumstances, there was someone whose circumstances were more challenging than mine. I began to realize just how fortunate I was. I had a wonderful family and terrific friends; I had a good job and strong skills; and I still had the opportunity to Shoot for the Stars.

Mark's death reminded me about perspective. It re-grounded me and forced me to really connect to what is important and who I am. I knew that I could never replace him or replicate our life together, but I could carry his wisdom and his love with me with every step forward. Life includes disappointments, tragedy, imperfections, and heartache. It also includes amazing triumphs, discovery, and great successes. Both offer valuable opportunities for growth.

After Mark's death, I realized that I needed to be closer to family. When two of my three children moved back to Indianapolis to accept positions there, I returned to Indianapolis to accept a position as senior vice president and US medical leader for biomedicines at Eli Lilly and Co. In that role, I was responsible for the launch of new medicines, real-world evidence-based research, relationships with large health systems, and patient assistant programs. It was another outstanding growth experience and wonderful to be back in Indianapolis.

After three good years, I kept hearing my parents' voices: Are you doing everything you can to make the world a better place?

I started to wonder if I was doing enough to apply whatever skills and abilities I might have to making an important impact, to making a difference, to moving the needle in areas that matter. My children all had excellent careers and were not financially dependent on me and I knew that I was never motivated by personal financial gain.

Headhunters had been contacting me about positions around the country, but one opportunity really resonated with me. So, in 2017, I accepted the presidency of Oakland University in Rochester, Michigan, a university of nearly 19,000 undergraduate and graduate students. One-third of our students are first-generation college students and one-third are Pell recipients. And, Oakland University had a new medical school in partnership with the Beaumont Health System. I was truly excited about the opportunity to have a significant impact.

Since becoming president of OU, we have increased academic success, scholarship, and community engagement and increased our focus on diversity, equity, and inclusion. Our campus has grown, institutional culture and morale have improved, and the entrepreneurial spirit is strong.

I am extremely proud of how effectively we have navigated the COVID-19 pandemic and we are now preparing for a close to normal fall 2021 semester. It has been exceedingly rewarding to work with a talented and dedicated team and to experience progress being made in so many domains. In spring of 2021, I was privileged to have my contract renewed by my board of trustees.

On Leadership

After spending the first half of my career in education, clinical care, and research, my career path shifted to administrative positions. I was fortunate to have had remarkable leadership opportunities, each of which was predicated upon those that came before. Initially, I was a section director in a department of pediatrics; then, I became an executive dean for research, the CEO of a large Children's Hospital, vice-president for research for a Big Ten University, the CEO of one of the nation's largest integrated academic health systems, a senior vice-president in big pharma, and now am the president of a research university.

In each of these positions throughout my career, I have described my leadership style as what Robert Greenleaf calls "servant leadership." In each administrative role, I've seen my primary purpose as serving the institution by setting the direction by defining aspirational goals, inspiring others to achieve these goals, and creating environments in which the institution will be successful and thrive.

As a physician, I learned how important it is to learn through observation. As a scientist, I know it's important to acquire data, be objective, let experiments tell the truth, and not let your preconceived ideas sway you. As a hospital administrator, I've learned how important it is to be a member of a productive team. As a parent, I want to create an environment in which my "children" will be maximally nurtured so that they will excel.

I don't claim to be the smartest person in the room. That's why I surround myself with experts and people who represent diverse perspectives. I like to bring groups of people together and then set Rules of Engagement that focus on Results, Trust, Commitment, Accountability, and Constructive Conflict.

I make it safe for my teams to be collegial collaborators and intelligent risk-takers. This can sometimes be tricky and difficult, but I encourage them to think big, be creative, take risks, and see failure as an opportunity to learn and evolve.

I have found that the Rules of Engagement are critical to success of high-functioning teams. If the goals are not ambitious, if they don't Shoot for the Stars, they may not be ambitious enough. Similarly, there is no harm in thoughtful risk-taking ideas and creativity balanced by being good stewards of financial resources.

My leadership style is a culmination of all of these experiences and approaches with an effort to keep enthusiasm high and to make the institution the best that it can be.

On Mentorship

To be successful and fulfilled, you should never stop learning, developing, and growing personally or professionally, and mentors provide incredibly valuable guidance. I know I would not be where I am today without great mentors, and I don't think you can ever have too many of them. I don't think mentoring is emphasized and encouraged as much as it should be in today's world.

I've found that no one person can serve all your needs, so I have crafted what I like to call a "mentor quilt." A mentor quilt is a support network of inspiring individuals who serve as advisors for how you want to live both your personal and professional lives. I have one mentor for research, one for clinical activity, one for work-life balance, and so on. I am always adding new ones – and I never let the others go. Find mentors and be a mentor. I like the warmth and comfort that I experience when I wrap myself in the thoughts of my mentor quilt.

On Work-Life Balance

When my children were young, the approach of summer always meant more activities, which meant it was a good time for me to take a look at my own schedule and make sure that I could effectively be both Mom and doctor. While not always an easy task, it is certainly one of the most important.

Work-life balance is fundamental to our physical, mental, and emotional wellness, as well as our productivity in – and satisfaction with – our professional and personal lives. In my experience, the key to balancing work and life effectively comes down to time management. I recall a proverb that says "Ordinary people think merely of spending time. Great people think of using it."

I sometimes say that "there is no such thing as work-life balance because we only get one life. . . . so, we have to learn to balance that one," Work drifts into our home life and our home lives drift into our work life.

Over the course of my life and career, I've found that the best strategy for time management is following the Pareto Principle, or what is more commonly called the 80/20 Rule. Most things in life are distributed unevenly, including our "To Do" lists. Applying the 80/20 rule, typically 80% of the value from our work comes from only 20% of the items on our To Do lists. So, focus your energy and time on the 20% of tasks that result in 80% of the value – the ones that yield the greatest return on investment.

Of course, just invoking the name of Pareto won't make the less-valuable 80% of tasks on your To Do list magically disappear.

You need a strategy for managing those items, as well. One of the most successful strategies I've used is the 4Ds: Do, Dump, Delegate, Delay.

- **Do:** This applies to those tasks that support your most valuable work – the vital 20%. Deal with e-mails, documents, phone calls regarding priority issues as soon as they come across your desk, your inbox, or your voicemail. I call this "handle paper once." This way, you stay on top of your priorities, you keep important projects moving, and you don't amass a daunting load to deal with at another time. That other time might be a long way off.

- **Dump:** If something comes across your desk that doesn't pertain to your priorities, doesn't require follow up, and doesn't support your goals, do you really need to keep it? Probably not. Dump it!

- **Delegate:** If a task requires attention or action but doesn't make your "Do" list, can/should someone else handle it? Is it on another person's "Do" list? If so, move it along.

- **Delay:** Very few things should make it to the Delay pile. But, on occasion, there may be something you want to review later. If so, file, print, or store it for another time.

Of course, there is no one-size-fits-all solution to time management or work-life balance. As our lives change, our priorities change and the balance we need changes, too. The 4Ds strategy has worked for me for many years, so I continue to use it. In fact, I revisit it almost daily to make sure I am on track. Find the formula and strategies that help you best use your time and achieve maximum work-life balance.

On Happiness

Over the course of my career, I've noticed that successful people are almost always happy people, but they are rarely content. If you let yourself be content, you welcome mediocrity into your life. If you are resting on your laurels, as Malcolm Kushner says, you are likely wearing them on the wrong end.

If, however, you find yourself in a place where you are just not happy with your job, I suggest trying out what I call the 4Ps:

First, **Push** and lobby for change that will change your circumstances.

If that doesn't work, **Put** up with it – accept the situation and decide to adapt to it. In other words, instead of changing the environment, change yourself.

Still not working out? Well, it might be time to leave, or **Pull** out. Sometimes leaving is the only way to move on and ahead.

And finally, no matter what, always find time to have fun, to enjoy life and to **Play**.

Find a position in which you can maximize your strengths to make the greatest contribution.

- Cultivate an environment where people feel encouraged and rewarded for creativity.
- Throw fear out the window — take risks!
- Embrace diversity in your colleagues and your organization.
- Realize that perfection is not success and failure is opportunity to learn and evolve.
- Accept that you will make mistakes. In fact, if you don't make mistakes along the way, you may not be trying hard enough!
- Find a suitable strategy for work-life balance. Work is important, but what else defines you?
- Create a "mentor quilt."
- Success breeds success, and leadership is about helping others succeed.
- Don't wait for opportunities to find you – seek them out and create them.

CHAPTER FIVE

Learning to Lead

By Donna Parker, MD

PERHAPS PEOPLE ARE BORN TO LEAD, but many do not recognize that potential in themselves without others continuously pushing them to the front. My career has been a lot of being pushed to the front with a bit of asking to move forward sprinkled in. When I complete a Myers-Briggs self-assessment, I clearly fall into the category of a "leader." It is interesting that I do not identify the constellation of character traits in myself which so clearly corresponds with those who like to lead.

Leadership has been defined as a process of social influence in which one person can enlist the aid and support of others in the accomplishment of a common task. What are those character traits? In no particular order, they are charisma, confidence, vision, interpersonal skills, vigor, enthusiasm, integrity, magnanimity, and fairness. These are the parts of me that have allowed me to be a successful leader and role model in medicine.

I left high school in Maryland and went off to Canada for my undergraduate education at McGill University. I am often asked why I made that somewhat unusual choice. I guess it was a peek into my nature even at 17 that I was a bit bold and confident with a good sense of adventure. I loved the idea of living in another country and especially living in a bilingual city.

What an opportunity that was. McGill was a tremendous growth experience for me because of the diversity of the campus and the city. My French became quite good, and I met people whose families were from all parts of the world. The rigor of the academics kept me focused and engaged. I was a part of a large student body, so I was able to remain rather anonymous, which if you ask me is the way I generally like it. My goal was to perform well and return to the United States to pursue medicine, and I did that.

I decided to attend the University of Maryland School of Medicine largely for geographical and financial reasons. It was time to move back closer to home, and as my state school it was economically appropriate. Perhaps if I had been thinking "leadership" then I might have courted the "higher profile" medical schools to augment my resume. However, I came to medical school with the hope of learning how to take care of patients without a real sense of what that meant over the course of a lifetime.

I was the prototypical girl who was good in science class, so I was steered toward medicine. Because I enjoy social interactions, the thought that I could engage with patients was on target. But at the time I had no aspirations to be a leader in medical education.

Questioning My Decisions

The transition to Baltimore was a difficult one for me. I had left a very cosmopolitan, multicultural city for one which seemed to me to be stuck at least a decade in the past. Most of my classmates were from Baltimore, and many of them had attended regional colleges and universities. I was clearly an outsider. However, I did meet a lot of fun and interesting people in my class, and I remain friends with quite a few of them. A handful are still on the faculty at Maryland.

About a third of my classmates were women. While we did not feel particularly marginalized, there were still vestiges of earlier times with the locker rooms in the OR at one local hospital labeled "doctors" and "nurses." We tended to laugh rather than become angry.

While medical school was intellectually fascinating, it was sometimes clinically harsh with tired residents and attendings not always seeming to genuinely care for or about patients. I found only a few people I would consider role models or mentors, and that concerned me. Had I made the right career choice? Clinical medicine was a theoretical good match, but would it be in practice? Were there other options I should be considering? The enthusiasm for my chosen work was not there. Through all these questions, my mentors remained incredibly supportive and over the ensuing years provided consistent advice and encouragement.

I was sent adrift into an internal medicine residency hoping for a spark. In the long hours, days, and weeks of residency, I learned that I enjoyed the fast pace and quick decision making required when working in the ICU (Intensive Care Unit) and in the outpatient clinic. In both areas, I also appreciated working collaboratively with staff to solve patient care problems. There was great satisfaction in seeing patients' lives changed in the moment in the ICU and over time in the clinic. I was easily engaged by patients' stories about who they were and how they led their lives. So, there was a place for me in clinical medicine. I just had to find the right situation. I was developing a vision for my future.

Adrift again, moving with my husband to North Carolina where he was beginning a fellowship, I had no job and continuing uncertainty about what sort of career suited me. I eventually secured a position at Wake Medical Center in Raleigh, which was a University of North Carolina (UNC) affiliate with medical students and residents rotating in both inpatient and outpatient areas. The position afforded me a lot of primary patient care responsibility along with a significant role in the training of the medical students and residents. It seemed like an ideal first job out of residency.

Finding My Place

Having once again been bold, picking up and moving to a new place with a new culture and values, I learned much about people and the art of medicine. I grew exponentially as a clinician by sheer volume and diversity of patient issues. HIV (Human Immunodeficiency Virus) was just emerging as an entity, and I experienced both the pain and reward of caring for young gay men who had left North Carolina for more tolerant places but were obligated by circumstances to return home to die.

Because of the vigor with which I approached my work, I was asked to co-manage the outpatient clinic and to coordinate our portion of the UNC physical diagnosis course for medical students. I also saw a need for organized pre-operative evaluations for patients at our site and started a clinic for that purpose. Looking back on this time, I enjoyed the spirit of the students, the constant learning through educating and creating order out of chaos. These have remained ongoing themes in my career since that time.

Recognizing where I found joy, as we were moving back to Baltimore to be near family, I began looking for a position that involved both administrative responsibilities and working with learners . As fate would have it, the position of Director of Medical Clinic was open at the University of Maryland School of Medicine (UMSoM). Fortunately, I had been a good student with strong inter-personal skills, so no bridges had been burned and people with whom I had worked as a student were still there to recommend my hire.

I must admit it was a little uncomfortable stepping into a new system and being immediately in charge. However, if handled well, those situations can be the source of much personal growth. I was very keen about the prospect of mentoring the internal medicine residents in their outpatient experience and felt I could develop a vision for making their experience better.

During this time, I learned that it is important to really understand current systems before implementing changes and to carefully assess what works well and what does not. The next step is to figure out who has power to make necessary changes if that person is not you.

I diligently kept abreast of policies, procedures, and curricula at other programs to incorporate innovative ideas. I attended national meetings to meet others in like positions. The internal medicine pro-gram director eventually asked me to coordinate all the outpatient education for the residents and to develop an ambulatory block rotation curriculum.

Upon completion of that task, I asked for a promotion based on my expanded duties and the structure of departmental education at other programs. That is how I became the director of ambulatory education. I believe if I had not asked for a different title, it would not have been offered. So, lesson learned: A little push can help to advance your career.

Concurrent with my return to UMSoM, the Admissions Com-mittee was expanding in size. I volunteered to join in order to increase my knowledge of the medical school administration and to participate in a process I considered quite meaningful. The associate dean had known me as a medical student, and I believe that facilitated the acceptance of a new faculty member. My diligent work, punctuality, and full engagement at meetings were recognized, and the associate dean also valued my integrity and fairness in thinking through situations that arose.

All of this led to an offer to be assistant dean a year later. This position was my first real foot in the door as a medical school administrator. I served in the Admissions Office and on the Admissions Committee for 13 years. I learned everything I could about the policies and processes of the office even though on paper it was just 10% of my time. Putting added effort into something about which you are passionate is the lesson here. The reward is the chance to spend more of your time doing those types of activities in future positions.

At this point, I had also reached the time in my life when I wanted to start a family. Trying to simultaneously begin an academic career created some challenges and surprises. Up to now, pursuit of a career was all I had ever known. I had never considered working less than full time, but while on maternity leave with my first child, it became quite clear that I could not be both the physician/educator and the mother I wanted to be with a full-time position.

My colleagues warned me that the Department of Medicine had never signed off on a part-time faculty member and attempting to be the first would be folly. Because I was so certain of my decision, I was prepared to look for a new job should my request be denied. Fortunately, after explaining that I could accomplish the important tasks working part-time, the department agreed.

Many people will tell you that working part-time means full-time work with part-time pay, and there is some truth in that. But for me, the biggest advantage was flexibility in my schedule. Although I cut back by giving up one of my two patient sessions each week and my inpatient attending work, I was able to do the rest of the work in the hours that suited my family. Being part-time meant no one harassed me for leaving at 3:30 to get to a lacrosse game. That alone was worth it to me, and I was lucky to have the financial resources to handle the decrement in pay.

My physician husband had a terrific job that could certainly cover our expenses if I needed a bit of time off before seeking part-time work that would accommodate motherhood. He was an important part of the decision making to devote more time than initially planned to our growing family. We now had two children, and I worked part-time for 18 years with gradually increasing work hours from 60% to 80%. I transitioned back to full-time work as our oldest daughter headed off to college and the younger one acquired her driver's license. The transition back to full-time work was a smooth and positive one.

The next twist in my career came about seven years after joining the faculty, when I accepted an offer to become the associate dean for student and faculty development. This was a newly created office, and that scenario presented both opportunity and challenges. I was initially offered the position at the assistant dean level, which would have represented a lateral move from a job I loved. I held out for the associate dean position with increased autonomy and the prospect of defining a new office.

The fact that I would be supervising two staff members meant that I would acquire more skills managing people and budgets. There were also a few existing education grants which had been handled by an office folded into this new one, so I had to quickly learn how to manage those. I created a faculty development curriculum and recruited faculty members to participate in teaching workshops and small-group sessions. The advising system for our medical students had also eroded, so I worked to create a new one, pairing a student and faculty member based on similar interests (academic, personal, or both).

The Student and Faculty Development Office was successful in many areas, but it really lacked a defined identity. Ultimately, it was bits and pieces of lots of programs. Looking back, I am grateful for having learned more about personnel management, budgets, and grants. However, I did not love the work and was ready for another change after a few years.

It took six years before I was offered the position of associate dean for student affairs with larger staff and more responsibility. My acceptance required quite a bit of pushing because the Office of Student Affairs (OSA) had several active issues that needed to be addressed in short order. I was also in the final stages of pursuing a new education grant with site visitors arriving imminently.

I understood that the path to promotion within the medical school was through grant and journal article writing, and that the move to OSA would put those activities on hold for several years, if not forever. Ultimately, I accepted the position because I felt that I had the organizational and leadership skills needed to substantially improve the office, and I cared about the education and well-being of our medical students. I set aside the immediate goal of promotion and moved to the position that I felt would provide greater personal rewards.

Asking for the proper resources to be successful is important in any job transition. As a condition of taking this new position, I requested the hire of an additional assistant dean of my choosing at 40% effort. He was a valuable and key addition to the office, bringing the level of staffing to what we needed to provide excellent student service. As other faculty who had been working in the office retired or moved on, I hired three more assistant deans. My aim was to always try to do more than my fair share of all the duties within the office to set an example, and to be a part of the team. Our camaraderie and teamwork created an environment that others dream of, and I feel truly fortunate to have all of them around. We made each other better.

I spent a total of 15 years as associate dean of student affairs, and I learned a lot about leadership in that role. Warren Buffet has said, "hire well and manage little." Having taken the time to intentionally recruit faculty and staff to the Office of Student Affairs who were committed to the mission and with the emotional intelligence to work with students and other stakeholders, most of my work was done. Instead of becoming overly involved in each person's daily activities, I set clear expectations, fought to provide necessary resources, and made sure to publicly acknowledge the amazing work that was being done.

As our school planned to launch the first major curriculum change in 25 years, I was poised to step into a new leadership role that would allow me to lead that effort. The education faculty saw me as the logical person to ensure the success of the project, and I stepped forward to make it known that I was interested in doing so.

Some negotiation was required for this promotion to occur, but in January 2019, I was named the school's first senior associate dean for undergraduate medical education. In this role, I oversee the Office of Medical Education, the Office of Student Affairs, the Office of Admissions, and the Office of Student Research. The vision was to organize these offices under one umbrella to work collaboratively and to share resources.

Growing and Helping Others Grow

Of course, the COVID-19 pandemic upended plans around the world. We were faced with launching a new curriculum based on active learning at a time when teaching was going remote. Much has been written about leadership during crises, and I found that reading quite helpful. My process was to consistently remind myself of our mission to provide an excellent education to our next generation of physicians, and the decision-making flowed from there.

Communication is always important, but with the physical distancing of the pandemic, finding ways to communicate effectively and with humanity became paramount. Our team was charged with being innovative and flexible in achieving our goals, and they all stepped forward to do that despite having busy and stressful clinical schedules.

I cannot overstate the importance of engaging in specific leadership training, especially for women. Each time a new opportunity is presented, asking for support for leadership training should be a part of that conversation. There are many wonderful programs in a variety of formats such that anyone should be able to find one that meets their needs and goals. The bonus to the actual training is the opportunity to network with other high-achieving women. It is incredibly important for us to support one another and to think of each other as we hear of opportunities.

A few years into my stint in student affairs, I began to provide mentorship and sponsorship very intentionally to other women at my institution who I thought had the capacity to become leaders. We would have casual lunches and conversations in groups and one-on-one just to talk about life, career paths, and what was happening on our campus. I made introductions between people with like interests with the hope that they would collaborate and expand their networks.

My work in undergraduate medical education is indeed a joy for me because of the opportunity to watch students grow into physicians capable of caring for others. However, the mentorship I have provided is another source of extraordinary joy for the same reasons. The ability to watch young female faculty grow into leaders is simply an honor.

The greatest lesson I have learned as I have moved up in management roles in academia is to never be afraid to take the lead if in your heart you know you have something to contribute and the skills to move others forward with you.

I cannot say that I know where my career will take me over the next decade, but I imagine that I will remain engaged in activities related to undergraduate medical education. In all endeavors, it is important to remain open to new opportunities, to continue to learn and grow academically and personally, and to follow your passion always.

CHAPTER SIX

Clinician to Environmental Activist

By Mona Hanna-Attisha, MD, MPH

I WANTED TO BE A DOCTOR AS FAR BACK AS I can remember, maybe from obsessively watching *M*A*S*H* reruns growing up. Or it could've been the story about my grandfather Haji that my mom used to tell me, when he fell out of a tree and doctors took care of his broken leg. Or maybe it was the early experience of being in a car accident and a caring physician who made it seem like everything was going to be okay.

In high school, I had some powerful experiences as an environmental activist, so I created an environmental health major, merging environmental science and pre-med courses. My passion for activism, service, and research was solidified in college, followed by four years of medical school at Michigan State University; my last two clinical years were in Flint.

It was at Michigan State University (MSU), as a College of Human Medicine Flint-based medical student, that I first fell in love with pediatrics and with the city of Flint. It wasn't a tough call which specialty I'd go into. As a medical student, you have to do rotations in a variety of fields, and as soon as I got to pediatrics, I felt like I was at home. Kids are usually looking for fun, and everything's new to them. No matter how sick they are, they still want to laugh and play. I was briefly tempted by obstetrics but noticed that as soon as my patients gave birth, I tended to forget about them; my attention suddenly shifted to their newborn babies.

A baby who is properly fed and loved and kept healthy and surrounded by people and communities that value and protect her has the best chance of becoming a healthy adult. This is what drew me to pediatrics. We pediatricians are at the pivotal intersection of clinical care and prevention. Every aspect of my job, from immunizations to emphasizing the importance of bike helmets, is not just about ensuring kids are healthy today. It's about tomorrow, next year, and 20 years from now.

We see life at its beginning, when it can be shaped for good. As Frederick Douglass said, "It's easier to build strong children than to repair broken men." Walk into the adult floor of a hospital any day, and you'll see beds of patients with problems like diabetes or heart disease that can't be fixed, because to do that you'd have to time-travel back to their childhoods and fix those too.

Tactical Decisions

As much as I love spending time with kids and seeing one little patient at a time, I wanted to have as much impact as I could — on as many lives as I could — so right from the beginning, I made a tactical decision to be obtain a public health degree in health policy and to be a medical educator rather than a pediatrician in private practice. That way, over the course of my career, I could share my passion for children's health and proven interventions with hundreds of new doctors who would go on to treat thousands of young patients, caring for them as I would and hopefully even better.

And that is what drew me back to Flint in 2011 to direct the MSU-affiliated Hurley Medical Center Pediatric Residency Program and to commit myself to training the next generation of physicians.

The year I came back to Flint was also the year that Flint lost democracy. The right of every American to have a say over their local government was taken away from Flint residents overnight. At one point, half of all African Americans in the state of Michigan were governed by emergency managers as opposed to 2% of Whites. It was grossly undemocratic and unjust, and would ultimately also be unhealthy.

To save money, the emergency managers severed a half-a-century relationship with fresh, pre-treated water from the Great Lakes and instead started drawing water from the local Flint river. The Flint river water was not treated properly. It was missing an important ingredient called corrosion control which made it about 20 times more corrosive than Great Lakes water. For over 18 months, this corrosive water leached lead — a potent and irreversible neuro-toxin — out of our pipes and into the homes and bodies of families and children.

When all this was happening, I was wrapped up in my world as a pediatrician, professor, and medical educator. In addition to being a busy medical professional, I was balancing being a busy mom and wife, driving my kids to soccer practices and Girl Scout meetings and juggling a million balls just like so many of you do now and will be in the future.

A Life-Altering Trajectory

My life changed when I learned that there was lead in the water. The corrosive water was eating away at our lead pipes. And knowing that there was lead in our water — filling baby bottles and sippy cups — ate away at me too. I literally stopped eating and lost 30 pounds. I couldn't sleep. I drank way too much coffee. I was feeling anger, fear, despair, guilt, and heartbreak — a roller coaster of emotions.

I knew it was not only a professional obligation, but my moral and ethical duty — my civic responsibility — to do something. I respect the science that has taught us that lead is a poison with no safe level. It erodes cognition and twists behavior. It can alter the entire life course trajectory of a child and a population of children. Lead poisoning is one of the root causes of so many of our inequities; it is a centuries-old failure of society to protect our children.

What's worse, the burden of lead does not fall equally on our nation's children; it is a form of environmental injustice, of environmental racism. Flint kids already had higher lead levels, just like kids in Detroit, Chicago, Baltimore, and Philadelphia. There kids were already struggling with so many of life's toxicities, so many obstacles to their success.

Academic physicians can have many job descriptions, including clinicians, researchers, educators, mentors, leaders, and advocates. My personal career as a medical educator, pediatrician, and researcher took a sharp turn from caring for one child at a time to suddenly caring for an entire population of children (from medicine to public health). My life took a turn I wasn't expecting, but fortunately my training and background had prepared me for that moment.

I knew that if I was going to make a difference in Flint, I would need science at my side. In an around-the-clock pace, I conducted the research to see if there was more lead in the bodies of our children. The results were heartbreaking and maddening and not surprising. Yes, there was more lead in our water and yes, there was more lead in our children.

Armed with the research, I literally walked out of my clinic, with my white coat on, stood up at a press conference, and shared publicly that our children were in harm's way. I demanded action. Academics do not usually share research at press conferences; research is supposed to be published in journals and presented at professional conferences. However, that peer review process takes a long time, and every minute that went by was a minute too long for Flint kids.

Even as I offered up scientific proof that children were in danger, my science was met with denials and attacks. For a quick minute, I regretted using my voice. I began to second-guess myself. I was scared and sick. I felt defeated and tiny. After all, I was just one person — one doctor — a small, brown, immigrant woman no less, going against powerful forces. I even thought to myself, maybe I should have just minded my own business. It would have been easier to keep my eyes closed and my voice silent. For many women leaders, the sense of "imposter syndrome" can be overwhelming.

Fortunately and fairly quickly, I realized this wasn't about me. Our work in medicine is about people. We need to constantly remind ourselves why we chose this most noble profession, why we went to school for so long (what often seems like forever), and why we wake up in the morning. It's not about the power or prestige or the paycheck; it's about the people whom we are privileged to serve.

Every number in my research was not just a number; it was a child — a child I probably cared for, a child I had taken an oath to protect. Grounding myself in my why — children — gave me the courage to speak out against a system that wanted me to stay quiet.

It took a while, but it was finally our persistence, teamwork, and science that spoke truth to power and helped expose the Flint water crisis. Within weeks, we were back on Great Lakes treated water and since then we have been building and sharing our model public health recovery.

I currently direct the collaborative MSU and Hurley Children's Hospital Pediatric Public Health Initiative (PPHI), a model public health program launched in response to the crisis. Through community and clinical programs, childhood health policy and advocacy, and robust evaluation, the PPHI works with many partners, including Flint's heroic parents and kids, as a center of excellence, with the primary goal of mitigating the impact of the Flint water crisis and serving as a national resource for best practices.

The PPHI is community-involved with the formalized and active PPHI Parent Partners Group and PPHI Youth Advisory Council. Our work is grounded in humble partnership with our community.

In addition to securing competitive grants and disseminating scholarly output, the impact of my work has been translated from academia to practice to policy, reaching children far beyond the city and state. For example, in an effort to address nutrition insecurity, I created a nutrition prescription program at our pediatric clinic that is co-located in a farmer's market. After robust evaluation proving the success of our effort on reducing nutrition insecurity and improving diet, a national nutrition prescription program was included in the 2018 United States Farm Bill. As such, there is now a $25 million national fruit and vegetable prescription program inspired by our work in Flint.

In addition, our work in Flint has shined a spotlight on inequities and injustices that so many children and communities face. The ripple effects of our work include an increased awareness of the ill effects of poor governance, science denial, public health disinvestment, environmental injustice, and systemic inequities. But more than anything, this work has reaffirmed the incredible power that we all have — especially as women physician leaders — to refuse the status quo and to demand better on behalf of our patients.

Wearing Many Hats

Lastly, when I went to medical school dreaming of becoming a doctor, I never thought I would also become an author. A stethoscope at the bedside can diagnose and heal and so can the power of the pen. As the author of the memoir *What the Eyes Don't See: A Story of Crisis, Resistance, and Hope in an American City*, I have witnessed the firsthand ability of storytelling to connect, inspire, and heal.

Medicine has had a long-standing relationship with literature and humanities; storytelling allows us to step into the shoes of others and strengthen our empathy. I have been humbled by the tens of thousands of individuals who have stepped into my shoes and embraced my story — a story that is fundamentally about all of us.

Besides being an author, I remain grounded in all the wonderful hats that we can wear as physician leaders. As my work progresses, I continue to strive to be a competent *researcher* who can use science to make the world a better place, a fearless *advocate* who always fights for my patients and my community, a compassionate *physician* who never loses sight that our patients always come first, a medical *educator* who understands that our impact is multiplicative when training the next generation of physicians, and a *leader* committed to paving the way for future female physician leaders.

Hospitals

"There is no question in my mind that physicians are uniquely positioned to lead healthcare reform and function as healthcare administrations at every level. Open the door and walk through the executive suite of your hospital or organization without fear. You belong there."

– Kathleen Yaremchuk

CHAPTER SEVEN

Life Is Not a Straight Line

By Kathleen Yaremchuk, MD, MSA

WHEN I FINISHED MEDICAL SCHOOL AND BEGAN residency, it never crossed my mind to consider the cost of the diagnostic studies that I ordered for my patients. As a physician, I believed my sole responsibility was to take care of the patient and do what I thought was necessary. It was the "administration's" job to keep the lights burning and deal with the financial aspects of running a hospital.

My career began as a general surgical intern at Cook County Hospital in Chicago, caring for the city's uninsured, where physicians were not concerned with costs of care or the financial aspects of the hospital. I don't think I ever saw an administrator during my tenure. The same was true as an otolaryngology resident at the University of Chicago. Although some patients were insured, we took care of everyone in the Emergency Department, including victims of the "South Side of Chicago Gun and Knife Club."

During rounds or when seeing uninsured patients in clinic, the cost of recommended procedures or the possible turning away of the patient who couldn't pay was not discussed. The "paperwork" under my purview then usually consisted of a consent for surgery and operating room (OR) forms required to board a case.

Following residency, I became a contract physician for the Great Lakes Naval Hospital in Illinois. With military salaries relatively low compared to private or academic practice physicians, the Navy had difficulty recruiting and keeping specialty physicians. I was hired by a physician group in Texas that provided specialty coverage for the military throughout the United States. Once again, I was in an environment that shunned discussion of costs or reimbursement since this was a single-payer system covering all healthcare needs of military retirees, active duty personnel, and their family members.

About this time, the national dialogue started on the rising cost of healthcare in the United States. I became interested in learning more about the infrastructure of hospital administration and researched available degree programs. In 1982, Northwestern University and the University of Chicago offered executive master's degree programs in hospital administration, so I decided to apply to both.

When I received the applications and request for college transcripts and Graduate Management Aptitude Test (GMAT) scores, I recognized how different the academic structures were between business schools and postgraduate training of medical school and residency. The GMAT covered topics far removed from my studies of gross anatomy, physiology, and surgery. To prepare for the GMAT, I enrolled in a review course like other prospective graduate business students.

I was ecstatic when my GMAT results scored in the 94th percentile. With a transcript from the University of Michigan's accelerated six-year Integrated Premedical-Medical Program, I felt confident that I would be accepted at both schools. My only worry was how to decide which program would best serve my future endeavors.

Imagine my surprise when not one but both schools rejected my application. Apparently an application from someone with a medical degree was so unusual that business school admissions offices had no idea how to evaluate the application. I had no recent classes in economics, social studies, or English literature, which was the norm for their other applicants. The fact that an individual in the top 5% of college graduates who had graduated from medical school was likely to successfully complete any graduate degree program was not considered.

Henry Ford Hospital in Detroit recruited me as an otolaryngologist. I had spent my clinical years there during medical school and enjoyed the large multispecialty group practice atmosphere. The Henry Ford Medical Group provided clinical care in the city and suburbs while maintaining an academic mission and commitment to the triad of patient care, education, and research.

Shortly after my arrival at Henry Ford I was appointed Division Head of Otolaryngology at the satellite clinic where I practiced. I hadn't thought much about the title and was actually amused when a secretary congratulated me on the appointment.

The division consisted of two half-time otolaryngologists and me. I didn't feel there was much to manage so the title seemed somewhat meaningless. What I failed to appreciate was that in addition to the otolaryngologists, there were audiologists, medical assistants, clinical service representatives, and hearing aid technicians for whom I was now responsible.

This position allowed me to participate in monthly division head meetings of all clinical departments. The forum discussed management issues and changes occurring within the Henry Ford Medical Group, and gave me exposure to the leadership of the satellite medical center as well as an opportunity to join other committees. By practicing at the site, I established my clinical credibility with patients and other providers.

I believe it is imperative for a medical leader to have a strong, positive reputation in their field of clinical practice. The commitment to patients and clinical expertise is used as an indicator of commitment to the institution and its mission. Time and again, my reputation as a clinician has been a guiding force in my administrative success.

The Henry Ford Hospital began in 1915 when Henry Ford bought the hospital from the city of Detroit for one dollar. The city administration lacked funds to complete the hospital and was glad to have the industrialist take it off of their hands.

Mr. Ford visited Johns Hopkins and the Mayo Clinic to better understand how to proceed with his vision of "the best hospital the city has seen." He readily acknowledged his lack of experience in building or running a hospital. He found he liked the multispecialty group practice clinic model of the Mayo Clinic and admired the educational rigor of Johns Hopkins, so he hired a surgeon from Johns Hopkins to become the first chief of staff of Henry Ford Hospital. The multispecialty group practice built then is now the Henry Ford Medical Group with more than 1,800 physicians and scientists.

When I joined Henry Ford Medical Group, the group employed 350 physicians and an equal number of residents and fellows. In metropolitan Detroit, the Henry Ford Medical Group pioneered the development of suburban ambulatory clinics that would provide care and direct admissions to the 900-bed tertiary care Henry Ford Hospital within the city.

Over time, an integrated delivery system developed, evolving into the Henry Ford Health System with acquisitions of an insurance company, several suburban hospitals, existing group practices, nursing homes, and home healthcare providers.

Expanding Experiences

For me, this growth provided exposure to areas of healthcare delivery different from my experience as a clinician. Moreover, a large organization like the Henry Ford Health System was able to offer its employees various educational opportunities.

In an employee newsletter, I discovered that Central Michigan University (CMU) offered a Master of Science in Administration (MSA) program with a core curriculum similar to postgraduate education in hospital administration. Meanwhile, our medical group's board of governors decided that a key strategy for future success was to develop a career path for physician leaders with an associated educational process.

I was halfway through the MSA at CMU when word of my participation in the program reached the chief medical officer of our medical group. I was invited to chair the Physicians Leadership Development Council, giving me access to all physicians in our large medical group who were interested in medical management.

Concurrently, my responsibilities as division head in otolaryngology-head and neck surgery grew as I demonstrated competence in the role of an administrator. I was named medical director for specialty services at the satellite medical center where I practiced. This gave me responsibility for 14 medical and specialty divisions and the ambulatory surgery center. I determined salaries and oversaw performance reviews, budget development, and implementation of new programs in a collaborative, matrix management process with the chairs of the academic departments. I thrived on improving services and solving problems. It was important to involve physicians in their practice and have them understand how to balance the budget.

There couldn't have been a better place for me than Henry Ford Health System. The concept of a vertically integrated health system that was being discussed nationally was actually being built in Detroit.

Serving Patients as a Hospital Administrator

After nine years of managing physicians, an opportunity arose as part of a joint venture with Henry Ford to become vice president of medical affairs (VPMA) at a 268-bed hospital in an impoverished area of Detroit. Here was a chance for on-the-job training in hospital administration. In this role I also served as medical director for five primary care clinics.

The hospital and primary care clinics faced the typical daunting problems associated with an inner city, including poverty, poor health status, high unemployment, and crime. The patient population served was largely Medicaid and Medicare with financial losses of $18 million the year I assumed the position.

As VP, I was responsible for hospital activities such as credentialing, utilization management, quality assurance, and Joint Commission for Accreditation of Healthcare Organization (JCAHO) standards. The ambulatory clinics had 250,000 patient visits annually and a budget of $10 million. Like many, I believe that problems can be opportunities. I regarded the problems here as potential learning opportunities. Moreover, I knew that by successfully solving these problems, my reputation as a "change agent" would be set.

The medical staff at the hospital was composed of minority and international graduates. Some questioned how a white female surgical specialist from the suburbs would fit into such a diverse environment. The title of VPMA did not ensure acceptance by the medical staff. I knew I would have to "walk the talk" to make converts.

My predecessors had been full-time administrators who never admitted or treated patients, so they were viewed with mistrust. I made it a point to conduct a clinic in the hospital, operate on patients, and take call for emergencies. This gave me access to the emergency department, operating rooms (OR), and hospital inpatient units. These are places where poor management and performance can cause exceptionally large problems in a hospital.

It did not take long for the grapevine to convey that I was a working VP. Influential members of the medical staff would talk to me on the inpatient units or in the OR lounge. If anything earns respect in a hospital, it is working shoulder to shoulder with the medical staff.

Seeking Small Victories

Over the course of two years, I learned about the politics of community hospitals and the issues of building a committed medical staff. I sought small victories by looking into areas with little or no resistance to change. I introduced critical pathways to the hospital by being a champion and discussing the subject with those influential physicians with whom I had built relationships.

Much like the military, it is difficult to recruit medical specialists to an urban facility. I discovered that the only neurologist on staff who would see our ambulatory patients was writing unnecessary prescriptions for narcotics. He would then ask the patients to return to his office after getting their medication at the pharmacy, ostensibly to make sure the prescription had been filled correctly. He would find an "error" and take the drugs from the patient. Because the patients did not pay for their medications, they were thankful for the so-called oversight. A nurse in my clinic tipped me to the scheme, and after an investigation I had to terminate the physician.

Another unfortunate experience involved a physician with the highest volume of admissions to the hospital. As the physician for multiple nursing homes, he would admit patients to our hospital, but never round on them, instead allowing his nurse to direct their care.

After documenting this physician's inappropriate care and charting irregularities, I suggested that the hospital CEO terminate his privileges. Unfortunately, that didn't happen and, as a result, I resigned from my position. When I received a call from the FBI and later read that this physician had been convicted of Medicare fraud, I knew that my education in hospital administration was complete.

Although ethically I had done what was right, raising that red flag ultimately caused problems in my career advancement. For several years afterward, my career stalled. I applied for positions and was never selected. I finally asked for an interview with the chief medical officer. Although the meeting was cordial, it was clear that there were "issues." It was an educational experience for me. I learned that by rocking the boat, I now had "baggage" and was perceived as a "difficult" person to work with.

Reinventing Myself

That meeting made it clear to me that I needed to reinvent myself within the institution. I found an opportunity as a medical director for an insurance company owned by Henry Ford Health System. It was a great position that allowed me to continue my clinical work while earning credits in "Insurance 101." I was introduced into the process of concurrent review for inpatients, prior authorization of procedures, and medical necessity versus patient preference.

Through concurrent review, I recognized that most hospitals function five days a week, yet charge the same inpatient rates for seven days a week. Most interventions occur during week days. Patients admitted toward the end of the week usually had to wait over the weekend for their procedures. The irony is that they were too ill to go home, but well enough to wait a few days for a necessary procedure. In my view, it seems that hospitals should charge, and insurance companies should pay, different rates for weekdays versus weekends.

The process of prior authorization was another eye opener. I would request a physician's records to determine the evaluation that preceded the decision to perform a procedure and receive a one word illegible note from the physician with a medical assistant's assessment of the chief complaint. I was surprised that the physician would charge for an office visit with such cursory office notes.

It was also apparent that direct-to-consumer advertising for procedures and medications was driving up the cost of care. When a maternity patient wanted an "underwater delivery" that she'd heard was better for the newborn, she demanded an out-of-state referral.

My response was a resounding denial of the request. While the consumer may feel that the delivery of her newborn into a whirlpool bath is a kinder way to come into this world, that is considered "patient preference," not "medical necessity."

As an active member of the Academy of Otolaryngology-Head and Neck Surgery (AAO-HNS), I had the opportunity to be appointed to the National Committee for Quality Assurance (NCQA) Practicing Physician Advisory Committee. This introduced me to the world of quality in healthcare — probably the single best use of my time with payback in ways I never could have imagined.

Several times a year in my role as physician surveyor for NCQA and member of the Review Oversight Committee, I traveled to health plans around the country, evaluating their performance on quality and service — two important areas in healthcare.

My time with NCQA helped me in my otolaryngology roles. I recently received a national award from the AAO-HNS for my community service associated with quality and have been named chair of the Advisory Council of Quality for the AAO/HNS.

My expanded experience in insurance, quality, and clinical care also helped me grow within the Henry Ford Health System. I became involved in the pay-for-performance insurance movement and Centers of Excellence designations. Within the Henry Ford Medical Group, I became the knowledge expert, negotiated with insurance companies, and submitted applications to regulatory agencies. Success begets success as I was recognized as someone with a unique skill set.

Added to my role then as vice chair of the Department of Otolaryngology in the medical group, I became vice president for clinical practice performance for the health system. This new VP title was actually one that I created to reflect the combination of quality metrics and cost effectiveness that payers were evaluating.

It was a bold move to develop a position and job description for something that never before existed. Acceptance of my proposal by the chief medical officer of the medical group was a significant learning moment: Look at who you want to be and what you want to do, and the rest is history!

Some suggest that I continue to take on "titles" and am involved in more things than most people can remember. I regard this as part of my nature, to be a learner. In each new role, I give what I have gleaned from every past position and continue to learn more. Nothing in life stands still, so as an individual, an administrator, or a physician, we need to continue to grow, changing what we do to stay relevant and provide a unique service.

I had never considered my future to be a chair of a department. In 2008, after our chair of otolaryngology moved to another institution, a search committee appointed by the chief medical officer and executive vice president of the Henry Ford Medical Group was set up to choose the next chairperson.

I was suddenly faced with the dilemma of applying for the chair position or watching someone else assume the role. Ultimately, I submitted my letter of interest along with 14 applicants from around the country. I wanted the most competent individual for the position to be selected and while I hoped to be the committee's choice, I decided that whomever they selected would be appropriate.

During the selection process, I was appointed interim chair for otolaryngology. I moved to the "corner office" and dealt with issues of the department while also serving in my role as vice chair of clinical practice performance and practicing clinically.

After a year, I was officially offered the position of chair of the Department of Otolaryngology-Head & Neck Surgery at Henry Ford Hospital. When I assumed the role, we had six otolaryngologists in the department.

Since then, we have expanded to 24 physicians and added the divisions of oral maxillofacial surgery and hospital dentistry, and built three new clinics with two additional ones on the horizon for 2022. All of this in the face of COVID.

An urban legend suggested that it is impossible to recruit professionals to Detroit because of its poor economic climate and bad reputation. Obviously, to recruit new otolaryngologists willing to commit their professional careers to the institution, the draw must be a world-class department. In the beginning, someone likened my tenacious recruiting efforts to that of a "rabid bulldog," but my persistence paid off. I now have people sending me their curriculum vitaes and approaching me for positions.

The phrase "timing is everything" holds true as well. In 2008, when I assumed the chair position, the economy was tanking, and Detroit had the dubious distinction of being the largest city to declare bankruptcy. As part of the financial restructuring, or "grand bargain," the city began rebuilding and changing its reputation. The city central became the "go-to" place for young people; now half of the staff and residents call it home. Another way to think of it is, "never let a crisis go to waste." For the city of Detroit, it was an opportunity to reinvent itself.

Within the 117 otolaryngology-head and neck surgery academic departments, or departments with residency positions, there are only six female department chairs. When I finished residency, 98.5% of the specialty was male. Currently over 50% of medical students are female and more than a third of otolaryngology residents are female.

However, there is still a hurricane-grade glass ceiling within the specialty for females. Of all medical or surgical specialties, the gender income gap is greatest in otolaryngology. I believe some of that is due to the difference in promotion to professor, chairman, and other leadership roles the salary gap plays itself out. Being from Detroit, I joke that all of the otolaryngology female chairs can still meet in a sedan and have not grown into an SUV to seat a quorum.

When we interview medical students for residency positions, it is an interesting dynamic. I believe a disproportionate number of females submit applications to our institution because we have a female chair and half of the faculty physicians are female.

Stars and Deal Breakers

As I recruit new residents and staff, I am committed to making each one a "star" within our specialty. My job is to help them be as successful as possible while furthering the reputation and goals of the department. It is a win-win from my perspective. To have a world class department, recruiting is incredibly important.

I had learned from my daughter, who was in human resources at Amazon, that it is not luck that gets you to increased stature. She shared with me that at Amazon, everyone interviews with five people — four are cohorts in the area and one is the "deal breaker." The deal breaker does not interact with the person being hired and has a more objective view of the candidate. If the initial four individuals in the department give favorable reviews to hire, the deal breaker can still disagree and their decision stands. The candidate does not get the position. The deal breaker uses the lens to view the new hire based on two questions: Are you better than the last person we hired and what skill do you bring to the team that we currently don't have?

Early on, I was desperate and went the route of the "warm body." The applicant was a board-certified otolaryngologist. When I started asking the two additional questions, I got a whole different set of applicants. They had the "fire in the belly" and the energy to do more than what is usually asked of them. The national reputation of the department has grown.

I explain our success in basketball terms. If LeBron James is the only star playing on your team, the team can only go so far. On the other hand, if you have a team of talented individuals who watch each other's backs and have goals that constantly change to achieve greatness, the sky is the limit.

I am the first to admit that I am not the star of the team. Rather, I coach and support talented individuals by giving them the substrate to grow and achieve their success. It is similar to the saying, "build it and they will come."

Several years ago, during an annual review by the CEO of the medical group, I was called on the carpet for going above his head regarding an issue I thought was unfair and detrimental to my department. I was essentially told that my chair position was at risk.

It was a beautiful Friday evening in August when I walked out feeling fairly dejected. I had grown the department, been recognized nationally, yet I was seeing the handwriting on the wall. I could have accepted the feedback and taken a less-active position to comply with the review. I considered the review unfair and thought about who was responsible for the job performance of the CEO of the medical group. It was the chair of the board of governors (BOG) for the medical group.

I called the current BOG chair and asked about the process to attain that position. It turns out, I had missed the deadline to submit the letter of interest, but he would make an exception. To make a long story short, I submitted the letter and won the election to become the first female chair of the board of governors.

In an ironic twist of fate, shortly thereafter, the CEO announced his retirement, so my initial reason for taking the position fell by the wayside. When I assumed the position, I was the only voting female member of the board of governors.

I never regretted becoming chair of the BOG. It has allowed me to pave the way for gender equity within the medical group and in leadership search committees. My platform has become one for underrepresented in medicine minorities and women. Recently, I started a list of individuals who have contacted me to ask advice on how to move forward in their careers, break through the glass ceiling and enjoy the journey.

This past year I submitted my name to the American Academy of Otolaryngology/Head & Neck Surgery (AAO/HNS) as a candidate for president. There is a fair amount of paperwork and due diligence that needs to be done before candidates are selected. I reached out to the current president to get his opinion of whether I was a worthy candidate. He was a friend, colleague, and we had served on the AAO/HNS Board of Directors together. He assured me that I was qualified and I submitted the necessary forms and releases.

In January, I noted a typo in an email from the AAO/HNS and I contacted the executive vice president to mention the error. I almost didn't send the email because I thought contacting the EVP for this was "below his pay grade."

He responded that he had taken care of the typo and mentioned that he was surprised I had not submitted my name for the president position. I was stunned, found the email with the attachments and sent it to him. He immediately texted me and asked that I call him. He reported that my application had "fallen through the cracks" and had not been forwarded to the nominating committee. He asked if it was ok with me that he send it as a separate attachment to the nominating committee with an explanation that I had followed the rules, but due to an internal snafu, it had not been included with the other candidate profiles.

Ultimately, I was selected as one of two candidates to run for president and ended up winning the election. I often think that if I had not noticed the typo, my candidacy and election would never have happened.

It is important to be passionate about your work and find joy in what you do. It's equally important to be able to invigorate those around you to be the best they can be. I am now in the mentoring, sponsorship, and "road plow" mode for women of all clinical specialties within my institution. I am also mentoring women within otolaryngology to assume chair and leadership positions.

Lessons Learned

A prime lesson in the field of medicine is to develop a passion for a particular area of clinical medicine and medical management, and accept opportunities to learn and treat them as tools in your toolbox. You never know where these paths lead. Most important, to build a positive reputation means to do the work, show up for meetings, contribute to discussions, and volunteer for assignments. Combining present knowledge with future learning will only add to your leadership skills.

I have also learned that others' perceptions of you can make or break your future career advancement. If this happens or you seem to have reached a "dead end" in your career, figure out a way to add new tools to your toolbox and then move forward. This sometimes means reaching outside of your current employment to professional organizations or societies.

There are always new ideas and analytic approaches to dealing with the healthcare system. By keeping yourself on the cutting edge, not only will there be opportunities to make yourself invaluable to your own institution, but to other healthcare organizations as well.

Finally, it is important to communicate your goals. The meeting before the meeting is the most important groundwork that can be laid to assure success. When the answer to a new idea appears to be "no," ask the question, "What would it take to make it happen?"

Personally, I have raised three children who have all launched successful careers. They were present when I received an endowed chair from Henry Ford Health System and a national award from the AAO/HNS. They recognize my contribution to medicine and are proud of their mother.

As many people do now, I met my current husband through an online dating app. He is a computer science PhD, who retired and owned a magic shop. Life is not a straight line and you never know where your interests will take you. Looking back, I would not have done anything differently.

There is no question in my mind that physicians are uniquely positioned to lead healthcare reform and function as healthcare administrators at every level. Open the door and walk through the executive suite of your hospital or organization without fear. You belong there.

CHAPTER EIGHT

Life Is a Series of Useful Lessons

By Patricia A. Gabow, MD

 IN 2012, JUST AS I WAS ABOUT TO ANNOUNCE my retirement as CEO of Denver Health, I received the invitation to update the original 1995 monograph *Women in Medical Management: A Mentoring Guide.* That update (*Lessons Learned: Stories from Women in Medical Management*) provided an opportunity for me to reflect on all the events, people, attitudes, and beliefs that helped shape my entire career.

I realized then that there are no major differences in the guiding principles of my personal and professional lives. The previous editions and this new one allow me to pass on the advice I have derived from many good and wise people over the years and share the lessons they taught. Moreover, now that I have spent the last nine years in retirement, I will add some new thoughts about what I call "my coda."

Because these lessons were not read from a book or taught in a class, they underscore that the first step to success is to seek friends and mentors from whom you can learn at every point in your life — nothing else will serve you so well both as a person and as a professional.

I decided to name the people who helped me as a kind of tribute to each of them. Some of them may have thought I was not particularly attentive to the lessons while they were being taught, and there is more than a grain of truth in that. Sometimes, I failed to follow the advice when it was given, and some lessons have "sunk in" slowly.

Nonetheless, having these lessons has been invaluable and it is in that spirit that I share them.

Although we cannot choose our families, we all know that they have an enormous influence on our futures. I was very fortunate to have an exceptional and warm extended family who taught me most of the important lessons for success.

My grandparents came to this country from Italy in the early 1900s. Both my grandfathers arrived as adolescents — alone and with nothing. Their experiences inspired me and taught me not to be afraid to take a risk. My mother reinforced this willingness to accept risk, encouraging me to attend medical school — something virtually unheard of in the rural Italian immigrant community in which I grew up. This reinforcement or restating of a lesson has been a common occurrence; wise people often seem to espouse similar philosophies.

My maternal grandfather was a wonderfully wise, peasant philosopher with insights into all aspects of life. He had an array of old sayings that embodied long-held truths. Let me share one that greatly influenced me from childhood through this day: "If you have a gift and you don't use it, no confessor on earth can absolve you." Hearing this repeatedly ingrained in me the concept that any talents a person has carry with them the obligation to use them in service.

More than 30 years later, Dr. Samuel Thier, another mentor, taught the same lesson. He believed that medicine was a learned profession in which practitioners are given valued information from the previous generation that we are to use, enrich, and pass on to the next generation without undue rewards. Lesson: Use your talents in service.

Using Your Gifts

My parents taught me that natural gifts and talents require hard work to be brought to fruition. In my school days, this was translated into "If you have the ability to get an A by working very hard, a B with minimal work is not acceptable." Lesson: Always do your absolute best.

My mother taught me another valuable lesson while I was in grade school. My school was in a rural area of Pennsylvania, and many children in my class were so poor, they often came to school day after day in the same dirty clothes. My mother, who was a schoolteacher, reached out to everyone, especially these children, putting into action what she told me: "Be nice to everyone, especially the poor children." Lesson: Reach out to everyone.

I have seen people in leadership positions, often physicians and academicians, who consider themselves above the crowd and deserving of different treatment than housekeepers, food service people, clerks, etc. This class mentality does not serve a leader well. This lesson, displayed at Denver Health in work and deed by so many employees so many times over many years, may be the single most important reason I have spent my entire academic career in a safety net healthcare system.

Still another lesson came from the older generation of women in my extended Italian family. By today's standards, they had tough lives. They had very large families; they did all the work themselves — the cooking, cleaning, washing, canning — on and on. I can't remember my paternal grandmother ever going on vacation or ever being taken out to dinner. My father was killed in World War II, and it was many years before my mother remarried. None of these women ever complained or were morose or bitter. In fact, they had great joy for life. Lesson: Don't whine — look at the good things in your situation. My grandfather had a saying that took this life view one step further: "Not everything bad happens to harm you."

Understanding the Truth

Sister Florence Marie Scott was my mentor during my four college years at a Catholic girls' school where, at least in those days, every class started with a prayer chosen by the teacher. Head of the biology department, Sister Florence, began every class with a prayer that ended, " . . . grant that I may understand the truth, and, when I understand the truth, fire me with the courage to use it."

As you enter leadership positions, you will confront difficult problems. In these instances, it is critical to try your best to understand the truth and not just accept what you'd like to hear. Leadership positions at any level tend to be addictive; you like the role. It becomes difficult to be willing to put the job (or for that matter, advancement to the next job) on the line by defending with vigor and zeal a position that you see as true, but is unpopular.

In some sense, I have come to believe people who have leadership positions should be those who don't want to keep them at any cost. These leaders feel free to make the right decisions even if it could cost them their jobs.

Sister Florence also reinforced the concept of risk taking. In those days, when nuns wore habits and were largely confined to convents, Sister was on the board of directors of the Marine Biological Laboratories in Woods Hole (the first and only woman at the time— let alone the only nun!). She spent every summer doing her research there. In this environment, she remained a nun—right down to wading in the water to collect specimens with her habit tucked around her legs. This sent a very loud and clear message: a woman can succeed in a man's world without changing who or what she is.

Medical school and housestaff training brought many mentors and lessons and much advice, but I will focus on two special mentors: Dr. Samuel Schrier, head of the housestaff program, and Dr. Arnold Relman, chief of medicine. They gave the same, very clear message: set high standards for people you supervise, and they will work to meet those standards. In a leadership role, clearly stating those standards and goals sets the tone for everyone in an institution and tells your employees you believe in their abilities.

Being the Best

I clearly remember another lesson taught by Dr. Relman. One day, making rounds, he said, "There are many forces conspiring to kill the patient; the doctor should not be one of them." Of course, no one was actually trying to kill the patient. The reference was about always giving the best care — no short cuts.

In a time when marketplace forces frequently result in healthcare institutions focusing on profits and not primarily on the best interests of the patient, this lesson must especially be embraced by physician executives. We have a professional obligation not shared by other non-clinical executives.

The corollary to Dr. Relman's lesson was to be the best physician you can be. From my perspective, being a good doctor may be the best possible training for being a healthcare executive—the operating principles are the same. To solve a problem, as in treating a patient, you need to make a diagnosis, develop a treatment plan, implement it, monitor the outcome, and change the treatment and/or rethink the diagnosis if you're not getting the response you expect. Sometimes, in both medicine and administration, you have to start out simply treating a symptom, but you shouldn't be fooled into thinking that the symptom is the disease.

When I was chief of medicine, I told the housestaff that it only took a few things to be a great house officer: listening to the patient, caring about the patient, being compulsive about getting the needed data, and being able to pick up the phone and ask for help when you need it. The same applies to being a good administrator, except instead of the patient, you need to listen to the people in the institution, care about its well-being, use data, and ask for help from your team and colleagues

When I started my working life at Denver Health and Hospitals and the University of Colorado School of Medicine, I was fortunate to have committed and exceptional mentors. From Dr. Schrier at the University, I learned to "hang in there." An example of this tenacity was his efforts to get a cigarette tax on the state's ballot to help pay for healthcare for the poor. He worked tirelessly on this for eight years. He responded to each failed attempt with a new strategy, and finally Colorado did get a cigarette tax which has provided many millions of dollars to healthcare in the state.

So the lesson is, if something is important to do, keep trying until you achieve it. In leading large, complex institutions, this is critical, because they change very slowly and with great difficulty. Persistence and long vision are necessary for success.

Watching Dr. Schrier recruit over many years, I learned another important lesson: surround yourself with the smartest and best people you can. People in leadership positions may feel threatened by those who are smarter or more talented than they are. This is a mistake. Having the best people on your team only makes you and your team better.

Another of his lessons was about pushing yourself. Many times, during the early days of my academic career, when I didn't want to try something new, such as starting a research lab or applying for a grant, I'd hear the message, "If you don't stretch, you won't grow."

The last lesson I learned from Dr. Schrier was about praising people. This goes beyond the pat on the back and the thank you note. Let me give you one example. When I was promoted to associate professor, Dr. Schrier wrote my parents a letter! My mother never forgot that. Personal caring like this creates a loyalty and esprit de corps on a team that is hard to beat. (Parenthetically, this is a recurrence of my mother's message about reaching out.)

Dr. Sbarbaro, my mentor at Denver Health and Hospitals, taught me two lessons when I first became chief of medicine: only touch the same piece of paper once (now you can translate that to if you read and email, answer it!) and don't be afraid to make decisions. He went on to say that if you never make a decision, you'll never make a good one. On the other hand, if you aren't afraid to make decisions, at least some of them will be right.

To succeed in this fast-paced life, you need to make as many decisions as are feasible on round one, move on, and don't agonize later. If the decision is wrong, learn from it, but don't wring your hands over it. This principle is another one that has strong grounding in the practice of medicine and its teaching tool, the mortality and morbidity (M&M) conference.

As chief of medicine, I always told the housestaff that they must expect to make some mistakes, but they should not make the same mistake twice. The M&M conference teaches that it is healthy to put those mistakes on the table and discuss them. We, in fact, did some administrative M&M conferences, and I think physician administrators should use this tool more often.

Dr. Sbarbaro taught me another important lesson: You can have a knockdown, drag out disagreement about an issue with someone, walk away, and not be mad — disagreeing about a matter is not a personal attack by you or on you.

Equally important to the lessons learned from mentors and colleagues are lessons learned from my husband and children. One cannot be guaranteed a wonderful spouse, but I have had this blessing. I cannot overestimate the professional accomplishments that have been made possible by having a stable and happy marriage. There are commonalities to this human relationship and your institutional relationships.

Many people move from one institution to another as a means of advancing their careers. Although this is a valid path, being at one institution for an entire career is not unlike having one husband — you really get to know and care about the institution in a very special way. For me, starting as an entry-level physician straight out of fellowship and moving through the system has been invaluable. You know the system from the bottom up, with all its strengths and quirks. Even more important, you know the people in the institution and in the community. You can be a family.

My husband, Hal, taught me that when you're uncertain about something, always assume the best. This especially applies to people. If you are fortunate enough to have children, they will teach more valuable lessons about administration than probably any other teachers — such great truths as don't nag, don't take yourself too seriously, don't sweat the small stuff, don't play favorites, one "bad" action doesn't mean someone is a "bad" person, put some sugar in the medicine, and give lots of hugs and kisses (figuratively, of course).

Finally, their admonition I like best of all is "get a life" — which, I think, means to see the big picture, get out of your little world. Or maybe it doesn't mean that. This, of course, is a critical point; you have to learn to live comfortably with ambiguity.

In addition to this long litany of what I have been taught by others, I actually think I learned one thing on my own (although, if I think about it for a while, probably someone taught it to me too). As I moved in my career from head of the renal division to chief of medicine to deputy manager to chief executive officer of Denver Health and Hospitals, it became apparent that my vision had to change for each new level of position. The higher you move in an organization, the broader your vision must become and the longer view into the future you must take. This is, in fact, the thrill of leadership.

In 2012, I found that the opportunity to continue to reflect on my career and its lessons was very timely. In 1995, when I first wrote about my transition from clinician to medical manager, I was at the beginning of my leadership career. With this latest update, I am nine years past the formal end of that career and have gained additional insights.

Four Decades, Four Lessons

When I retired, I had been at Denver Health for almost 40 years, was CEO for 20 years, and saw age 70 in my not too distant future. With these years of added perspective, I still affirm all of the leadership lessons I wrote about in 1995 and 2012. I have lived them and used them over more than four decades and they have stood the test of time. I will underscore four of them.

1. There are many lessons to be learned from wise people—some family and some strangers, some younger and some older, and some physicians and some politicians. No matter what your age or your experience, never stop listening to those who can teach and inspire.

2. If you have some success as a leader and have an opportunity to provide influence, try to understand the truth and have the courage to say what must be said.

3. Remember the words of one of my mentors, Dr. Relman: "As physician executives, we are here first and foremost for the patients, not to enrich ourselves or our organizations."

4. My grandfather always reminded me that patience is a virtue — it is also a necessity for leaders. Few, if any meaningful accomplishments happen quickly. Transitioning Denver Health from a department of city government to an independent entity was more than a five-year journey with twists and turns. The effort was transformational; stopping at some turn would have cost Denver Health its future.

Embedding Toyota Production Systems or Lean into Denver Health and reaping the benefits was a multiyear journey. Yet, it too was transformational and stopping at some barrier would also have cost Denver Health's its future. Over time, as efforts reach fruition, the barriers seem to fade from one's memory and only the accomplishment stays vivid. (I suspect this is a particular quirk of the lens of time.) Take on the hard tasks and see them through to the end.

While these lessons from my early years remain guideposts, the later years also added new ones that relate directly to leading a large and complex organization.

One of the main obligations of a leader is to create a vision for the organization—a vision that inspires, a vision that is good and noble, a vision that imparts to all employees the belief that they can do great things. During my leadership at Denver Health, our vision was to be a model for the nation — both audacious and good at a time when our country sorely needed models (and it still does). The vision for an organization must be transformed into a path of actions that the leader and those she/he leads can walk.

Leaders of large enterprises must put out many fires every day. Without a path to walk to a greater end, it is easy to feel frustrated, beleaguered, and burned out. It is this advancement — no matter how small — along the path to achieve vision that gives the work joy. Leaders, like parents, must walk the path they espouse. They must be role models in their professional and personal lives; they must do what they want and expect of others and avoid doing what they do not want others to do. Leaders must commit to organizational transparency and openness. Information is power and it needs to be shared.

In 2012, I wrote that the hardest lesson for a leader must be knowing when to leave. I cannot say I learned it; I can only say I made that decision. But I know deciding to leave my leadership position and Denver Health pulled at my heart strings. Perhaps, in the end, truly loving your institution and loving what you do every day, is what it means to be a leader.

My Coda

Like many people of my vintage, I find that "retirement" doesn't really capture the rhythm or activity of the phase of life that follows the period of being an organizational leader. Although I used the term "retirement" in 2012 when I was ending my time as CEO of Denver Health, I now think that "coda" better captures the last nine years.

The dictionary defines coda as "something that serves to round out, conclude, or summarize and usually has its own interest." Each of these components has been realized for me during this time. While they represent both maturing of past efforts or new areas of focus, all the lessons that I articulated previously remain relevant for me now.

And I continue to pass on these lessons to others. Prime among these lessons was my grandfather's saying, "If you have a gift and you don't use it no confessor on earth can absolve you." When we leave our position as an organizational leader our gifts don't vanish. In fact, our coda period may give us the time to use them more.

Fulfilling the definition of coda, I have rounded out my career through four activities: board service, writing, lecturing, and mentoring. I have been privileged to serve on several boards, including the Robert Wood Johnson Board of Trustees and the Lown Institute Board, where I am now chair. This has enabled me to continue to think about health and healthcare and to interact with smart, concerned, and committed people.

I have written two books that served to summarize much of the learning and experiences I described in the previous editions. *The Lean Prescription: Powerful Medicine for Our Ailing Healthcare System* (2015) detailed the principles and essentials of Lean (Toyota Production Systems) and the Lean transformation that my team led at Denver Health. Most recently, I published *TIME'S NOW for Women Healthcare Leaders: A Guide for the Journey* to pay forward to the next generation of women all the guidance others had given me as well as my own learnings.

These books and my interest in the social determinants of health have afforded opportunities to speak to different audiences, teaching them and learning from them. This has been so rewarding, I am starting my third book.

As I look at healthcare today, I have many concerns about where it is and where it is heading. One has to be dismayed by the fact that we spend twice as much as other developed countries but have poorer health for our population. The continued melding of big business with healthcare through for-profit and private-equity acquisitions raises urgent questions about how these fit with the long-held core value of putting the patients' interest above our own.

The coda period for me indeed has had its own interests, which blossomed with the newly found free time. My husband and I have hiked, soaked up the culture, and enjoyed the food in most of the European countries—what a privilege. The newfound time has provided opportunity for spiritual growth and reflection. I am now in the fourth year of a bible study course and have discovered the solace of daily meditation.

But this time has also made it clear that there is a conclusion, a very real coda both to institutional leadership as well as to each of our lives. If you have spent many years leading an institution, as I have done, it is difficult to no longer influence its culture and decisions. This feels like a loss. As a reality of life's coda, we have lost both sets of parents and many dear aunts and uncles. But my husband and I have been blessed to be together and to see our two children become admirable adults and to have married wonderful spouses. This has added much joy to this life period.

Any physician who has traveled the path of learner, practitioner, and leader and has lived to have a coda period has indeed experienced a priceless treasure. I am grateful to have been one of those.

CHAPTER NINE

Be Yourself, Everyone Else Is Already Taken

— OSCAR WILDE

By Jayne McCormick, BSN, MD, MBA

"There are no constraints on the human mind, no walls around the human spirit, no barriers to our progress except those we ourselves erect."
— RONALD REAGAN

I'VE ALWAYS WANTED TO BE A DOCTOR. When I was young, I always watched the doctor shows on TV. I loved Chad Everett on "Medical Center"! My personal barrier was that I hated school. A recurring challenge for me, as I have come to realize, is that I get bored easily and, as the expression goes, I don't "suffer fools gladly."

My parents wanted me to have a good Catholic education. I hated it. A bunch of well-meaning women who were never trained to teach, had poor relationship skills, and provided poor role models. No intellectual stimulation. My first challenge and lesson: fight for what you want. Don't be complacent, especially about your education. I campaigned one whole summer and talked my parents into letting me go to public junior high. I was the first in my family to do this. That was my first big achievement.

Public school was better. By 12th grade I was bored again, so I talked myself into becoming a nurse, even though I really wanted to be a doctor. I figured four more years was all I could stand. So initially, I was erecting my own barriers. Some of us like to do things the hard (and long) way. I'm certainly one of those people. So instead of taking eight years to get to the end of medical school, it eventually took me 13.

Mabel was my first role model. Mabel was my grandmother and about the only medical person in my family. Business careers are big in my family. She was a nurse in 1910, during a time when very few women had careers. One Memorial Day, as we visited my grandfather's grave, she told me she had been tending that grave for over 50 years.

I had a huge "aha" moment: she had been a widow longer than she had been married. The fact that she had a successful career during an era when most women were housewives that allowed her to remain independent and provide for her family made me realize that I should never depend on anyone else to provide for me. I had to be self-reliant and find a reliable career for myself.

She was an incredibly strong woman. She was the one everyone admired and looked up to and called if they were ill or had a problem. Mabel persevered till age 95. She was a huge influence on me.

BARRIER: LACK OF ROLE MODELS AND CHALLENGES

"The strongest principle of growth lies in human choice."
— GEORGE ELIOT

Looking back now, I don't regret taking the longer path through nursing. It was a great five years. The experience gave me a nursing perspective that as a healthcare leader I now find invaluable. Nurses are our frontline and I have walked in their shoes.

Initially, I loved medicine and taking care of patients. I worked in a burn unit and fell in love with the multidisciplinary team approach. Surgical residents rotated through the unit making major decisions about patient care. I realized that I wanted to have more influence on my patients' care. It was a critical care unit; we also staffed our own operating room. I fell in love with the comradery of the OR and the excitement of critical care.

After a year or two, however, I realized nursing wasn't satisfying enough for me. Even though I had already started my master's in nursing, I wanted to be more involved with creating treatment plans and making decisions. I also felt a void of having no mentors whom I could relate to in nursing.

A surgery resident unknowingly made a huge impact on my life while we rode on a ski lift one day. He advised me against going to medical school and on to a surgical residency. He told me the work would be too hard. His implication: a woman wouldn't make it. The gauntlet was thrown down! Challenge accepted; decision made.

BARRIERS: TIME AND STEREOTYPES
AGE IS NO BARRIER

*"Don't presume to tell me what I will and
will not do. You don't know me."*
— TITANIC

Another hurdle: I had to go back to school before I could even apply to medical school. You would think that nursing school would have been great preparation. Unfortunately, I had to go back and take classes in physics, calculus, organic chemistry, and English. I decided if I did well and persevered, it would be an omen that I should go on to medical school. So while my friends were all getting married and starting families, I went back to undergraduate school. About that time, I realized I was becoming pretty driven.

I remember an earlier discussion with some of my high school girlfriends who all had big career plans. They were shocked that I wouldn't consider marrying a manager of McDonald's. They thought I was a snob. I wasn't; I just didn't realize yet that if I married, I wanted someone who would respect me and whom I would totally respect. A good career was extremely important to me and I wanted my husband to have a strong one as well. I wanted us to be equals.

Again, self-reliance is an important value for me and has been part of my success. Interestingly enough, none of those friends focus on their careers now. They have chosen to focus on family. I believed then, as now, that you could have both and be satisfied with both.

*"I don't believe you have to be better than
everybody else. I believe you have to be better
than you ever thought you could be."*
— KEN VENTURI

It was difficult to pick up and leave my friends to go back to school full time, but I loved the intellectual challenge of medical school. Dating, however, was tough. The guys were pretty intimidated that I wanted to be a surgeon. My ambition didn't go too well with their egos. Interestingly, the other students thought I was so old. I was a whole five years older.

Even though in the late 1980s, 40% of my medical school class was female, there were no women role models on the faculty. In fact, my surgery chairman told me that women shouldn't go into surgery. Oh my God! It was like waving a red cape in front of me again! No way would I back down now.

Would you believe that when I went to interview for residency positions, one of the male physician interviewers asked me if I had ever sewn clothes growing up? As if this was a qualification? I wanted to ask him how much he had done in high school. Needless to say I didn't rank that program.

I ended up going to Eastern Virginia Graduate School of Medicine for my surgical residency. I tried to interview at the other two surgical residencies in Virginia but at that time they rarely considered women. At Eastern Virginia, I finally found some mentors. There were no female professors or attendings when I first started, but there were several female senior residents (one per year). One of my chiefs was a woman. Finally someone I could look up too.

Also on faculty was a Black male trauma surgeon who was quite amazing considering this was the South. He was one of the best teachers I ever had, a real mover and shaker. He kept you on your toes. He told me no female had ever made it through their trauma rotation as a chief without calling in sick. In other words, women were weak.

So what did I do? I volunteered to take the hardest rotation that year. Because we were short a resident, I worked consecutive 36-hour rotations for more than a month and never missed a day. No 80-hour work weeks then. I have a habit of proving things (and competing with) myself.

It was also an unwritten rule that surgery residents didn't miss any time for childbearing. So being a fool, I timed it so my first child would be born just after I finished. Pregnancy as a chief surgical resident was no fun! Oops! My water broke three weeks early, in the OR during a thoracotomy. Of course I finished the case and finished the year.

ASSET: WORK-LIFE BALANCE

"If you obey all of the rules, you miss all of the fun."
— KATHERINE HEPBURN

I married during my residency. I swore I would never marry another physician. And I didn't want children. I didn't want interference with my career. So, who did I marry? I ended up marrying a "fertility" doctor. Fate was laughing at me! The best laid plans . . . My husband, whom I met as an intern, has not been a barrier; he understands my world. He has always known how important my career is to me and has never questioned or been threatened by it. He is always supportive and very willing to share.

He has taken on child rearing responsibilities when needed. He's not stuck in traditional marriage roles. We share many of the same interests. I love the outdoors, physical fitness and animals. Work life balance is so important. I have been able to achieve that. I do work very hard. But as they say, I play hard. Mucking out stalls, breaking horses, holding onto a hormonally crazed stallion during breeding season, and hiking in the Sandia Mountains helps me maintain balance. What I initially thought would be a barrier has become very important to my "success." It has also reminded me to be flexible and to change with life's circumstances.

RIGHT PLACE AT THE RIGHT TIME
FINALLY SOME MORE MENTORS!

"You must be the change you wish to see in the world."
— MAHATMA GANDHI

My first year as a "real" surgeon was in academics in Virginia. Research and teaching aren't my strength, although I loved working with the residents. They keep you mentally sharp. I helped cover the trauma service. Though initially it was exciting, the thrill was soon gone.

That year allowed me to learn the academic view of medicine, which I have also found very helpful in my healthcare career. I often find my hospital systems competing with academic medical centers. It helps to understand "where they are coming from."

However, at that point, I liked building longer-term relationships with patients. After my husband completed his fellowship, I moved on to private practice in Nebraska. While there, I became involved in elected medical staff positions. As they say, I became an "accidental" leader. (I kept making the mistake of saying "yes.") I loved it.

I had two female chiefs of staff in particular who influenced me: an eclectic psychiatrist and a down-to-earth, do the right thing kind of radiologist. They both encouraged me to get involved in physician leadership. I started seeing the bigger picture in healthcare. I realized there is more to medicine than taking care of patients, one at a time. I began to embrace the vision of physicians as a key group needed to create affordable, quality, healthcare.

Clinically, however, I started to get bored again. After my thousandth cholecystectomy, I was wondering what's next. Around that time, I helped care for several cancer patients, none of whom had experienced what I considered a "good death." I learned about hospice. I started educating myself about the new specialty of hospice and palliative care medicine.

People can have a good death and actually live longer if we focus on quality of life and not quantity of life. I realized there was a huge need for end-of-life care in our society. Many people are unaware of the benefits of hospice and palliative care.

I started gaining a non-surgical perspective in healthcare. Ironically, at about that time, the medical director of my affiliated organization's hospice died (from cancer). I became the hospice medical director. This move had a huge impact on me. It was one of my first "paid" management/leadership positions and has truly added an important, "medical" viewpoint to my leadership portfolio. I loved it so much that after several years, I decided to leave surgery. The new field called to me. I become a palliative care doctor. I became double boarded in surgery and hospice and palliative care medicine.

OPPORTUNITY: RIGHT PLACE AT RIGHT TIME
BARRIER: MISPERCEPTIONS

*"My darling girl, when are you going to understand that
'normal' isn't a virtue? It rather denotes a lack of courage."*
— Practical Magic

Fate again stepped in. My organization hired a new CMO who
was one of the most strategic people I have ever met! He preached
a new vision of healthcare. He understood the importance of paid
physician leadership. He was willing to invest time and money in
physician leaders. He had a new idea for quality officers at each
of our metropolitan hospitals. I was the first woman he asked to
become one.

New challenge? Different path? Of course I would take it. My
surgical partner thought I had lost my mind. How could I "throw
away" all those years of training in surgery? My other colleagues
thought I had gone to "the dark side" and wasn't a real doctor any
more. It blows my mind how many doctors think that just because
you are paid by a hospital or health system that all free thought has
flown out of your head! Huge barrier, but I have learned that with
time, through relationship building and the development of trust,
those misperceptions can be overcome.

Around that time, a chief quality officer for the system was also
hired. Now we had two strong physician leaders. Both were men
and both had a huge impact on me. The CQO was a great mentor
who was actually looking out for me. He was interested in "growing
me" as a leader. A rare opportunity arose. I was in the right place
at the right time. The CMO was developing a physician executive
leadership/MBA program with Gallup University and the University
of Nebraska. I was asked to take part in the pilot group. There were
only nine of us in that class, all physicians. Working full time, raising
two teenagers, and going to school for an MBA was going to be very
difficult, but I figured this opportunity might not present itself again.

It is one of the best things I ever did. I grew so much! The first
unit in the course was "knowing self." I believe that to be a good
leader you really have to take a good look at yourself, warts and all.

That program encouraged me to be very introspective. As part of the course, we did an analysis that involved the "strengths-finder" program. It affirmed that my first strength is "responsibility." This is a huge part of why I am so obsessive about getting things done. The course teaches you that a strength, if not controlled, can turn into a barrier.

I'm also an "achiever"—I always have to move on to the next challenge. As a "learner," I need "input," which is why I constantly require so much data. I am also strong in "harmony," which I think is one of the most important things I have learned to utilize. If you don't take the time to build relationships, forget it. Few physicians have this strength, and I have seen this deficit adversely affect my mentors.

The third unit in the leadership portion of the course was learning the global perspective. This portion was important and eye opening. We traveled to Thailand and looked at medical tourism. One beautiful facility (Bumrungrad Hospital) was Joint Commission certified, had staff with a great service orientation, and provided high-quality care at a much cheaper price than the U.S. Huge "aha"! We Americans always assume incorrectly that our healthcare is better!

LESSON LEARNED: SERVANT LEADER OPPORTUNITIES EVEN IN ADVERSITY

"A woman is like a tea bag; you never know how strong it is until it's in hot water."
— ELEANOR ROOSEVELT

When I completed my MBA in 2009, my children were so proud of their graduate. Shortly after, my professional world imploded. My mentors, in their attempt to improve quality and move the organization forward, I feel, forgot to build relationships and listen. I read a recent article on the negative aspects of silence in the work place.

To this day, I believe I should have been more vocal and courageous. I began to see that my leaders were heading down the wrong path and I wonder what would have happened if I had been more vocal in trying to get them to stop and build more relationships. These two physicians had great vision, but without relationship skills and the ability to listen to others, they sank. A big upheaval

occurred. The medical staff voted no confidence in the administration. The CEO, VP, CMO and several others "resigned." The
organization became so afraid of physician leadership that, in my
opinion, they were taking "two steps backward."

This was a huge learning experience for me! With time, despite
the personal and professional setback, I was able to learn and grow
from this tough experience. I realized that I wanted to continue to
be a physician leader. Collaborate, listen, change course when you
are wrong; trust and relationship building is what it is all about.
Unfortunately, to continue to grow professionally, I realized I would
have to move elsewhere.

HUGE PERSONAL BARRIER: IT'S ALL
ABOUT WHO YOU KNOW

*"Life is a banquet and most poor
suckers are starving to death."*
— AUNTIE MAME

For a woman to pick up and leave for a new job opportunity, I feel,
is a lot harder than for a man. I had several barriers. My daughter
had one more year in high school where she was valedictorian and
a cross country star. Could I ask her to leave that? My husband was
willing to stay, bless him. Even my closest friends and family couldn't
believe I would "leave" my family. People constantly asked my poor
son how he was doing without his mother. Military men leave all
the time, but don't get all these questions.

It was and continues to be extremely difficult to live apart from
my family who are my support system. However I believed strongly
that this opportunity came at the right time. Or maybe not exactly
the right time, but when a great opportunity arises, I believe you
have to grab it or be left behind.

A colleague I had befriended while I was earning my MBA called
about a position in New Mexico. I've learned that networking with
colleagues and staying in touch is critical for career advancement.
This was the opportunity to become CMO for three metropolitan
hospitals in an eight hospital system. It was an opportunity for
career growth and probable advancement in the future. It was also

in a location that called to my outdoor nature. (I knew that kind of opportunity wouldn't come along very often.)

I interviewed twice and was turned down because they were rethinking the position. I was devastated. I felt I was perfect for the role. After a few months, rather than giving up, I began looking at other opportunities. Several months later, the New Mexico organization called me back. They had decided that the original job was too big for one person and instead divided it into two jobs. I was asked to return to interview for the metropolitan CMO position. This experience underscores the importance of not burning bridges, even when you are disappointed.

> *"We make a living by what we get, but*
> *we make a life by what we give."*
> —Winston Churchill

I had a very fulfilling seven years as a leader in New Mexico. My mentor, who happened to be a woman, left after a year or so of working under difficult circumstances. Again, it was an opportunity for learning. The system eventually hired my supervisor , who was not experienced and was a poor mentor, although he did allow me to be independent. Without a mentor of my own, I was able to find satisfaction by becoming a mentor to others. I even helped to develop formal mentoring/coaching opportunities for providers who were having difficult times with their relationships.

I was given quite a bit of responsibility over several areas of hospital medicine, including hiring, budgets, and program development. Some of my accomplishments included stroke certification, expansion of the neurology group, the hiring of a neurosurgeon and neuro-interventionalist. I was also the head of medical staff affairs and helped to open up two new hospitals. We developed our own credentialing verification organization. In addition, we developed a system peer review group for the six non-Albuquerque/regional hospitals so they could have access to experts within the system.

The most difficult part of my role was guiding the medical executive committee when they had to remove a provider's privileges because they had caused harm. I was yelled at by the best of them.

I found that if you treated everyone by the same rules, treated people equally, and never made it personal, things would work out. I, along with the hospital attorney and president of the medical staff, was actually sued in federal court , even though we had all done the right thing.

For me, it has always been about putting the patient first. Integrity, fairness, and consistency were most important to me. One difficult situation I had to overcome involved pressure from two high-level leaders who wanted me to bend our credentialing rules to hire candidates they wanted on staff.

I thought of our patients and what harm could occur if we didn't maintain our high credentialing standards. Once a physician is on the medical staff, it can be very hard to correct. I had to be able to live with myself, so I resisted the pressure. It was so important to me to treat everyone equally and to do what I said I would, even if it might jeopardize my job.

"Sometimes knowing what to do is knowing when to stop."
—BILL CRAWFORD

Over time, I again began experiencing a sense of boredom. I realized that if I was going to advance career-wise, I would have to move. My current environment had become very male dominated. When my boss was hired, there had been no question about considering a female candidate. I was told the CEO had already picked someone he "liked" vs. considering who was the best qualified. Additionally, I had lost some of my drive, partly because I was pretty satisfied with what I had accomplished. And I missed patient interaction.

I had been doing a small amount of clinical work but realized I wanted to do more. I felt I was ready to "pass the baton" and retire from leadership. I remained long enough to transition and train the people who would be taking my place. Ultimately three different individuals were hired to take on the various responsibilities of my job! That made me feel pretty good: it took three people to continue doing the job I had been doing alone. The hand-off went well.

I returned to being a full-time hospice and palliative physician. Although I told the hospice leadership that I didn't want a leadership position, the lead physician kept calling to "run things by me." I finally agreed to take on the role of president of the medical staff at the new hospital for a year until they could get their own leaders in place. I stayed on several committees. I was frequently asked to teach students and new hires.

And then COVID hit. We transitioned to mainly video visits. I had already been thinking about retirement; video visits just weren't satisfying for me. They were better than phone calls, but I missed the face-to-face offered by in-person interactions. The fact that there were some very qualified candidates available to replace me made my decision to retire much easier.

That is the other lesson that I think is important. If you care about the job you are leaving, you should do everything you can to make that transition smooth. You should also make sure the programs you have helped to develop can continue.

I guess it is in our nature to leave some sort of legacy. I am proud of my contributions both programmatically and as a mentor. I have been able to mentor multiple new female and male physician leaders. I even encouraged my daughter to pursue an MPH, as well as an MD, because I knew it will assist her if she chooses to pursue leadership in the future.

She was already organizing her fellow medical students to work in the COVID vaccine clinic at the university. She is a resident now but I believe it won't be long until she becomes one of our next leaders. . . . Healthcare is at such an exciting crossroad! I am OK passing on the torch of leadership!

Thinking back:

My greatest barriers:
- Personal attributes
- Misperceptions
- Sexual stereotypes
- Lack of strong role models

My greatest assets:
- Strong, independent personality

- Continuous need for intellectual challenge
- Taking advantage of being in the right place at the right time
- Diverse medical background/perspective
- Mentoring
- Ability to adapt and change
- Work/life balance
- Clinical experience before becoming a leader
- Consistency: doing what you say you will do to maintain integrity and trust.

"Do not go where the path may lead, go instead where there is no path and leave a trail."

— RALPH WALDO EMERSON

Chapter Ten

Finding the Right Niche

By Elaine E. Batchlor, MD, MPH

I NEVER THOUGHT I WOULD BE A HEALTH system CEO.

A doctor, yes. That I knew from a young age. But a hospital and health system leader? Someone who stands in front of television crews and legislative caucuses?

Not in a million years.

Here is how it began: in the shelter and quiet of a public library. I was just a girl, growing up Black in an almost all-white community. Libraries were my sanctuary; I read voraciously about anything and everything. It was there that I encountered the novel *Dear and Glorious Physician* by Taylor Caldwell. It was a fictionalized account of St. Luke, a physician in ancient times devoted to healing, expanding knowledge, promoting public health and battling socioeconomic causes of disease and disability.

This characterization of medicine inspired me and formed a lasting framework for my subsequent education and career. Decades later, it still fits my view of who I am and what I do as a physician executive.

Of course, I had other models. My parents were social activists who took me to the Poor People's March in Washington as a 10-year-old girl. My uncle, a self-styled revolutionary, fed me books by Stokely Carmichael and Angela Davis.

Looking back, it is clear that my primary influences were people who not only believed in things, but who took action to make those things happen. Ultimately, I would come to this realization: I wanted to heal bodies, but I also wanted to heal the systems and attitudes that make us sick.

Not that this path was abundantly clear at the beginning of my career. Like most medical students, I had a vague notion of the specialty I would pursue — internal medicine — based less on personal ambition and more on the intellectual culture associated with this specialty.

After completing my residency, I signed on for a fellowship in rheumatology, ultimately spending five years at a county hospital affiliated with UCLA.

Sometimes we make conscious choices that propel us on our path. Sometimes a mentor or an experience comes along at just the right moment, pushing us toward where we were probably heading anyway. UCLA Harbor was a combination of both.

The hospital had a strong training program, but it was also a typical county hospital. I had a front row seat to the problems that the poor experience in attempting to access medical care. I also experienced the frustration of a physician attempting to provide care within the constraints of a suboptimal system. I saw ways in which the system could be changed to better serve its mission of caring for the poor. At some point, I was struck by a thought that began to recur: I might accomplish more to help my patients by attempting to reshape the system than by caring for them one by one.

I was fortunate to have a rheumatology program director who shared a broad view of the mission of medicine. He guided me toward working on a health services research project with colleagues at UCLA's Schools of Medicine and Public Health.

Shaping the Future of Healthcare Delivery

During the research year of my fellowship, I tested the impact of teaching rheumatoid arthritis patients to participate in making medical decisions with their doctors. Seeing those vulnerable patients gain a voice in their treatment — many of them for the first time in their lives — was inspiring. Conducting research that could translate those poignant moments into a better way of doing things, even more so.

The year following my fellowship, I joined the faculty at UCLA Medical School to continue work on the project. My agreement with the Division of Rheumatology was that I would build a career doing health services research in rheumatology. I would strengthen my training for such a career by completing a master's level program at UCLA's School of Public Health. The end goal: to help shape the evolution of medicine and healthcare delivery through research.

At this point, I made another choice that altered my life's trajectory: I enrolled in a public health program that focused on health services rather than epidemiology and research methods.

Epidemiology would have been more valuable training for a research career, but health services was what appealed to me. Health services focused on themes that excited me: the history of medicine, the evolution of healthcare financing and organization, the sociopolitical forces influencing healthcare policy, and the challenge of providing care for poor and underserved communities.

I was surprised that I enjoyed being a student again; learning new things invigorated me. The ideas and experiences of my fellow students, mostly other professionals who shared similar interests, stimulated me.

While I pursued a degree in public health in order to advance a career in academia, by the time I completed my MPH, I questioned whether I wanted to remain in academia. I was comfortable knowing the expectations of me as an academician. However, the pace was too slow. My extrovert self also found it too solitary a pursuit, with too much time devoted to writing papers and grants.

I wanted a job where I could more directly affect the care that people receive, as well as one in which I would accomplish my goals by working closely with other people. It was why, soon after I completed my master's degree, I enrolled in a residency in preventive medicine.

I remained on the medical school faculty, but my thoughts were drifting elsewhere. I took every opportunity to visit physicians who were public health officers to learn about their jobs. I took the state exam for public health officers. I waited for a public health officer job opening.

Then the phone rang. It was a medical friend asking a trajectory-changing question: did I want to work as a physician administrator in a staff-model HMO?

My cautious, conscious mind was hesitant. Stepping away from academia would be risky — my colleagues told me that if I left I'd never get back in.

However, my subconscious mind — the one that had, from an early age, propelled me outward to a broader understanding of healthcare — was interested.

Naysayers tend to make me defiant. I trusted my friend and I liked the physician executive running the HMO. I decided to take the risk.

The job turned out to be a wonderful opportunity to discover and develop management and leadership skills and to work on improving healthcare operations. My responsibilities entailed managing physicians, other healthcare professionals, support staff, and the operations of a busy outpatient clinic.

I learned the value of teamwork and of continuous quality improvement. An engaged and empowered staff began to make progress on long-standing challenges, such as ensuring medical records availability, reducing wait times, and improving patient satisfaction. I also learned how to work effectively with practicing physicians, helping them understand and embrace the importance of customer service and cost-effective clinical practice. I enjoyed the opportunities for continuous learning and working on activities as diverse as capital budgeting, architectural plans for new building, and clinical practice.

After two years with this health plan, I accepted a position as medical director for a network-model HMO. I viewed this as an opportunity to learn about a different type of delivery system and to continue to broaden the scope of my responsibilities.

The transition was easier this time because I knew I was on the right path. This — the world of people and practice, of putting new ideas into play and measuring the results — was where I was supposed to be.

I continued to work as a health plan medical director for three different health plans over the course of six more years, taking on larger roles with each shift. Then opportunity knocked again.

If I have learned anything in my career, it is that doors often swing open where you least expect them. In this case, the door came in the form of a phone call from the CEO of a statewide healthcare foundation asking me to go to work for him as a program officer focusing on healthcare system issues.

Once again, I hesitated. A foundation? In a different city? I was not convinced that I would enjoy working in a not-for-profit organization, outside the mainstream of the healthcare system. In a way, it seemed like a step back toward academia, toward ivory-tower research and reflection, constantly studying the problem instead of solving it.

Once again, I decided to take the leap. And once again, I was glad I did.

Here is why: Our perspective is heavily influenced by where we sit. My perspective broadened during the time I spent outside the trenches of healthcare. It also taught me not to fear change in my career. Each risk I took resulted in a fuller, better understanding of the issues I cared passionately about.

Looking back, I realize now that the critical element in my career growth was exactly that: taking risk, not making the safe bet, staying with the natural progression.

The five years I worked at the foundation gave me the time I needed to reflect on how the healthcare system and its parts could improve. I collaborated with academics, industry stakeholders, and other experts to chart how healthcare businesses function and how they could work better. I pursued and helped secure funding for innovative ideas to improve various aspects of the system. We addressed issues such as workforce development and deployment, provider payment, quality and performance measurement and the structure and financial performance of healthcare organizations. It was challenging and fun to figure out how to use foundation resources to leverage change.

Foundations generally achieve their goals by working through other organizations and people. While it was nice to be the person who decides which issues and organizations to fund, after five years, that restless, questing part of me emerged again — the part that wanted to jump back into the fray.

As I weighed these issues, Mother Nature threw a spanner in the works. I always had a vague idea that I would like to have a family. Like many professional women, however, I was more invested in developing my career and I put off having children. Fortunately, I met my husband just in time. So, at an age when my peers were preparing to send their children off to college, I got married and had not one but two children — twins.

Starting a family had an impact on my professional life that was both surprising and predictable. Every mother knows she will have to make accommodations, but nothing really prepares you for how your life will change. Even if I had just one child, I am sure I would have grappled with the need to redefine my priorities. Two adorable, demanding children sped that process up. After some soul searching, I realized that I wanted to be available for my children.

Finding the Balance

My passion for working in a role where I could help improve healthcare had not diminished. I just faced the classic dilemma that (few fathers, but) nearly all working moms face: I needed a job that would allow me to balance career and family.

Fortunately, the right opportunity presented itself and when it did, I jumped at it. A regional Medicaid health plan called L.A. Care Health Plan needed a chief medical officer. The job was family-friendly, served a vulnerable population that truly needed and deserved good care, and required both medical and managerial experience.

What it lacked, apparently, was prestige. Just as I had been warned not to leave academia, I was warned that going to work for a Medicaid health plan would box me into the world of publicly financed healthcare, as if I was entering a career ghetto. The warnings were telling in terms of the value they placed on the lowest tier of our multi-tiered health payment system.

Once again, I ignored the naysayers. Once again, the risk paid off. L.A. Care was a deep-dive into critical health issues facing our nation. Long before the Affordable Care Act, the organization was striving to improve and expand systems of care for underserved communities. It was a tremendous opportunity.

Little did I know it was a prelude to an even bigger opportunity.

Eight years into my time at L.A. Care, the phone rang again — a recruiter was seeking seven people to take on a task few wanted or thought was possible: to start a high-quality hospital in South Los Angeles. It was a high-profile project with even higher risk. But I had already become accustomed to that. A few months later I became a board member of what is now MLK Community Healthcare. Within two years, I accepted the role of CEO.

Of course, the naysayers once again predicted career doom. For once, however, they may have had good reason.

If you are from South Los Angeles, or you know its history, you know why so many people thought I was committing career suicide.

South LA, to outsiders at least, seemed to be a place of intractable problems. Watts and Compton are widely known for all the wrong reasons. The community has suffered repeated riots, economic depression, social isolation, and all manner of neglect, including lack of basic healthcare infrastructure. The old public hospital had closed in 2007, largely due to quality lapses. It was, and still is, a poor community where most people were covered by Medi-Cal.

No wonder people thought I was crazy, trying to start a private nonprofit hospital in a place like this. Do not do it, people told me. It will not end well.

You can probably guess how I responded.

Where others saw risk, I saw opportunity. Once again, I was taking on a new challenge. The hospital was the result of a unique public-private partnership that gave my leadership team management control over a publicly funded facility, but required all of our powers of diplomacy to build bridges with our public partners. The structural challenges facing us required strong outside-the-box thinking. It was clear that Medicaid was not a sustainable payment base for a high-quality health system.

It was the kind of work I wanted to do ever since I read the story of St. Luke. Here was a vulnerable community and a blank slate upon which I could write my vision for a new kind of healthcare — one that insisted upon excellence for the most vulnerable, despite the obstacles that our health system throws up.

Getting to Yes

When this book was last published, I was just embarking on this new challenge and encouraged readers to check back in a few years — "I'll let you know how it turned out."

Here's that update:

Since opening in 2015, MLK Community Hospital has changed the way people think about safety-net hospitals. We are one of only 6.5% of hospitals in the nation to achieve HIMSS-7, the highest level use of health information technology in a hospital. We are in the top 10% of hospitals nationwide for patient satisfaction. We have received multiple "A" grades for patient safety from the Leapfrog Group. Politico has called us "the hospital of the future."

Along the way, I surprised myself by doing something I never thought I wanted to take on, and doing it well: fundraising. Following my instinct for partnership, I quickly developed a strong working relationship with Dyan, an experienced fundraiser who shared my passion for doing the hardest thing along with my zeal for setting something right.

With her, I discovered that generosity is an opportunity. When presented in the right way, to the right people, asking turns from risk (hearing no) to strategy (getting to yes). My partnership with Dyan has turned out to be one of the most enjoyable and productive aspects of my job.

Last year we became a health system, designed to provide community-based prevention and disease management. MLK Community Healthcare now includes a multispecialty medical group, multiple practice sites, a population health program, integrated behavioral healthcare, street medicine for homeless patients, and a graduate medical education program.

A core theme in my career is one I suspect is central to the careers of many innovators and entrepreneurs: We do not listen to those who say something cannot be done.

What I found instead is that taking the unusual, the difficult, and the less-attractive path often offers amazing opportunity. Finding and working at places with the right scale has contributed to my satisfaction — large enough to have resources and to make impact, small enough for autonomy and flexibility. Finding challenges worthy of meeting has been key to my success.

Big challenges typically are not solvable through conventional means. They force us to think outside the box and consider new approaches. They hone our critical thinking skills. This makes us adaptive. Working at a start-up organization has given me a unique opportunity to stretch my creativity and innovation. I have done that even in the area of financing, turning a federal program traditionally used to fund low-income housing to funding healthcare for the most vulnerable.

Importantly, the risky choice also gives us the opportunity to live our values. Even if you do not reach all of your goals, you will remain faithful to the passion that brought you to healthcare in the first place.

I am a medical doctor who has worked in many different domains: academia, the private sector, health plans, and now a hospital and health system. I am also a woman for whom sexism (and racism) was part of the norm in my advancement.

Sexism affected me as I took on larger leadership roles in healthcare organizations. Colleagues doubted, second-guessed, and even attempted to undermine me. It made my work more stressful, and it constrained my opportunities. But it also made those opportunities others might pass on look like the jewels they turned out to be.

Every step of the way I was told that my career would suffer if I made a wrong turn. As far as I can tell, that hasn't happened yet! Each turn has been the right one.

Given the size of the challenges confronting us, we need more people — more women — who are willing to do the things that seem impossible to do. Together we can create the possible.

Chapter Eleven

Medical Manager: Was It Worth It?

By Selma Harrison Calmes, MD

THIS CHAPTER IS ABOUT MY 20 YEARS AS A department chair in anesthesiology in two public (county) hospitals. In many ways, my experience as a female medical manager was unique, but I hope the lessons learned will be useful to others.

My management experience was different than most because it focused on anesthesiology and operating rooms (ORs). At the time, the surgeons ruled, and there was little interest at the hospital level on intelligent use of OR time, resources, and revenue generation.

I decided to be a physician after having polio at age eight during one of California's many polio epidemics. I was hospitalized for months. The trauma of being hospitalized for polio then is only now being realized, as recently published patient memoirs vividly document the psychic trauma and family disruption.

Like most polio survivors, I ignored the psychic effect of hospitalization and the residual physical effects of the disease. Super-achievement was also a by-product of polio; most survivors are classic Type A personalities. Although I'd been paralyzed initially, I eventually managed to pass as "normal" in spite of a slight limp. Nevertheless, trying to do so took enormous physical effort.

My family was already stressed before polio. My mother was an "Army brat," whose goal in life was to be a colonel's wife and have beautiful children. My father was the son of a Swedish immigrant steel mill worker. After working in the same steel mill, he joined the Army, was able to go to West Point, and launched a successful military career.

In 1944, he was killed in action in Germany, leaving my mother a 26-year-old widow with three children under age four. I was the oldest; the youngest was only three months old. In contrast to the many programs to support families of those lost in current wars, in World War II, there were few resources to help families like ours, except for a small monthly payment from Social Security. You were just on your own.

Like most women of the time, my mother was totally unprepared to make a living and raise three children alone. I realize now that she was probably too depressed to give her children the emotional support we needed after the loss of our dad; she was struggling herself. As we grew up, money was always very limited.

Academic and athletic achievement was expected as a way out of poverty and to repeat the pattern of our dad's life achievements. Despite the fact that being a smart female was definitely discouraged in the 1950s-1960s, I managed to make it through a prestigious college on scholarships by living at home and taking every possible student job. I was fortunate to get into medical school with the help of my organic chemistry professor.

Although it was physically stressful, I loved medical school and I loved being a doctor. The interactions with patients, especially children and their families, solving the puzzle of what was wrong with the patient, as well as the "doing" in surgery and anesthesia were exactly what I wanted.

I decided on anesthesia during a pediatric internship, on the advice of the women pediatricians with whom I worked. They felt that anesthesia was a good specialty for a woman with children because the hours were allegedly better than in other specialties. I later found this to be an urban legend!

At that time, most hospitals had moderate surgical schedules, and OR work generally ended in the afternoon. However, cases often ran late or emergencies rolled in and sometimes fellow anesthesia staff got sick. So there were many times when I was up all night on-call.

Today, because the OR is usually the only profit center for institutions, ORs are pushed to turn out as many cases as possible as efficiently as possible. ORs now typically have at least two shifts for elective surgery, and all the emergencies then follow.

The modern practicing anesthesiologist usually doesn't get dinner until 8:30 p.m. or later, and then start the emergency cases. Room turnover time (the time to get the OR cleaned and set up for the next case) is tracked, and care of a patient with an anesthesia problem can be marginalized due to this "production pressure."

My management training began while I was trying to be a wife and mother AND a physician. I'd married a medical school classmate after freshman year, had a baby during internship and then another during residency, so anesthesia's disruptive work hours became difficult. It took a household staff of five (four were part-time) to meet all my family's needs and an accountant to deal with all the workers' paperwork. In desperation, I started reading basic books about management, hoping to manage my life more easily and make room for some fun.

About this time, I also wondered how women physicians in the past had managed their families while practicing medicine. This led to a strong interest in the history of women in medicine, an area that has become an exciting academic endeavor for me. Incidentally, the answer to the question about how past women physicians managed is that they were unmarried, stopped practice once they married, or had live-in servants.

My first job in anesthesia was at a children's hospital in central California, where I was one of three anesthesiologists. After seven years, I'd done everything you could do in pediatric anesthesia at the time, so I looked for a new opportunity. Opting for academics, I took a part-time job as the first pediatric anesthesiologist at a university hospital in Los Angeles, about 200 miles away. My success teaching there two days a week ultimately led to a divorce and a move to Los Angeles with two children.

In those days, the academic promotion system was secretive, and the importance of research was not made obvious to women who were told that teaching and clinical care were sufficient to excel. Male physicians, on the other hand, seemed to get picked up and mentored by senior colleagues with research labs. After seven years in this position, I learned that my failure to produce research papers meant no promotion.

My next position was as the first specialty anesthesiologist in the state's largest HMO. Daily work assignments were on a strict rotation basis, and I often missed doing the difficult pediatric cases. This was a dysfunctional department filled with many non-performers, including a physician who resented my recent academic experience (I was still on the lecture circuit when I started there). This doctor was an uncontrolled, equal-opportunity, and highly experienced bully, my first experience with this problem since medical school.

As I studied the day-to-day processes within the department, I recognized areas that needed change and thought about potential solutions. These were my initial insights into how department management might work and the first time I considered a management role for myself.

After failing to make partnership in that organization, I participated in the job fair at our specialty society's annual meeting and quickly received an offer to become chief at a public hospital in central California. Although I hadn't held any prior medical management position, I felt what I had learned while trying to balance medical practice and home life (two children and a husband) would serve as good training for the role.

Like my previous organization, the quality of staff and practice structure was less than optimal, reflecting anesthesiology in that era. The hospital accepted both indigent and private patients. Anesthesia staff were hired by the county at a low basic salary, which was to cover care to the indigent patients.

A practice plan existed for private patients who were billed at the usual private fees. That revenue was not shared, but went directly to the anesthesiologist involved. With fierce competition for the private cases, it was hard to find physicians willing to take on county patients. Changing to shared-private practice revenue, common today among anesthesia groups, would mean disrupting the entire practice plan for all the other specialties and was not possible.

One of the most difficult physicians under my supervision was actually mentally ill. He often left his anesthetized patients and wandered in the hallway. At the time, there were no national standards for anesthesia monitoring. Fortunately today, there are clear-cut monitoring standards, including continuous presence of the anesthesia providers in the OR. This doctor ended up harassing me for years, making threatening phone calls and breaking into my computer. This was extremely traumatizing.

The medical director who had recruited me was my mentor, the only one I've ever had. He introduced me to the American College of Physician Executives (ACPE) which has since been rebranded as the American Association for Physician Leadership (AAPL). Although he stayed at that hospital only one year, I continued to attend ACPE seminars and read helpful books.

There were few anesthesiologists in ACPE then, which would have been useful, because our management problems were and are unique. Anesthesiologists have since formed their own management organization, and many have or are seeking MBAs. We are also taking on leadership roles in the entire perioperative process, preparing patients for surgery and doing postop care, especially in ICUs.

After two years, I moved back to Los Angeles to become chief of anesthesia at another county hospital that was part of a five-hospital system. My charge was to get the anesthesiology department affiliated with the associated medical school. That meant recruiting higher quality anesthesia staff — a difficult task given the low salaries.

Much of my administrative time was spent on personnel and budget issues. At one point, the county had an acute budget problem, and I had to lay off half the staff. Union rules required that anesthesiologists from other county institutions be transferred to our hospital, replacing those who were laid-off. All were inadequate clinically, and numerous clinical disasters followed.

Trying to deal with this situation was another time-consuming battle, especially because the medical director at the time did not appreciate the need for competent staff. The surgery faculty was also an issue. They were more interested in doing private cases at their academic hospital, leaving surgery residents in charge of some critically ill indigent patients.

Despite the many obstacles and without a mentor or formal management training, I was slowly able to affect improvements, developing a responsive, communicative, helpful, available department — the only one like that in the hospital at that time. The fact that our group was primarily female might be a good lesson for male medical students and faculty!

Among the positive changes was a medical student rotation that became extremely popular. We also accepted a high-quality CRNA school that had lost its academic home, allowing us better, higher-quality staffing to get the cases done. We initiated a Preoperative Evaluation Clinic staffed by a nurse practitioner we trained. Eventually, we took over many aspects of preop patient preparation for surgery, including cardiac evaluation.

Once I discovered the usefulness of data and the ability to analyze it in Excel, I began keeping basic OR statistics, then added in our quality improvement (QI) data. When an OR scheduling system was to be implemented, hospital administration put me in charge, much to the surgeons' chagrin. They never really utilized it; the chair of surgery told me, "I don't believe in data!" I, however, could hardly wait until the end of the month when we could run the statistics to see how we were doing! Although I never received credit for these efforts, I feel validated by the fact that today, data management is a vital skill for medical managers.

Meanwhile, in my personal life, polio was rearing its ugly head again. Post-Polio Syndrome (PPS) symptoms (increasing weakness and fatigue in those who had polio[1]) suddenly appeared. There symptoms are aggravated by stress — unavoidable in my position. A major stressor was an unsupportive medical director. Also, anesthesia involves a lot of physical work, and as my symptoms increased, I had to spend less and less time in the OR.

Eventually I was forced out of the chair position and into a lateral move to hospital QI. That same week, I discovered a major problem in my marriage. Devastated and totally burned out, I retired in 2007. After 42 years in medicine, I spent the next two years doing nothing but working in my garden, enjoying its beauty and the natural world.

After that two-year break, I returned to medicine, taking on a part-time position as the anesthesiology consultant for the Los Angeles County Department of Medical Examiner/Coroner. (This is the only US coroner department to have such a position; I was their second anesthesia consultant.) This interesting job involved analyzing records of patients who died during or after anesthesia, trying to determine if death was related to anesthesia management. This gave me another opportunity to make a difference in anesthesia care; cases with poor management must be reported to the state medical board.

The job turned out to be much busier than I'd planned, and going to court for hearings and malpractice cases was sometimes unpleasant, but my experience in management helped me handle the multiple aspects of the position, including organizing data and writing well. I developed a database of cases and summarized causes of deaths from anesthesia in Los Angeles County, the nation's most populous county. This information has been used to educate coroner staff about anesthesia-related deaths.

During this time, anesthesia and surgery were changing rapidly, and new surgical methods and anesthesia drugs led to new ways for patients to die during or after the operation. Newer operations, such as radical cosmetic surgery (for example, liposuction, sometimes over most of the body), and laparoscopic (lap) band surgery to prevent obesity were becoming prominent.

These were procedures done in less costly non-hospital facilities, such as a surgeon's office. Newer anesthesia drugs (propofol, among others) added more deaths in these office operating rooms. The singer Michael Jackson was among those who died from propofol. It was overwhelming dealing with the hordes of international media descending on the coroner's office.

In my role, I focused on being easily available for consults and gave case conferences with coroner staff presenting their findings. I gave conferences for academic anesthesia departments and presented at national anesthesia meetings. I also wrote a chapter for a book by the department's specialty consultants (Sathyavagiswaran L and Rogers CB. *Multidisciplinary Medico-Legal Death Investigation: Role of Consultants*. Elsevier Academic Press. London; 2018).

Coroner staff's knowledge of possible anesthesia causes of death greatly expanded as our communication increased. It was gratifying to develop this new role, and I grew to greatly respect the hard-working and dedicated pathologists and their support staff, who play such an important role in determining causes of death.

Although I retired from this coroner position in 2017, I still maintain a presence in my previous academic anesthesiology department, serving as advisor (both official and informal) to young women faculty. I often speak to anesthesia organizations about what I found and how anesthesia care might be improved.

Challenges and Rewards

In summary, I consider myself a pioneer as a leader and medical manager within the field of anesthesia. There were few women in my day and fewer as chiefs of anesthesia departments. Now looking back on my career, I sometimes wonder whether it was worth trying to be a medical manager.

Overall, despite the stresses coming from working in systems chronically stressed by budget problems, aggravation of my PPS, with resultant medical complications, and deterioration of my relationship with my husband, I would still have to say "yes, it was worth it."

I had a deep personal commitment to public hospitals and indigent care dating from my polio experience when I was a patient in a public hospital. Working within that system I encountered many difficult situations, but there were also amazing and satisfying rewards.

For example, in my role as chief of anesthesia, I was able to hire more competent staff who helped to improve the overall quality of care. As the reputation of the department grew, I helped attract many medical students (both male and female) to anesthesia, all of whom saw a department run primarily by women physicians who functioned as a smooth team and gave top patient care. There was no other department like it in the university's environment. This has been a gratifying legacy.

Although this has been a difficult and stressful career, there have been many high points. The medical director who was my nemesis is long gone. My mentee (she was chosen as chair when I left that position) now is the hospital's medical director and discovered the huge mess her predecessor left behind. Some of the medical students who rotated through our department did their anesthesia residencies at our academic hospital and now work as anesthesiologists at that public hospital. Anesthesia residents now rotate through, so the academic affiliation was achieved. And, the patients are still getting great anesthesia care.

Policies, such as facilitating breast feeding, which I implemented to meet the particular needs of female staff I had hired, are still in place. Sexual harassment issues continue to be quickly and effectively dealt with. These are just a few of the reasons for women physicians to consider medical management careers. I believe we bring a unique perspective that can translate into better care for patients, as well as a better work environment for healthcare workers including fellow physicians.

Lessons Learned

Lessons I learned that might be useful to others include the great importance of data (be the data person in your organization and understand the information), look at the big picture (it's easy to miss a good solution if you don't) and use your staff to help generate solutions to management problems. One of the best days for me was after an ACPE program on this. I gathered some staff to discuss a scheduling issue. With only minimum input from me, they came up with an excellent solution! It was so easy, the staff felt empowered and bought into the solution.

Perhaps the hardest lesson I've learned is the importance of communication. You can never communicate too much, in my experience. Although we might think intelligent people who made it through medical school would understand something with one announcement or notice, that is not the case. It takes multiple repeats, in varying ways, to get the message across. I used to get upset with people who missed an announcement/new policy or whatever, but that's just the way it is and we have to keep communicating.

Moreover, the staff has to sense your dedication to this. One of the best things I ever did was to post weekly announcements on the main bulletin board. While our hospital was recovering from a major earthquake, I put up announcements every few hours (things were changing rapidly) at the central location where department staff gathered. This turned out to be a critical step to get us functioning as a group after the disaster.

Finally, one of my "hobbies" is to research and write about the lives of early women anesthesiologists. This has led to some gratifying projects. My first biographic subject was the anesthesiologist Dr. Virginia Apgar, who developed the Apgar Score for newborns. I've gone around the world to talk about Apgar! I hope other women physician managers can enjoy a hobby like this and tell the stories of early women physicians, who struggled with even more restrictions than those of us today.

REFERENCE

1. Jubelt B, Agre JC. Characteristics and Management of Post-Polio Syndrome. *JAMA*. 2000; 284(4): 412-4

CHAPTER TWELVE

Every Physician Is a Leader

By Asha Padmanabhan, MD

AS AN IMMIGRANT WOMAN PHYSICIAN (I CAME to America from a small town in India at the age of 28), an introvert who preferred flying under the radar, a mom with young kids who felt that every moment not spent at the hospital should be spent with my family, leadership was not on my radar.

Until it all changed.

The treasurer and VP of our anesthesia group had just announced that he was leaving the practice. Of the three remaining partners, of which I was one, none of us had any idea about the group's finances. I had been a partner for less than a year, and during that time, none of the financial information had been openly shared, and I didn't know enough to ask.

Unable to sleep one night, I wondered who would take over the responsibility? How would we run this practice? Billing companies, insurance companies, contracts, payroll, etc. Who would manage that? Who would make sure our nine physicians and 27 CRNA employees would get paid? I knew I would have to do something.

At that point I did not consider myself a leader. I was happy being a new partner in name only, happy providing the best anesthesia care I could. As soon as my car left the parking lot, I was content to put everything work-related out of my mind and focus on being a good mom to my two young kids. As an introvert, I had never spoken up for myself in my career.

When the three remaining partners met the following day, I found myself volunteering to be treasurer. My other two partners had no interest in the role. The minute I raised my hand, I felt sick. How could I do this? I knew absolutely nothing about finances. I had never balanced a checkbook or managed an account. I had gone from my parents' house, a sheltered young woman living at home during medical school, straight into marriage right after graduating, to a husband who managed all our finances.

But I'd raised my hand and now I would have to live with the decision.

Looking back, it was the first time I realized that when you are offered an opportunity and don't know how, say yes and figure it out later.

The first six months were among the toughest of my life. I began learning all aspects of practice management, from billing to contract negotiation, to payroll and even HR. Because this was before online searches, my best resources turned out to be our vendors. Long meetings with our billing specialist and our CPA became routine as I grappled with the new terminology.

I had to let go of my reluctance to talk to people and learn to reach out. I started attending conferences and learned to ask questions, even when I felt foolish, assuming everyone would think me stupid for not knowing the basics. I did all of this while still carrying a full clinical load.

Two years in, just as I was feeling comfortable, starting to enjoy the challenges, the rug was pulled out from under me. The CEO asked for a meeting with the three partners. We'd been in negotiations to renew our contract with the hospital and had several meetings with the CFO. In preparation, we'd hired an expensive outside contractor to assess the fair market value of our practice. He met with the C-suite and came up with a proposal on how many ORs we could staff and the budget required.

So when the CEO's administrative assistant asked for a meeting for the following day, we assumed it was the follow-up to our previous meeting. Instead we were informed that the hospital had decided to award the contract to a large national group. No discussion about an RFP (Request for Proposal) being put out, no opportunity for our group to put in a bid. This was a done deal. He gave us our 90-days' notice. Our only options were for everyone to be employed by this group or leave.

After getting over the shock, we entered into discussions with the incoming group. The three of us decided, naively in retrospect, that we'd do our best to make it fair for all our employees. Long story short, the partners were offered a better deal which would severely undercut the other employees. After several weeks of negotiations, the three of us decided to gracefully bow out, allowing our employees to stay or leave and not enforce the non-competes we had in place. Several employees benefited by the temporary large increase they saw in their salaries.

Looking back, with 20-20 hindsight, I see so many mistakes we made as three good clinicians with little leadership and management skills. Still, I take comfort in the fact that I did my best and could sleep better at night with a clear conscience. We helped the employees, even if it wasn't the best for us personally.

Lessons learned from this experience:

1. Raise your hand and volunteer even if you feel unprepared. When opportunity knocks, open the door. You never know how your life will change for the better until you do.
2. The business of medicine — billing, coding, HR, contracts — are all skills that can be learned by physicians. Be open to asking for help. My biggest learning came from sitting down one on one with our CPA, billing company, and attorney rather than from the practice management courses I took during this time.
3. If you are in a leadership position, or if you want to be in one, build relationships and network within the hospital — with the C-suite and with fellow physicians. If I had done this, I might have been better prepared. Instead, I left it to my partners, believing they were better suited to the task, not recognizing that it wasn't their strength either. I had let my own insecurities and impostor thoughts get in my way.

Being Open to Change

The next phase in my journey started when I took up a position as a staff anesthesiologist. At first, after the trauma of the previous months, it was a relief to focus on just being an anesthesiologist and taking care of my patients, not having to worry about payroll and HR and everything else I had been immersed in for the past three years.

However, I soon recognized that some of the processes were not working efficiently. Although I knew I could make them better, now I didn't have the power of a title. I went to my boss, but his priorities were different. I realized that for all the stress and anxiety of my previous three years, I did enjoy the power of being able to make decisions and improve processes. I enjoyed being a leader. It was challenging, stimulating, and rewarding.

Recognizing how little choice or say I had as to where and how I wanted to work, I began looking for a new opportunity. I found an ad for a chief of anesthesia position on a hospital job posting site for an employee of a large national anesthesia management company. Never having been chief or had that level of responsibility, I hesitated. How could I dare to apply? No way would I be considered. Yet, what did I have to lose? I sent in my application, secure in the assumption that I would never hear back.

I was shocked when asked to set up a phone interview within a few days. I was completely honest about my management experience as treasurer. The regional director interviewing me asked how I would handle conflict; would I step up or step away? I responded, "If you'd asked me this three years ago, I'd have said I hate conflict and I avoid it as much as I can. But the last three years have taught me how to handle it, how to challenge when necessary and how to negotiate when I can." I believe that that may have clinched the deal. After several more interviews, I was offered the position.

Lessons learned:

1. Leadership and being in control of certain aspects of your career are addictive.
2. Sometimes, being stuck in a situation is worse than the pain of stepping out of your comfort zone. If an opportunity is presented, take a leap of faith even though you may think you would fail.

Being Chief

The next five years were a roller coaster of highs and lows — one moment believing I was a good chief, the next, that I was terrible.

I walked into a practice where the outgoing chief planned to step down after eight years in that role. The staff physicians had all been there for more than 10 years. For most, this had been their first and only job out of residency. Everyone was used to a certain way of doing things. There was a hierarchy with the OR manager the center of the power dynamic.

And here I was — a brown woman, a newly minted chief, a reticent introvert who disliked conflict, and yet who looked at the way things were being done and recognized opportunities for change. The set-up was perfect for me to be met with resistance, even for small changes I wanted to make.

In my previous job, I was used to having, if not full support, most certainly friendly co-operation from the OR staff. My first day in this hospital showed me how different things were going to be. Unbeknownst to me, my credentialing process was not complete. The final rubber stamp was still required.

My director suggested I could still start my first official day. Although I wouldn't be providing anesthesia care for a couple more days, I could get oriented. While I was in the OR, one of my new colleagues had difficulty placing an IV. I asked if he wanted help. "Sure" was the response. No one in the OR said anything as I placed the IV, but a few hours later, I received a phone call that the CEO wanted to see me. I assumed he wanted to welcome me on my first official day. He did, but then asked if I was aware that I shouldn't have touched the patient since I hadn't yet been "officially signed off on." I was mortified. In the moment, in that OR, I hadn't stopped to think. I was trying to be helpful. I should have known better.

What really upset me was that the OR nurse who saw what was happening never said anything. Instead he took the issue to the OR manager, who didn't confront me either, but chose instead to pass it on to the CEO. I learned a harsh lesson that day. Up to that point, I'd been fortunate to work with people who worked well with me.

Even though this new staff and manager didn't know me, I expected the same sort of team work.

Being an inherent people-pleaser, I found it a hard lesson to learn that not everyone would automatically like me just because I was nice to them. I didn't realize that my failure might be something some people might look forward to.

The next day at work I took a deep breath, quietly determined. I would be a good chief, I would be fair to everyone working with me, I would give everyone the benefit of the doubt. I understood that I would likely make decisions that might be unpopular, but I told myself that I was not in this job to have people like me. My director had taken a chance on me, giving me this opportunity, and I would do my best to be the kind of chief I would like to work for.

I remained in that position for five years. There were many hard lessons and bitter realizations, but equally, many learning opportunities and personal triumphs.

Eventually I felt vindicated when fellow physicians, OR nurses, and even the notoriously hard-to-please OR manager told me I had positively changed the culture by bringing in open dialogue. Previously, rumor, innuendo, and miscommunication or deliberate miscommunication had created a sense of distrust and antagonism between the OR staff and the anesthesia department. The fact that they knew I was open to criticism without getting defensive, that I would listen, that I was not interested in attaching blame but in finding solutions, all helped to build trust and professional collegial relationships.

Lessons Learned:

1. Say "yes" to opportunity even if you don't feel ready.
2. Don't assume everyone has your best interests at heart BUT always go in with the intent to do your best, be open and willing to take feedback that hurts without getting defensive.
3. Treat everyone fairly, have an open door policy, be willing to assume responsibility for the mistakes you make (and you will make many).

4. Do not try to fit a square peg in a round hole. In other words, do not try to change your personality to fit your or other people's assumptions of how a leader should look or act. Work with your strengths and you will be more effective.

The Winds of Change

For those who have read Dr. Selma Calmes' chapter, you may note a number of differences between her experiences and mine. This is primarily because the specialty of anesthesia has been undergoing a slow but inexorable change for decades. I saw this when my company lost our contract to a large management company. Up until then, once you finished residency, you either took an academic position or went into private practice.

After a three-year stint in academic anesthesia as part of the Johns Hopkins system in Baltimore, I moved to Florida and joined a private practice group that contracted our services with the hospital. The promise of a partnership was alluring even though it meant a lower salary for the initial years with no guarantee of being offered a partnership at the end of the three years.

The first year I took up the treasurer position, I learned that our group, as with most private practice groups in the area, could only function with financial assistance from the hospital. The economics of working in an area where most of our patients did not have private commercial insurance, with Medicare payment rates for anesthesia only 33% of commercial payers, meant that reimbursement for anesthesia services was not adequate to pay salaries to anesthesia staff. Most private practice groups survived on stipends given by the hospital.

Although I didn't realize it at the time, when my small private group lost our contract to a large management company, this was the beginning of a wave that today has taken over the practice of anesthesia not only in South Florida where I live, but is slowly spreading across the country.

Although management groups had been around for a while, it's only in the last dozen years that they have either taken over, merged with, or acquired most private practices. By employing many physicians and nurses, these groups' economics of scale allow them to offer more attractive contracts to hospitals. For physicians, that means private practice opportunities are almost non-existent in South Florida.

No longer are there partnership track positions with the promise of being in control of some of the financial aspects of your career. There are several large management companies that employ physicians and nurses and contract anesthesia services to the hospitals. When I applied for the chief of anesthesia position, it was as an employee of another large physician management company. This entity is now the largest employer of physicians and allied nursing staff in the country.

What Next?

Early in my tenure as chief, I attended the annual weekend retreat that the large anesthesia management company I work for had for chiefs and vice-chiefs from all over the country. I remember how hard those two days were, not knowing anyone. Being an introvert, I couldn't force myself to introduce myself to anyone. There were so few women attending. We would pass each other in the halls, smiling sheepishly as we hurried from session to session. It was a very lonely experience.

When the time came for the retreat the following year, I wanted to make this a better experience. I asked the organizers for a list of female attendees. I sent emails, asking the women if anyone wanted to meet up for coffee. The response was astounding. Everyone wanted to. We set a time and met outside a coffee shop. We actually had to make more room for the number who showed up.

We compared notes, vented to each other about the hurdles we faced, many of which stemmed from being female and the perceptions of being a female leader. As the conversations ebbed and flowed, I realized that each of us was desperate for this camaraderie. As a female leader, I had certainly felt very lonely. But I assumed that was just me — every other female leader I met seemed so put-together and confident. Now I realised we shared so many common experiences and challenges. We came away from that meeting energized and promising to keep in touch. Realizing the power in a community, I was determined to continue to create this not just for me, but everyone present that day.

Unfortunately, the following year, the organizers refused to release an email list and I couldn't set up a formal meeting. However, as it turned out, that meeting was another turning point. Every physician and allied clinical staff being recognized with awards in different departments and clinical specialties that year was male. So were all the speakers for the conference. Some of the female chiefs and vice chiefs I had met the previous year were outraged. Several of us took up the baton to ensure there would be more gender parity going forward. As a result, a movement was created for diversity, equity and inclusion.

Lessons Learned:

1. You are not alone. There are other women who are experiencing some of the same challenges you are. Reach out and form a support community.
2. The ripple effects of something you create can go far and wide beyond your wildest dreams.

And Then the Next Steps: What If I Could?

During the time I was making forays into community building for women in leadership in the large management company I worked for, I realised that we lacked the resources to find help. Each of us lived in a silo in our own hospitals, without a network. We didn't play golf like our male colleagues or have the unique male bonding rituals. Most of us were raising young kids. At that time social media like Facebook was still not as prevalent as today.

I had so many questions myself: How do I tackle a particular management situation? How do I find information about this position I am interested in? How do I learn what to say in certain organization meetings?

I thought, if I have all these questions, I'm sure many of my female colleagues must as well. So I decided to start a blog. I contacted women physicians who were in leadership positions in different parts of the country, none of whom I knew personally, and interviewed them by phone. They shared their journey, including the challenges they had faced, how they worked through and overcame them. As I talked to them, I built relationship and a network of strong supportive women. I now have a podcast along with the blog.

Lessons Learned:

If you want to learn something, never hesitate to ask. One of my early interviews was with Dr. Mary Dale Peterson, who at the time was the treasurer of the American Society of Anesthesiologists (an organization of over 60,000 anesthesiologists). She went on to become the president of the organization in the most challenging time of COVID. Her warmth and willingness to help is something I will never forget, nor is her advice to "get to know your organization's finances. If you can figure out the money, you will succeed"

When Status Quo Is not Enough

While I was busy with my blog and podcast, work as chief of my department settled into a routine. While things on the surface seemed fine, I was restless. I felt I needed something more. I had attended our state anesthesia society meetings for several years and noticed the lack of women physicians on the board.

Not ready to do anything about it, I still faithfully attended the meetings, learning the language of governance and lobbying. It was an eye-opener. Sheltered as I was in my clinical practice with a distaste for all things political, I was shocked to find out how much state and national healthcare policy was intertwined with political parties. Slowly, I got more involved in committees, realizing that few physicians actively worked with legislators.

As I became more involved with the FSA (Florida Society of Anesthesiologists), I saw how few women there were on the board. At the next annual conference, I organized a panel for women physicians, inviting them to learn from other women physicians who were in leadership. The response from the attendees was tremendous. This became an annual feature at our subsequent meetings, bringing more and more women physicians together. I was building a community again.

Simultaneously, somewhat jaded from medicine and wanting an interest outside of my profession, I decided to start a business with a direct sales skincare company. Why, as a physician who hated the word " "sales," had no social media presence or skills, and no social network outside of medicine, would I consider this? At that time, I needed to be more than "just a doctor." And I wanted an income stream outside of medicine. An online business that I could fit alongside my full-time medical career and commitments and my family seemed something worth exploring.

That "little" skincare business ended up teaching me more about myself, about entrepreneurship, and about having a supportive community than anything else in my life so far. Apart from business skills and entrepreneurial skills, it taught me more leadership skills and team building than some of the courses I have taken. It taught me to work on my personal development. And it brought some of my joy back in practicing medicine.

Lessons Learned:

1. Some of the lessons you need to learn to become a better person will come from the most unexpected places.
2. Keep an open mind. Don't let other people's judgments and expectations of you steal opportunities that could change your life.

Being True to Yourself

A few years into my involvement with the FSA, I decided to run for an elected office on the board. The first year I ran, I had no idea what was involved. When it came time to present my candidate speech, I was unprepared. I mentioned my few committee involvements and how I would like the opportunity to serve. Of course I didn't win.

I decided to run the following year. I had a better idea why this position was so coveted: it was a lead up to becoming president of the entire organization, a seven-year step-up journey. The older White males still intimidated me there, and I hadn't yet built many relationships. I lost.

By the third year, I felt I had a real chance. I'd put in enough time in the trenches, had a stronger voice, and knew the difference

I could make. I lost by a narrow margin. Several people encouraged me to try again.

The next year, a month before the elections, I asked an older and wiser colleague if he had any advice that would help me win. He said: "Asha, you need to be one of the boys. Go out with us for drinks, let people get to know you."

While I recognized the importance of letting people get to know me, I felt that there had to be ways other than "going out for drinks." Did I even want a position that may or may not depend on my acting like "one of the boys"? Maybe this wasn't for me.

I called a female physician friend who was one of my strongest supporters and told her I planned to drop out of the race. I was truly conflicted. I thought I was letting my female colleagues down. If I didn't run, there would not be another opportunity for a woman on that all male board for several more years.

I decided to run, but on my terms. I wouldn't try to change myself into becoming "one of the guys." For the first time, I asked several colleagues to support me. Previously I'd been too embarrassed to request help. This time my speech was prepared and was based on my strengths, on how I was good at building community and consensus, which was what our society needs. I won despite having a strong opponent!

Lessons Learned:

1. Be true to yourself. Step outside your comfort zone when necessary but do it for the right reasons in the right way.
2. Don't be embarrassed to ask for help. In the past, I assumed I should be elected simply by being seen and recognized for my efforts.

The Journey Continues: Getting To Know Myself

Five years after taking up the chief position, circumstances outside of my control led to a parting of ways from that hospital. I accepted another position as medical director at a different facility. Compared to my previous job, this was as different as night from day. The manager and director as well as the staff were more cooperative and willing to work as a team.

Still, the baggage I carried from the circumstances of leaving my previous job was painful. I had lost my sense of self-worth as well as my confidence in myself as a leader. Outwardly, I was content. I couldn't have asked for a better job and better people to work with. Yet I knew something wasn't quite right. It came to a head when I felt a situation at work was unfair. I felt that I couldn't negotiate for myself despite having taken several these courses in negotiation skills. I felt like an impostor again.

I decided to consult a coach, hoping to learn how to negotiate for myself. Within three sessions I underwent a personal transformation. I started recognizing my thought patterns, learning why I act and behave the way I do. I learned to recognize my strengths and work with them.

Coaching helped me bridge the gap between who I was and who I wanted to be by taking all the techniques I'd learned over the years in the abstract and showing me how to apply them. What had earlier been "book learning" that I'd tried to emulate, I could now apply specifically to me.

As I grew personally, I saw this as the missing piece to my desire to be a mentor to other women physicians. I decided to learn to be a coach myself. I took a course that offered a certification. Now I coach early- and mid-career women physicians in leadership development so that they can step confidently into administrative and leadership roles.

Lessons Learned:

1. Every physician is a leader.
2. The key to becoming a better leader is to manage your mindset.
3. Self-confidence comes from knowing yourself, from becoming aware of your thinking process and being able to manage in the moment.
4. Coaching is something every woman physician (and every physician) should consider to reach their full potential.

New Realities

As Dr. Selma Calmes, one of the pioneers for women in leadership positions in anesthesia alluded to in her chapter, there were very few women in management and leadership positions when she became one. Sad to say, today, even though there are many more women in the field, our numbers in leadership roles still fall far short of what they should be.

In the last several years, more than 50% of anesthesia residents are women. Yet, there are fewer than 20% of female professors in academic institutions or chiefs of departments. Women chiefs of anesthesia in private practice or in large national groups, like the one I work for, are still few and far between.

Added to the difficulty of rising in leadership are the changes in practice models. Certified Registered Nurse Anesthetists, who for decades have worked as part of the anesthesia care team, have been fighting to provide anesthesia care without physician oversight and supervision. In a few states, they have succeeded. In several others, the physician supervision requirement has been taken over by any physician (surgeon or gastroenterologist, usually). Imagine a surgeon performing surgery and simultaneously supervising the CRNA providing the anesthesia care.

Part of my duties as a physician leader within the community and within the Florida Society of Anesthesiologists is advocating for my patients and for preservation of physician-led anesthesia care. I spend a significant amount of time working to educate politicians about how removing the physician from the anesthesia team would be detrimental to patient care.

Last year, the Florida legislature passed a law granting independent practice to Advanced Practice Registered Nurses (APRNs) in several specialties, including Family Practice. CRNAs were excluded. However, this is a yearly struggle that our specialty faces every legislative cycle. The role of physician extenders taking over the practice of medicine is expanding rapidly.

I worry where this is leading. When I chose to become an anesthesiologist, I never envisioned the need to explain why having a medical doctor (rather than a nurse with far less comprehensive medical training) in charge of someone's anesthesia care is so important. Yet that is what I find myself having to do, over and over. Is it a losing battle? I hope not. My hope is that the young physician leaders coming up will join the fight to keep anesthesia care under the direct supervision of anesthesiologists.

Bottom line: I would not trade in my years of enjoying my clinical practice, my leadership journey, and my personal growth in that journey for anything else. I'm a better human being and a better leader, a better mother and wife, for having faced these challenges.

CHAPTER THIRTEEN

A Journey with Passion and Purpose

by Eneida O. Roldan, MD, MPH, MBA

*"Far and away the best prize that life offers is the
chance to work at work worthy doing"*
— THEODORE ROOSEVELT

THE DRIVE TO KNOW MORE, GIVE MORE, AND make a difference has been my primary motivator in both my professional and personal lives. Since childhood, I was inquisitive, always thinking outside the box. I refused to accept the status quo on any matter that came my way. Although my ways were often unpopular and uncomfortable to the mainstream, the overriding quest for knowledge made it all worthwhile.

In this chapter, I share my journey as a leader in healthcare. That journey focuses on the value I, as an executive, place on soft skills (also called Emotional Intelligence). These have helped me master challenging career transitions by increasing self-awareness, knowing the best "fit" for my talents, keeping a positive attitude, embracing change, and finally overcoming adversity.

All of these skills have ultimately helped my personal growth. You will not find here a guide on how I became an executive using hard skills. I assume those physicians/professionals reading this have mastered those skills through many years of schooling. This chapter will document my personal journey. While it may seem unconventional, there are lessons for anyone transitioning from clinician to physician leadership roles.

My career in medical management really began in childhood. As my first mentor, my maternal grandmother taught me never to accept the status quo. Although I didn't know then that someday I would make the transition from a "white coat" to a "suit," her early lessons became the core for my belief that any successful transition or change in life is a choice. That choice should be made with a foundation of purpose to better who you are or want to become; with direction that has both conviction and support from others including mentors and family; and with a clear focus on goals while staying true to your values, never compromising integrity, honesty, or ethics. This has played a major role in my journey.

Change is inevitable. It is how you deal with it — the loss of the known to an unknown — including the chaos of transition — that makes you successful. I knew I wanted to go to medical school at the age of eight. I was inquisitive, always seeking answers and interested in how the human body works.

I graduated from medical school and entered the most basic science specialty, pathology. Colleagues and mentors alike asked why I chose that field. They told me I was a "people person" and that pathologists worked away from people, behind the scenes. Facing this stereotyping/status quo challenged me to teach those questioning my choice that it is far too easy to think inside the box. If I had then, I would have missed a wonderful opportunity.

Much to my surprise, pathology offered a great foundation for a career in management. It taught me to work in teams and that technology has an important role in medicine. It also provided the opportunity to learn to budget an organization.

Running a lab is all about knowing how to implement quality standards for products and services, working as part of interdisciplinary teams, and producing a product with the highest standards at an affordable price. I didn't choose pathology knowing this would be a great field to acquire the knowledge that would help me as a medical manager. I simply chose the specialty that satisfied my quest to learn the origin of disease processes and mechanisms in depth.

Nurture Passion, Fulfill Purpose

During my residency program, I was fortunate to find another mentor. She was a faculty member and the director of the Department of

Pediatric Pathology. She taught me that without passion there can be no progress in your life's endeavors —personal or professional. Passion allows you to share talents, while complacency and apathy constrain progress and growth. Passion opens your world to new ideas and enables you to accept change with an open mind. Her words embodied the role passion can play in different aspects of the journey. It is with both passion and self-awareness that we begin to understand who we are, where we are going, and if we even like our direction.

My mantra became: "In the face of change, conviction, purpose, and passion, provide the drive to accept a transition in pursuit of a different direction and opportunities." I vowed to be open for any opportunity that would nurture passion, fulfill a purpose, and represent a positive change of direction. I also focused on nurturing my soft skills.

In every journey, we encounter opportunities. What's important is to have the proper foundation to recognize them and be ready to seize them. After having been successful in private practice for 12 years, I decided to pursue formal education in public health and entered a master's program focused on developing public health programs. This provided an opportunity to engage in population-based medicine and, more importantly, to learn how to make these programs administratively and operationally successful.

After graduating in 2002, I realized I needed more formal financial acumen, so I enrolled in a Physician Executive MBA (PEMBA) program at the University of Tennessee Haslam School of Business. This turned out to be the best decision I made in my transition to administrative medicine. As my network grew inside and outside of medicine, business world contacts called to engage me on projects integrating medicine and business. I was suddenly learning business firsthand.

One of my earliest projects was for a group of entrepreneurs who needed a physician with business knowledge — someone who could speak the business lingo while integrating concepts of medicine into business. From this experience, I learned "speed to market" and "carpe diem" (seize the day) as well as concepts that I currently use in my new endeavor. I was well on my journey of transition.

Subsequently, I was offered the role of president and CEO for a local community hospital that had recently filed for bankruptcy protection. Located in Miami, Florida, the facility was the first Hispanic hospital opened in the city at the beginning of the Cuban exile in 1963. Every important Cuban community leader had some personal connection to it.

Being of Cuban decent, I was especially passionate about wanting to do my part to save the hospital. At the same time, I was aware that if the outcome was not positive, I might not be able to remain in the Miami area and pursue a career in hospital administration. Staying true to my mantra, I accepted the job, which turned out to be an incredible learning experience. The board and I ultimately transitioned the hospital out of bankruptcy and sold it, thus preventing closure and the loss of services to that community.

As a result of this success, the local community came to view me as a capable administrator. After passing the gavel on to the new president and CEO of the community hospital, I realized I wanted a greater challenge. Never did I imagine that I would be asked to join Jackson Health System as the administrator of their flagship hospital, Jackson Memorial Hospital. This was the same medical center where I had studied and become a trained physician.

This became another journey of passion and purpose as well as the chance to use both hard and soft skills for the betterment of many. To be able to serve the place that made my physician journey a reality was truly a wonderful opportunity. But not everything that shines is gold. There are many who agree that I took on one of the hardest jobs in the country, not only because of the extraordinary challenges that are part and parcel of any ailing hospital system, but because as the appointed "savior" of a public organization, I had to juggle city/county/state politics while trying to focus on my purpose.

Within the first eight months of my tenure, the president and CEO of the Jackson Health System announced his departure. I was seen as the heir apparent. Once again, I faced another change in direction. I had to make a decision as to whether or not I would consider the role of president and CEO of the entire system. After much thought, but with a continued desire to grow by challenging myself,

I decided to announce my candidacy. This decision resulted in the most challenging and eye-opening experiences along my career path.

Jackson Health System is both a public health system and an academic medical center. It is one of the largest public health systems in the country and the largest in the state of Florida. Its funding depends on public dollars, local economy, and hospital operations. Unfortunately, my announced candidacy and subsequent confirmation coincided with unprecedented flux in healthcare and a serious downturn in our country's economy.

Difficult Decisions

The challenges I faced in this role would mold the rest of journey. The most important and difficult lesson I learned was that while my goal was for the betterment of the patients and the community, there were other drivers well beyond my control. Once that became clear, I came face to face with a dilemma familiar to many administrators: what to do when personal ethics conflict with policies and politics of those who have ultimate control? In my case, both the environment and circumstances were not aligned. However, it was an incredible opportunity to learn how to navigate a different world, offering so many lessons that would help in the next phase of my journey.

As difficult as it was to acknowledge, I had to accept the fact that ultimately my own direction had to change. I had done the best within my power; it was time for me to move on to my next role. I decided not to renew my contract. Leaving the position was difficult, since Jackson was and continues to be a special place in my career journey. It molded me as a physician. It held special memories that today are still with me.

I was offered the opportunity to stay in an administrative role at UM and at FIU College of Medicine, but I decided to take time to reconnect with who I am. I wanted to own a piece of what I could create. I became chief executive officer of a start-up company focusing on telehealth — an area in which I was able to provide solutions to many of the problems within the healthcare delivery system.

This opportunity offered flexibility, innovation, integration of all my skills (medicine, administration, and network), and a huge potential for growth. It also enabled me to continue teaching at the FIU College of Medicine — an important part of my transition decision. I wanted to share my given talents.

Naturally, this new role was not without challenges or problems, but having the tools to face them and the ability to accept transition made any change more bearable. I learned a lot and met individuals who were successful in business and invested in new ideas and innovation.

I was still teaching as founding faculty at FIU, so one day, I met with the dean of the College of Medicine. I told him I wanted to develop, to innovate, and keep my passion of life-learning. More importantly, I wanted to continue teaching and to mentor. He offered me a full-time position as associate dean of international affairs to lead the International Visiting Medical School Program (IVMS).

After eight years, this program has evolved into a best practice, offering qualified medical students around the world the opportunity to gain US experience before entering their specialties. Currently there are 348 global university partners in 62 countries. The program has hosted over 4,000 students. I am very proud of this endeavor which aligns with FIU's global strategy initiative. It gave me the impetus to attend an executive program at Thunderbird School of Global Management. My Certificate in Global Negotiations has enhanced my ability to negotiate contracts with global partners which I continue to this day.

Three years ago, I was admitted to an 18-month senior-level management program at the University of Pennsylvania Wharton School of Business. There, I met very successful individuals whose passion for knowledge was equal to my own. I found new friends and new colleagues across the globe. The knowledge I acquired in Thunderbird, a school ranked in the top five for global management, along with what I learned at Wharton, helped me negotiate a very favorable contract both financially and professionally that will last at least 10 years.

Continuing a Life's Work

During my time at Wharton, I suffered a great loss. My mom passed away from complications of a stroke. Amid so much advancement in medicine, I was angry that although she had the opportunity to seek the best care, she died doing it her way. Having always shied away from doctors, she left her fate up to destiny.

Although difficult, I had to accept that this was her wish. I understood that the same woman who guided me, taught me how important life-long learning, self-love, and passion are to know your purpose in life, had physically left my side, but not my heart. It was her and my grandmother's guidance that made me who I am today.

My mom's purpose in life was to give and serve others. She worked hard and always did chores by herself. Seldom would she ask for assistance. I was sad that she didn't live to see yet another milestone in my life. She was always so proud to see me receive another diploma, another award, so the completion of this program and attaining an alumnus status at Wharton made it all so much more special. It is never too late or anyone too old to continue to thrive.

The year my mom passed away, I decided to travel to Cuba. I felt an urgency to physically know my birthplace. I left Cuba when I was two years old and never returned. Visiting was an emotional experience. Having this opportunity was a true blessing. Everything my mom and grandmother stood for came to fruition. My family left their country to be adopted by a country they love, the United States of America, a country that offered all the opportunities to make dreams a reality. They taught me that through hard work and passion, one can reach the highest levels.

My family left everything behind except their passion, their education, their values, and an urgency to serve and give back. These are the values I own today and passed on to my children. It all made sense. So, to honor my mom and my grandmother, I decided to gift an endowment at the College of Medicine. This scholarship awards a minority, passionate, life-learner, and leader. The scholarship has entered its third year. The first recipient had a very similar story to mine. Her grandmother and mother were her first mentors. To be able to give is one of the most humbly experiences.

Six years ago, another opportunity came my way when the dean offered me the role of chief executive officer for the Health Care

Network at Florida International University where I have been for the past 10 years. The mission was to restructure the entity and realign its mission and vision. The skill set needed for success encompassed all my life learning.

Since its inception, I have built a team of highly dedicated professionals who share the same vision and more importantly values needed to succeed: loyalty, hard work, dedication, trust, and common purpose. A six-year performance report recently presented to the Health Care Network Board of Directors was excellent. It was not about me but about leading a group of individuals marching in the same direction with a common purpose and a foundation of trust. For any leader, that is a gift.

My role as a physician executive continues to grow. In addition, I have other roles within the College of Medicine (Herbert Wertheim College of Medicine) as associate dean for international affairs, associate dean for the Master of Physician Assistant Studies as well full professor in the Department of Pathology. In these roles, I still mentor both students and faculty. As associate dean of the Master's in Physician Assistant Studies, I have been able to meet the aspiring physician assistants and help them navigate the world of healthcare from the eyes of a physician. In this current healthcare environment, it is critical to develop teams in which we are all called to be leaders.

In 2020, the world changed. The global impact of COVID-19 devastated millions. It fundamentally changed how we do things not only in our daily lives, but also in our professional journey. Hundreds of physicians chose to leave medicine for fear of their physical safety and that of their loved ones. Yet, in every crisis, there are opportunities and a silver lining. Young people are applying to medical school in greater numbers than ever. And many of them aspire to become physician leaders.

Most recently, the university president appointed me to the University Health Care's COVID-19 Task Force. This offered the opportunity to collaborate with local government to advance testing and vaccinations to our community at large as we face this devastating pandemic.

There has been no greater challenging but important time to be part of medicine than now. The pandemic has taught us much more than the pathogenesis of the virus. It has taught us how deep rooted our needs as human beings are; how much we take for granted. We now understand how difficult it is to feel human in isolation. We understand the importance of others in our lives. This pandemic has changed us. Some of us have lost friends and colleagues but remain steadfast in our commitment to others, especially the most vulnerable.

For me, it gave me the chance to return once again to the frontlines. I took the opportunity to calm the anxieties of other clinicians, to be a voice of reason to those asking for answers. Understanding that *knowledge is power,* I collaborated with experts I might not have otherwise personally known. One of the many lessons learned was how to adapt during a time when events around us were changing daily.

Amid such a chaotic time, we need more physician executive mentors to develop the physician executives and leaders of tomorrow. We need them to share their journeys, their failures, and their successes. More importantly, we need them to lead and, during crisis, be a giraffe not a turtle. A giraffe sticks his neck out, not knowing if there is branch that may hurt him. Leaders are giraffes. Turtles hide their heads. We have many turtles and not many giraffes. That's why it is so important to support our future physician executives.

A Life's Journey

During the journey of life, we get to meet individuals who tell us a word, a phrase, that may not mean much at the time; however, years later it surfaces. I was fortunate to meet a very successful businessman who said the following: "When one is young and full of dreams, we work hard to get to our goals; the next phase in life, you build a family and enjoy the fruits of your labor; the last phase, we seek to leave a legacy. A legacy is giving back. In giving back, you feel gratitude for the opportunity to make others shine. This is the culmination of happiness."

Although I am working as hard as ever, I intend to leave a legacy — a legacy of passion, values, giving, and serving. As I look at my career, I have laid down the roadmap that can fulfill this dream. It all starts with that first mentor, someone who supports you, who cares, and who is not afraid to give you tough love. Years later, the mentee becomes the mentor. You guide by your experiences, but you let the mentee grow through failures and successes and teaching them the difference. I am proud to have mentored two of the young leaders featured in this book: Drs. Sosa and Gonzalez, who participated in FIU's 4th-year elective Seminars in Physician Leadership.

As I look at the past 10 years since I wrote the chapter for the first edition of this book, I stop and ponder the many things that life has prized me with both in my personal as well as my professional life — from fulfilling professional goals, to stepping up to serve in the unknown, COVID-19 pandemic, to becoming a grandmother four times, to the tremendous loss of my mother, to visiting my homeland for the first time, and finally the culmination to give back through an endowment and life-long mentoring. Words cannot express the gratitude I feel.

The journey has been long, the work has been hard but through perseverance and faith, all became possible. Especially during the past 20 months, when the world was impacted with COVID-19 pandemic, the losses for many have been numerous, the work exhausting, but the lessons learned priceless.

My professional life has truly been a roller coaster of great opportunities, growth, hard work, and the honor to serve; facing continued challenges and unknowns yet finding energy that I thought I had lost. There has been no better time to show resiliency, conviction, and firmness on values and purpose. During these past te10n years, I have continued to grow professionally, spiritually, and amid a great loss, feel humbled that at this stage of my career, I was still called to serve.

Finally, the balance of work and family is important to complete a successful journey. Being the wife of a surgeon and the mother of three, I know this all too well. It is very lonely at the top. A family bond built on unconditional love and support along with my faith has kept me grounded and given me the strength to continue to face challenges.

Maintaining an open dialogue with my husband and children and prioritizing tasks allowed me to continue moving along my career path. I can share my doubts, my weaknesses, and my difficulties openly without fear of rejection. In doing so, it gave me the energy, courage, and hope needed to face another day.

Even though there is more acceptance of women in management today, the issue of balancing work and family is, unfortunately, still primarily a woman's issue. For a physician executive, there will be times when family may suffer for the sake of work and vice versa. Having a supportive family will provide the wherewithal to face any adversity.

Some say that the pandemic caused a lack of trust in the "white coat." We cannot let this be a deterrent to the many great things we have done for others. That is our strength, that is our purpose. At this point in time, physicians have the opportunity to take the lead role in changing how healthcare is delivered. Those entering the world of management have an important role to fill.

I believe physicians — women and men — are the best equipped to manage change in healthcare. Below are some points that summarize my advice to those physicians who wish to become successful in the world of medical management, especially in a world where the only constant is change. This is a world that may not be comfortable at first, but in which there is much to gain, personally and professionally.

- Never negotiate your values. Keep them firmly grounded.
- Never shortchange your quest for knowledge. Formal education and experience are key to success.
- Never accept the status quo even if it means going against the mainstream.
- Learn from others. There are many mentors. Grow your network.
- Keep your options open. Every opportunity is a learning experience. Choose the right "fit" for you.
- Never take family for granted. Their love and support is unconditional.
- Enjoy the journey. It is not a destination. Keep the passion!

Provider Groups

"If you are not at the table, you may be on the table."

"It is not always lonely at the top."

– Josephine Young

CHAPTER FOURTEEN

Having Fun While Trying to Have It All

By Josephine Young, MD, MPH, MBA, FAAP

AS A YOUNG CHILD, WHEN ASKED WHAT I wanted to be when I grew up, I usually replied that I wanted to be a pediatrician and help people. This was often followed by advice to consider becoming a nurse or social worker or physician's assistant instead. The implication being that, as a girl, I should not be aspiring to be a doctor, but instead focus on something less challenging if I still wanted to have a family.

Despite this, with my parents' full support, I followed my heart and decided in seventh grade to become a doctor. Almost 30 years after that decision, I was a seasoned pediatrician and the chief operating officer of an 80-provider private pediatric group. On the way here, I have been in solo, group, and multispecialty practice in nonprofit, academic, and private settings while enjoying a busy and fulfilling life as a wife and mother.

My husband and I both graduated from medical school in 1991 and were married during the week in between our respective medical school graduations. After two years spent dating from afar, residency as newlyweds felt like another iteration of a long-distance relationship. Even though sharing a home, our three years of residency were frequently spent apart on-call every third night on different nights, in different hospitals, in separate programs. By our senior resident year, we decided that it was time to start our large family. Happily, our oldest was born during my chief resident year.

After residency, I spent almost two years in solo medical practice in a nonprofit clinic working with a team of mental health clinicians.

While there, I also served as adjunct faculty for pediatric residents. As detailed below, I resigned from this position due to administrative issues. I transitioned briefly to a combined short-term pediatric private practice and pediatric continuity clinic attending role while awaiting my husband's gastroenterology fellowship completion.

We soon moved to Seattle for his first faculty position. Within a few months, while pregnant with our second child, I entered a general academic pediatric fellowship. Three years later, I had obtained both my MPH and my subspecialty board certification in adolescent medicine. Upon fellowship completion, and while expecting our third child, I returned to private practice in a large multispecialty nonprofit group. I remained there for two years before coming to my current practice. During this period, we had our fourth child.

As expected, a dual-physician marriage imposes significant demands on time and commitment to outside responsibilities. This is especially true as both of us have substantial administrative roles with broad scopes of involvement. While frequently challenging, our profound understanding of each other's professional needs allows us to work with more synergy, less misunderstanding, and more patience. Nevertheless, even with mutual support, intense days are still encountered.

Looking back over the years, in spite of having worked in multiple settings, I always anticipated staying long term in each position. However, when organizational priorities undergo substantial change or new opportunities present themselves, it is important not only to be open to options, but also to have the courage to make significant changes. As I adapted and worked in different roles, I have learned important lessons, some more hard-won than others. Here are a few lessons I would like to share:

Never go to a meeting for which you do not know the agenda.

Corollary: **Never attend a meeting to which you do not know the range of attendees.**

This lesson was learned early during my chief resident year. Quite unexpectedly one day, my co-chief and I received a phone call from a faculty member requesting our presence at a meeting that afternoon. Although not apprised of the agenda, we naively never thought to ask. Hours later, we walked into a meeting attended by several other faculty members and proceeded to be berated for our handling of a recent housestaff matter. The critique was unwarranted, but being unprepared, we did not have the data at hand for an effective rebuttal.

Since that experience, I always insist on knowing the agenda for any meeting I am asked to attend. As a corollary, I also insist on knowing who will attend the meeting. This serves to minimize surprises or ambushes and also allows me to invite additional attendees to balance the meeting if needed.

When built into a habit, these questions about agenda and attendees become very natural to ask at the time of the meeting request. If the gathering is scheduled for a day or more ahead, it is also reasonable to ask for written confirmation including the agenda and list of attendees.

Titles matter.

Corollary: **Unless volunteering, ask for compensation before accepting new responsibilities.**

When offered my first job out of residency, I was told that while I would be the only doctor on staff, I would not have my predecessor's title of Medical Director because the clinic was in the process of restructuring. Not one to be concerned about titles and organizational hierarchy and not a deliberate negotiator, I was naively ready to agree to the title of staff physician. However, something made me ask how my responsibilities would differ from the previous medical director. Possibly caught off guard, the response was that there would be no difference. Now fully aware of the power play at hand, I suggested that I hold the title of Medical Director until such time as formal changes had been made. Reluctantly, there was agreement.

Two years later, significant management issues came to light that necessitated my direct involvement with the board of directors in a confidential meeting. Attempts were made to bar my access to the board with statements that I had no right of independent access.

After a detailed search into the archives, I retrieved the founding charter and the original organizational chart that defined my right as the medical director to have direct access to the board. Shortly thereafter, I was asked by the board to assume additional administrative responsibilities, to cover for departed staff including the administrator, and handle all aspects of management, essentially re-building the clinic.

Focused on my dual responsibilities, I waited until the bulk of the urgent work was completed before asking for compensation for these duties. The board denied my request and told me that I should have asked for this prior to doing the work. This was another hard lesson learned: If I expected compensation for extra work, I needed to make the expectation known and negotiate for it up front rather than waiting for someone else to notice.

Several months later, a new administrator was finally hired in replacement. Contingent upon her acceptance of the job were demands that would specifically decrease administrative transparency and accountability. Although this job had a perfect blend of clinical, teaching, and administrative duties for me, I found that the intended organizational structure and oversight was not aligned with my priorities for high-quality patient care and institutional integrity. Therefore, I tendered my resignation, giving them three months' notice to optimize stability for the clinic, and joined the faculty of the university where I had trained.

Throughout this experience, I was fortunate to be mentored by the university's pediatric department chair. As a woman in a prominent leadership position, she gave her time generously, sharing her wisdom and advice. Most importantly, she helped me develop an objective process to examine the situations at hand and determine a course of action that was both prudent and congruent with my management approach. This was the first time that I experienced direct personal mentoring, and she helped me to appreciate the value of asking for and accepting help.

Since then, I have come to fully understand the importance of titles in an organization's hierarchy. It has nothing to do with ego. Rather, a title generally gives the title holder access to information about the organization that he or she would not have without it. Moreover, with a higher title, there is greater access to potential key information that allows for the ability to anticipate and strategize, and to better understand the actions and motivation of other stakeholders in the organization.

As a result of this understanding, I no longer accept new positions without reviewing the organizational chart and knowing where the job title fits. I have also learned to make a conscious decision before taking on new responsibilities as to whether I am investing my time to learn a new skill and whether I need to discuss compensation before I start. This approach has alleviated any sense of unmet expectations.

Define your management philosophy.

A writing assignment during my MPH coursework required that I detail my management philosophy. Although many students complained, the professor emphasized that without the ability to clearly articulate a management philosophy, one couldn't know if their actions are consistent. Having already spent several years in management, I pondered my experiences and decided to sum it up in two words: "Respect and Autonomy." As a manager, I believe it is imperative to have *respect* for each individual regardless of his or her job title. In addition, once given the expectations and resources to fulfill a job role, managers need to foster *autonomy* within their staff as much as is feasible within each job description.

That MPH assignment was 14 years ago, and it was truly one of the most memorable and useful tasks that I was assigned during my postgraduate training. I have no doubt that each emerging manager needs to have a defined management philosophy that should be thought about often and amended as necessary with increased experience.

If you are not at the table, you may be on the table.

Early in my management career, I held leadership roles without clear job descriptions and therefore had limited access to knowledge and information. Having learned that accurate information was imperative for success, I concluded that the best way to get information is to be in on the discussions. Offering to help and being willing to serve on committees are some of the easiest ways to get information quickly.

In a large organization where there may be as much circulation of rumor as fact, it is useful to be part of multiple forums to best assess the accuracy of the available information. After participating in several arenas, I also learned that being at the table meant having a say in the destiny of my department. Without that participation, our needs were not taken into account and decisions made on our behalf often had unintended negative consequences. It is certainly better to be at the table than on the table!

Find your voice.

Although a very successful student, I was rarely one to raise my hand. I was confident in what I knew, but never felt the need to demonstrate my expertise to others unless I was directly asked or challenged. This approach did not hamper my ability to graduate as valedictorian of my high school, but did negatively impact my success on hospital rounds, and was definitely not credibility-enhancing in management discussions. While I readily learned to contribute to clinical and middle management discussions, the development of my executive voice and presence was a more conscious endeavor.

In engaging an executive coach, I worked with her to find my "executive voice" and learn to wield it. I first had to acknowledge and accept that my current title and position comes with power — the power to question, to influence, and to act. To be effective in my job, it was imperative that I own this power and use it wisely or someone else would, and perhaps not as judiciously.

Several years into my role year as chief operating officer, I was comfortable speaking my mind in a variety of settings on a variety of topics. Aside from being more familiar with the topics and issues at hand and having the increased confidence that comes with experience, I had the comfort of owning my position and title. Where I once downplayed the significance of my executive position, I no longer felt apologetic about my administrative role. Instead, I embrace the possibilities of the unique contribution that I am able to make as a physician executive and use the opportunities to communicate effectively from a position of strength.

"Do something each day that scares you."

— Eleanor Roosevelt

While I don't do a scary thing every day, I do periodically seek out new challenges when I begin to feel comfortable in my primary job. This helps me stay at the top of my game, avoid complacency, and remain humble and honest with myself about how much more I still have to learn.

For example, I challenged myself and joined the board of directors of a medical professional liability company. It was in a related field, but in an area that I knew almost nothing about. After a full day of board orientation, meeting with each member of the C-suite executives, I gained a clear understanding of the strategic challenges facing the company. More importantly, I came to understand that the skills and knowledge I had acquired as a member of a successful senior management team translated well to another industry.

While I still had to learn the specific technical content of the insurance industry, I already possessed the skills required for strategic planning, assessment of competition, understanding of information technology needs, and marketing and business development. Moreover, as a senior manager in my own organization, I had a greater understanding as to the separate and complementary responsibilities of the board and management, and what specific roles each should play to optimize the functioning of the other. Most importantly, I appreciated what the board needs to leave to management to operationalize and execute, and when the board needs to be clear in its strategic planning and direction.

A strong mentor is a gift.

At several key times in my life, I've been fortunate to benefit from the guidance of a mentor. The willingness of someone experienced and well respected in their field to reserve personal time for me was greatly appreciated and needed. I used the opportunity to ask questions, explore hypothetical situations, and simply to listen — to listen carefully and discern the pearls of wisdom born of challenges large and small; to understand that there is another way of approaching something.

The best mentors have been people who offer concepts to consider and not rules to follow, a compass, not a map. Early in my career, it was harder to appreciate philosophical advice. Sometimes it was easier to just have someone tell me what to do. It would have been easier, but clearly not better. I always learned more when I fully considered the points and counterpoints involved, made a decision for myself, and experienced the consequences.

As I have taken on the role of mentor myself, I recognize that the opportunity of mentoring is perhaps a greater gift because it is learning at a higher level. In fact, in the role of mentor I have learned as much if not more than I have as the mentee. This is likely because being a mentor necessitates greater introspection, personal accountability, and consistency of behavior. However, I could only function in this role after having had strong mentors who taught me what to expect.

Being a mentor is unlike any other relationship. It is different from being a friend or a supervisor. As a friend, my primary role would be to support my friend's desire to make changes. As a supervisor, I am charged with keeping my employee accountable to stated responsibilities and provide additional opportunities for growth. The primary investment is in the individual as an employee, limited within the parameters of the organization's needs. As a mentor, my investment is in the individual as a person, the result of which may extend beyond the needs of the organization if the mentee is also an employee.

In my personal experience, the beginning of a mentoring relationship can be either a formal request for mentoring, or more frequently, the product of multiple informal conversations around aspirations. There is the recognition that there is a potential within the mentee to achieve something significantly beyond his or her current endeavors. This may have been something consciously or sub-consciously desired, but typically unspoken until that point.

Once identified, it is now up to the mentee to engage and decide whether this is a goal to pursue. If there is the agreement, then the relationship is set as I provide my commitment to nurture that potential to fruition, even if that ultimately results in the mentee taking a position in another organization.

To me, the agreement is a key element because it advances the foundation of trust that is necessary for the mentorship to flourish. Without this trust, I will be unable to successfully challenge my mentee to reach outside of his or her comfort zone to gain new experiences, build confidence, and most importantly engage in honest self-assessments and further goal-setting. In addition, the explicit agreement assures that the goals represent an alignment with the mentee's desires, and not my personal goals for him or her to achieve. This conscious awareness and separation is needed so that there are no unrealistic or unspoken expectations at play that may result in misunderstandings or miscommunication. To be done well, mentoring is a slow and steady process, not to be rushed but readily cultivated.

I come to work to relax!

I have often joked that I come to work to relax. That's because my real life as wife and mother of four is far more demanding and challenging to manage than any project at work, no matter how difficult the issue. Early on, I felt guilty about being a working mother, worrying that the pursuit of my own career would equate on some level to neglecting my children, and that they would grow up either resenting it or feeling an element of loss.

Even as a child dreaming about my future, it was always a fantasy of working full-time and being an involved mother once I was home. There was never any doubt that I would not be working. And yet, when I had my first child during my chief resident year, I gave more thought to being a stay-at-home mother than I ever thought I would. I felt guilty about turning over her care to someone else. If not for the fact that I was obligated to return to my chief resident year, I might have pursued a longer maternity leave. For each child, the weeks leading up to the end of my maternity leave were the hardest. Those emotions did not lessen for subsequent children, even though I knew that it would work out well once the transition was made.

Because I am reserved by nature, it was several years before I considered being candid about my internal conflicts in being a working mother. However, the experience of sharing with others allowed me to verbalize my own personal reality. I concluded that in many ways, I was a better mother when I was working. I appreciated my children more. I was able to focus on them more when I had been away. I treasured more the day-to-day achievements. I am sure I was more patient with them when I had not been there the whole day. And yet, the ultimate test of what I would choose if my career and motherhood met head-to-head came during a very inauspicious summer morning a number of years ago.

I was at a routine prenatal ultrasound when we were told that our fourth child had a complex congenital heart defect. In the weeks that followed, through literature searches, consultation visits, and long nights filled with uneasy thoughts and dreams, my husband and I eventually settled on a plan to have our son's delivery and subsequent surgery at a world-renowned university hospital that was out-of-state. Faced with an uncertain future that may not allow for out-of-home childcare, I carefully considered my career.

I was frank with our CEO, our chief personnel officer, and our chief medical officer about the very real possibility that I might not be returning to work, and that it was even less likely that I could return to resume my role as the site medical director of our largest clinic. They were incredibly supportive, exploring the option that the position be held in reserve for me by having an acting site medical director. I agreed, appreciative of their overwhelming support and grateful for having an ideal job.

As I anticipated my last day at work before maternity leave, I imagined I would be emotional and maybe a bit conflicted. However, when that day arrived and I realized that I might be walking away from my career permanently, there was no ambivalence. In fact, I felt a great sense of peace. There was a remarkable clarity in my vision, knowing where I needed to be and what I needed to do. I knew then that no matter how much I enjoyed my job, being a mother came first.

Two weeks later, our child was born. He had open heart surgery at nine days old and was discharged from the ICU at three weeks old. We were on a flight back home, all six of us, within 24 hours. I had very minimal contact with my practice in the early months, but as the situation improved, I started attending phone meetings during baby nap times and slowly started to work on projects from home.

At seven months, my son started full-time daycare as I returned to work. It was then that I also started a support group for families affected by congenital heart issues, which continues to this day. Within the group, we share a bond as heart families. Being on this journey together, rather than individually in isolation, makes all the uncertainty and challenges much more bearable.

I have come to realize that much of my guilt as a working mother was self-imposed and now understand that children who are cared for by loving adults will thrive in the environments in which they find themselves, even if it is not always in the company of parents. I have devoted as much time as I can to actively participate in their lives, whether in the classroom, on the sports field, or at the dining table over homework. But the best conversations have always been during my hours as a "chauffeur." That's when we discuss the compelling questions that reflect the most important issues in their lives at that moment. Being able to be present at those times has been priceless.

It is not always lonely at the top.

One topic of some controversy is whether it is acceptable to be personal friends with a direct report, and by extension, with those who report to them. There is no doubt that some level of personal engagement enhances work relationships, but should that extend to a personal friendship?

In general, a level of professional friendliness is more than sufficient for a successful work relationship; yet, if it is desired, I feel strongly that it is possible to have personal friendships at work, even in a management position. However, there needs to be an awareness of the inherent risk in being friends with your direct reports because you hazard the real or perceived loss of objectivity as it relates to that individual. Moreover, the subsequent decisions that are made may be subject to greater scrutiny or possible misinterpretation. This is a risk that can be largely eliminated by not pursuing a friendship, but it is not completely removed because there may be incorrect perceptions that arise of their own accord.

Still, I believe friendships can be successfully pursued if there is confidence in being able to handle the risks. For me, the friendship must not influence my ability to provide feedback, pursue accountability, impose disciplinary action, or assign resources or opportunities. I approach issues and consequences from a factual, principled basis. That is, I first examine the situation, whether positive or negative, for its objective elements. Then I determine the relevant consequences that need to be applied. These are based on principles embodied within existing policies or guidelines or are extrapolated from precedence. In this approach, the specific individual, and thereby the relationship, is secondary to the decisions that need to be made.

These complex relationships do require that greater care and conscious awareness go into seemingly everyday decisions. The friendship should be neither secret nor flaunted, but publicly acknowledged when relevant. Social opportunities, especially those of general interest, should be offered equitably to all direct report peers whenever feasible.

Some may consider this degree of effort more work than a friendship should entail, not worth the risks, or unwise to pursue. It may therefore be prudent for those individuals to avoid developing friendships at work. As for me, I have met many remarkable individuals in my days at work, and while I continue to navigate these relationships mindfully, I know that these friendships have enriched my life both personally and professionally and find all the effort quite worthwhile.

Maybe you can have it all.

So the question remains: Is it possible to have it all? I would like to believe that it is, but not always all at once. Aside from the basics of time management, prioritization, and organization, it comes down to some blind faith, a realization that I don't have to do it alone, and a good dose of personal forgiveness.

It is the ability to recognize when some things are good enough and which elements demand flawless execution. It is the willingness to stay up late on more than a few nights when it is needed, not have a spotless house, and know when to walk away from the work for a little while in order to center myself.

I am frequently asked how I stay so positive and keep from burning out. My answer has been the same over time: I trust my internal gauge as to whether I am having fun. If I am not, it is time to take a break and recharge.

Looking to the Future

During the nine years since the publication of *Lessons Learned: Stories from Women in Medical Management,* I returned to school to earn an MBA from the University of Washington in an 18-month program focused on technology management. I intentionally avoided a physician-oriented healthcare management MBA as I wanted to experience a traditional program enhanced with an entrepreneurial focus.

My private practice underwent a CEO transition due to retirement, and experienced significant leadership style changes concurrent with unprecedented staff layoffs at the onset of the pandemic. I was recruited by a local Blue Cross plan to join them as the medical director of commercial markets, working with large local and national accounts.

This is the next iteration of a dream job in being able to simultaneously use my clinical skills, population health focus and business experience on a daily basis to benefit patients from within a whole new sphere of influence. I serve as an experienced physician voice, advising decision makers on the clinical implications of business decisions being considered, so that the needs of the patient (or member in insurance terms) are ever present and top of mind.

At this writing, my husband and I have two employed college graduates, a junior in college, and a junior in high school. Our youngest had his successful second open heart surgery in the short pause between waves of the COVID pandemic. Some extended time spent together as a family, due to remote work and school during the pandemic, gave me what felt like a second chance to be a stay-at-home mom. Because of a lack of business travel, it was the most extended period of time my husband and I had spent together in our 30 years of marriage. As our family was blessed with health during this time, it was a fulfilling period to reinforce our relationships and focus on gratitude for simple pleasures.

For the first time in decades, I have not had direct reports; however, I continue to mentor colleagues interested in exploring their potential and advancing their career. I also started a virtual monthly Women's Leadership Circle meeting that brings together women across different industries, at various stages in their career, to have an open agenda discussion about the experiences and challenges most relevant to female leaders.

The changes of the past several years have also tested the premise of whether it is possible to be friends with direct reports while remaining an effective leader. The friendships with my previous team members have outlasted the employment and it is clear, in retrospect, that the trust and mutual respect within these friendships was part of the synergy that allowed us to achieve more together than otherwise expected.

Throughout my career, I have been grateful at every step for the opportunities presented, the experiences gained and the potential to benefit others. I do not know the tenure of my career, nor the ultimate breadth of my work, but I remain open to discovering where and how I can advocate for the best outcomes for my patients, build the strongest teams, and continue to have fun along the way while still being present for my family!

CHAPTER FIFTEEN

Pearls Are a Woman's Necktie

By Grace Terrell, MD

I GREW UP IN RURAL NORTH CAROLINA IN THE 1960s, the oldest of four children. I was a classic tomboy, spending most of my free time playing outside with my brothers and cousins when I wasn't working in the garden, feeding the livestock, going to school and church, or watching favorite TV shows.

My first years in school were stressful for me, because temperamentally I was different from the other girls. As a result, I was picked on by the boys, and became disruptive in class. I dreaded report card days, when my all-A record was inevitably spoiled by that D-minus in conduct.

Although the bullying I experienced in school was quite severe, as I gradually became more confident of my own talents and self-worth, it actually made me fearless. Later, as a medical student and resident, behavior others would interpret as harassing or abusive just rolled right off my back.

Reading finally saved me from perpetual misery at school. I devoured books by the dozen and developed a love of reading that has remained an important part of my life. My parents knew they had their hands full with me, so they made sure I had lots of activities to keep me focused.

Starting at age six, I participated in scouting, choral music, piano lessons, oil painting, and plays. Though not typical then, this was very much like the activity-filled lives of many children today. I even had my own horse, named Daisy. Since none of my other siblings liked to ride, some of my best memories are of my Dad and me riding our horses together.

The culture in which I grew up drew clear distinctions between the roles of girls and boys and I often felt uncomfortable with those traditionally assigned to women. I didn't want to learn to cook, sew, or homemaking and I didn't want to become a secretary, teacher, or nurse — the only careers I thought available to women. Although I had the highest grade point average in my class, I was told to learn to type. That way, "if I had to work," I could always get a job.

Prior to Title IX, there were few sports opportunities for girls. I was jealous of my brothers' participation on baseball and football teams. I wanted to be an athlete, but year after year I was cut from the basketball team, the only sport open to girls at the time. Despite many hours of practicing alone, my petite and clumsy self couldn't seem to master the game.

Luckily, I discovered running. In ninth grade I tried out for track and excelled, lettering in it. The following year, there were not enough girls trying out to form a team, so I ran on the boys' team. I ran the mile and the 880. Every boy I beat would promptly quit the team as a matter of pride rather than wait to be cut. As a result, I was middle of the pack at the first of the season but dead last by the end.

As a young person, I began to become a student of human nature. This was in part a result of experiencing so much death in the people I was close to, including family. First, my grandfather died of a cardiomyopathy at age 59. Not long after, my third grade schoolteacher died of metastatic breast cancer in the middle of the school year. My other grandfather died of coronary disease when I was in eighth grade, and one of my grandmothers died of colon cancer when I was 15. My last grandparent died of a stroke when I was 19.

My parents are only 20 and 22 years older than me. As I think back now, they had lost all four of their parents before they were 40. They were wrestling with all the issues of young adulthood while deeply grieving. In the midst of all that, they were able to create a family life that emphasized the moral imperative to make one's life meaningful in a loving and supportive environment.

The message I heard from my mother, whose own life choices had been theoretically limited by economic circumstances, was "you can do anything you want to do, Grace, so long as you set your mind to it." This existentialist message I have taken to heart.

Like Barack Obama, I graduated high school in 1979. This was the class that divided the baby boomer from generation X. I believe our values are boomer: focused on hard work, achievement, finding meaningfulness in our careers and life choices. But our circumstances are X-er: attending high school during recessionary, Watergate-driven cynical '70s, graduating college in the midst of the Reagan recession of 1983, entering our 50s after the 2007 crash.

From a leadership perspective, this historical margin creates the possibility of a group of individuals who are simultaneously idealistic and cynical, hard-working and somewhat self-centered. That juxtaposition allows a certain degree of conviction mixed with energy, perseverance, and caution that may be just what is necessary to lead us through our current national challenges.

In 1979, I won a Morehead scholarship to attend the University of North Carolina at Chapel Hill. At that point, the scholarship had been open to females for only three years. The scholarship allowed me to obtain an incredibly rich undergraduate education. During the summer months before college, I participated in an Outward Bound program in Colorado. I got to ride a plane for the first time and spent four weeks in the Rockies in a challenging physical and mental environment. Other summer experiences included working for a police department in California, a law firm in North Carolina, and, in 1982, during the Falklands War, working for the Liberal Whip's Office of the Parliament of Great Britain.

In college I ran on the women's track team for a year and participated in crew another year. Track turned me into a life-long runner. Choosing a major was difficult because I wanted to learn "everything." I ultimately majored in religion and English, with enough economics courses to nearly declare a third major.

More importantly, college is where I met the love of my life. Tim is the fifth of six children. Both his mother and father are physicians. Like me, he grew up in a large, close-knit family. We had both grown up on farms where we lived with grandparents in the same house. Our families were intensely committed to Democratic politics in an increasingly conservative state and equally involved in church — his were sixth-generation Quakers, mine were Southern Baptists.

College for me included student government, track, and crew. For Tim it included managing the kitchen at his fraternity, delivering pizzas for Dominos, working as a camp counselor, exploring the new field of computer science with punch cards, algorithms, and programming. We both majored in religion because it was the most intellectually comprehensive department in the university.

A week after we graduated in 1983, we married. In the midst of a recession, we had about $500 between us, no jobs, and liberal arts degrees in humanities. A year before, almost on a whim, I began thinking about medical school. The idea of taking a deep dive into the natural sciences, which I had not really studied since high school, with a career focused on helping people seemed appealing.

Tim's mother, Dr. Eldora Terrell was a role model. She showed me such a life was possible. In an era in which women's choices were supposedly fixed, she had six children, practiced internal medicine, founded a clinic for uninsured patients in the community, took a public stand for integration in the Civil Rights era, was active in her church, served as a medical director of a nursing home, a college board trustee, chief of staff of the hospital where she attended patients, and still managed to can green beans, make strawberry jelly, harvest asparagus, and ride horses to help with the cattle round-up on the weekends. Through her, I saw how the professional role of physician actually frees women from certain social constraints.

Ten days after graduating and three days after getting married I was in summer school studying physics. That wasn't the only course I had to take before applying to medical school. There were two physics courses, two organic chemistry courses, and some biology. Then I had to take the MCAT and do well in order to be accepted.

From 1983 to 1985 we lived in Richmond, Indiana, while Tim pursued a master's degree in Quaker history at Earlham School of Religion. We had a three-room cinderblock apartment in an undergraduate dormitory where I worked as head resident. My salary was $3,000 dollars a year. We ate for free in the campus cafeteria. I thought it was the coldest place in the universe.

At age 22, I found myself married to a creative, idealistic, and definitely unfocused man, working in a job where I was responsible for students only a few years younger than myself. They challenged me, insulted me, and generally pursued their own agendas. They didn't know that I had a recent "grand past" as a Morehead scholar, intern to Parliament, and UNC varsity athlete. To them, I was either the person who let them into their dorm room when they lost their key, the one from whom they hid their marijuana, or the person who was supposed to settle their roommate complaints.

For intellectual enrichment I took a "wives' course" on John Updike at the School of Religion. It was awful: faculty wives crocheting and talking about their children's preschool experiences.

Tim was trying to find himself and I was trying not to lose myself. I focused upon those science courses at the college that I needed for medical school. Fortunately, I could take these for free as part of my employment. In addition, I decided to expand my general knowledge base.

First, I found a Cliff's Notes pamphlet and looked at all the great books listed on the back page. Then I started from the As and read each work of literature, from *Absalom, Absalom* on down the alphabet. After that I read all the works of philosophy I could locate, including all of Hegel, all of Kant, all of Kierkegaard, and so on.

I told myself I was doing this before I went to medical school because then I wouldn't have time to read for pleasure. In retrospect, though, I was probably depressed. Training and running a triathlon finally got me out of my funk. I took the MCAT, interviewed, and applied for several medical schools. I was accepted at Duke and entered in 1985.

Tim and I traded places in the fall of 1985. Suddenly I was the medical student, with purpose and focus, and he was looking for a job. He worked as a bartender in the Duke faculty lounge for a bit, and finally landed a job counseling Native American high school students, helping them get into college through the North Carolina Commission of Indian Affairs. For the first two years we scraped by on his $13,500 a year salary. Then we decided we just had to have a baby.

Katy was born at the end of my third year of medical school. I took eight weeks off, then did my fourth year "in reverse," taking the sub-internships at the end of the fourth year rather than at the beginning.

The year Katy was born, Tim decided to return to school for a master's degree in the burgeoning new field of computer science. He took all of his classes on Tuesdays and Thursdays so he could be home with the baby on the other days. On Tuesdays and Thursdays, my sister, a freshman at UNC drove over to Durham to watch the baby, while Tim drove over to NC State University to take his classes.

After I graduated from medical school, I stayed at Duke Medical Center an extra year and did an internship in pathology, reasoning that without night call, I could be with the baby at home giving Tim time to finish his degree.

My year as a pathology intern still seems surreal. Like many working mothers, I felt the pangs of guilt every morning as I left my daughter at home. It didn't matter that her father and aunt were available as primary caregivers. Katy walked early, talked early, and was like a little Tasmanian devil full of energy. I hated missing any part of her development, although her irregular sleeping and eating patterns kept us all perpetually exhausted.

I spent my days doing surgical and autopsy pathology. The autopsies on fetuses and children were particularly difficult for me. I still remember how I felt entering the autopsy suite to view one particular case. The little girl was almost the same age as my Katy, her body in a nightgown, still clutching a teddy bear.

Like many internships of that era, the pathology department at Duke was not a particularly warm environment. Because the program directors knew I did not intend to remain in pathology as a specialty, they focused their mentoring energies elsewhere.

When some of the physicians learned of my plan to practice general internal medicine, I began to experience discrimination for the first time. Duke was not primary care friendly. One professor told me that I should leave and find some primary care program in a community setting, that as a "real" academic institution, there was no place for a generalist at Duke.

That year, while in the surgical suite, I accidentally severed the artery and nerve to my left index finger on a formalin-hardened surgical specimen. The injury required hand surgery. For eight weeks while the re-anastomosis healed, I was unable to cut surgical specimens. When I returned to work the day after my surgery, an upper level resident yelled at me for a good 30 minutes, making it clear that my injury was going to make life difficult for the other pathology interns. The department administrator was equally unsympathetic; his only concern that this might bring OSHA down on the department.

Once Tim finished his degree, we knew we needed to make a change. I was accepted into the primary care track in internal medicine at NC Baptist Hospital in Winston-Salem. I completed my pathology internship on June 29, 1990, and began my second internship July 1. That was the start of the second craziest year of my life.

We were living with Tim's parents in High Point, North Carolina, about 20 miles from Winston-Salem. Tim got a job in public health sciences in research computing at the medical school. Our household was not exactly mainstream America. We had four generations, including Tim's 94-year-old grandmother, my busy internist mother-in-law and father-in-law, Tim, me, and Katy, the quintessential "terrible two" year old. The four dogs in the house added to the chaos. Still, it was wonderful having the security of two salaries for the first time after eight years of marriage.

Like every other medical intern, I rotated through cardiology, heme-onc, general medicine, emergency medicine, and the other specialties with every second or third night call. I do not remember that time as being difficult or abusive. I was excited to finally learn my craft in a residency environment that was both rigorous and supportive.

I developed a very close relationship with Dr. Bryant Kendrick, a chaplain at the medical center who managed the internal medical primary care track. He became my real mentor, helping me process my continued "strangeness": we focused upon medical ethical issues, the excitement engendered by the Clinton era anticipated healthcare reform, and the spiritual wholeness of the doctor-patient experience.

After 14 months of living with Tim's parents, we had saved enough for a down payment to purchase our first house. It was on a wooded lot with a stream, a tree house, a swing set, and an elementary school and playground next door. We balanced our roles as young parents and professionals, began paying off our student loans, and spent our free time together hiking, parenting, exercising, and keeping up this new house.

In 1993, seven months pregnant with my second daughter, Robyn, I completed my residency and began private practice with my in-laws. I took my medical boards that September, before promptly going into labor. The next eight weeks were some of the sweetest of my life. I took maternity leave and was able to walk Katy to the neighborhood school for her first days of kindergarten. I also got to spend some very quiet and special time with my new little girl.

Although as grandparents, my in-laws were both interested in the welfare of their new granddaughter, as medical practice partners they were equally eager for my return to work. This was the period when primary care started to lose status and get slogged by the economic forces of managed care. Our once-a-week call meant covering seven internists, three nursing homes, and unassigned hospital cases.

These were also the days before hospitalists and before nurse triage. The paradigm was still for the internist to be the center of all activity in the middle of the medical universe, despite the degradation of both reimbursement and status. It was far more brutal in many respects than my residency, but also more rewarding.

The intensity of the experiences with patients in the office, the hospital, and the nursing home in that era has been unsurpassed. It was comprehensive, and I had been trained to be effective in a multitude of settings. In areas where I had not, the 40-year experience of my father-in-law and mother-in-law filled in the gaps left in my training. It helped me understand the real role of physicians: to listen, to act, to help, to heal.

About six months after I had joined my in-laws' private practice, administration at High Point Regional Hospital, where I admitted patients, began discussions about the creation of a PHO (physician hospital organization) as a response to anticipated changes in the healthcare environment from managed care.

The chief-of-staff, Dr. Al Hawks, gave a passionate speech about the need for collaboration and cooperation and a steering committee of seven was formed. The three specialists and three primary care physicians nominated to form the steering committee were all established male medical staff members.

Almost as an afterthought, my father-in-law nominated me. Over the course of the next 18 months, we met every Thursday night, sometimes until one or two o'clock in the morning, to create what ultimately became Cornerstone Health Care.

Most of us were junior partners in our practices. Because we were young and less established in the community, we were more willing to be reckless. We figured out our governance and income distribution and began developing a culture based less on autonomy and more on collaboration. We also focused on investing in information, technology, and advanced models of care delivery.

Cornerstone Health Care was established October 1, 1995, from the merger of 16 practices in High Point, North Carolina. In 2000, I became CEO. During that time, I saw my daughters grow to young adults, my in-laws retire from medical practice, and my practice merge with two other Cornerstone internal medical practices to become the first NCQA-recognized level-three Physician Practice Connection Medical Home in our state.

Cornerstone grew from the original 16 practices in High Point, to 93 locations throughout the Piedmont Triad region of North Carolina, with over 300 providers practicing in 10 separate hospitals that were part of six separate health systems.

Our company's focus was to be the model for physician-led healthcare in America. We were committed to transform our model from a volume-based system to one that was value-based, leading our market in innovative approaches to a sustainable 21st century healthcare delivery system.

From 2013 through 2017 Cornerstone and I gained a lot of national prominence and, some would say, notoriety.

In 2013 Cornerstone Health Care developed innovative care models in primary care, cardiology, oncology, pulmonology, and dual-eligible populations, and moved all of our contracts to early value-based models. Within 18 months, we had lowered the cost of care by 20% and in 2015 won the prestigious AMGA Acclaim Award for its highest-performing medical groups.

We spun off our infrastructure into a company called CHESS, which was invested in by LabCorp, Wake Forest, and now, Atrium. That company, for which I was the first CEO, remains an under-recognized powerhouse in value-based care, managing over 150,000 lives in high-performing risk contracts in Medicare Advantage, NextGen ACO, and commercial contracts. I remain on the board of CHESS and am proud to see the vision we had for it a decade ago is coming to fruition as "the market catches up."

Under my leadership, Cornerstone made the move to value-based healthcare earlier than much of the rest of the market. Our rationale was built upon our confidence in our ability to provide higher-quality healthcare at a lower cost in a physician-led independent medical group.

We went all in, but the market did not. Payers talked a good game about wanting to move to value, but they were as ill-equipped to do so as the high-cost hospital systems. As the payers dragged their feet in providing value-based reimbursement, the move to value strained our finances and local hospitals quickly took advantage by hiring our physicians feeling the strain of our financial commitments. In 2016, Cornerstone lost its independence, becoming part of the Wake Forest Health System, which is itself, now part of the multi-state Atrium Health System.

By 2016, the other physicians at Cornerstone had had enough of me and I was mentally exhausted and quite heartbroken at the public animosity I experienced in the local medical community to which I had dedicated 23 years as a practicing physician and CEO of Cornerstone. I had a new ambiguous role at Wake Forest within the confines of CHESS, and I was certainly not culturally well-suited for the Wake Forest environment at that time.

Two women academic department heads at Wake took me out to dinner and told me about their own challenges, emphasizing that Wake was not a good environment for women leaders. Although now Dr. Julie Freischlag is the CEO of Wake and much of that culture has changed, at the time, the entire executive team at Wake consisted of white men. Two of them, Dr. Russ Howerton and Terry Williams, are very good friends of mine, but that did not make my ability to navigate the Wake environment any easier, an environment that felt as sexist and unwelcoming as any I had ever experienced.

In 2017, I could stand it no longer. I accepted a position as CEO of Envision Genomics at the Hudson Alpha Institute of Biotechnology in Huntsville, Alabama, a startup founded by the legendary team featured in the Pulitzer prize-winning article and subsequent book *One in a Billion* that made the first diagnosis of a rare disease in a child using genomic sequencing technology that resulted in a life-saving cure.

Our startup company had a revolutionary information technology that could use whole-genomic sequencing to diagnose heretofore rare and undiagnosed illnesses. Although I practiced primary care medicine every day, I, like most physicians, was not very knowledgeable about the capabilities of cutting-edge genomics. To get up to speed, I used my reading superpowers to read every textbook on genomics I could find and quickly got a professional certification in genomics from Stanford University through their online learning platform.

Upon arrival at Envision, I wrote a business plan built upon the unmet needs of patients with rare disease and went to the market to get out a minimally viable product. Compared to the resources of Cornerstone and Wake, Envision's resources were minimal. I learned the world of venture capital, startups, biotechnology, pitch decks, and fundraising.

Once again, I was in a company trying to do something ahead of the market. Payers would not reimburse our technology and potential health system partners were not interested in any technology, no matter how much it improved patient care, if they didn't make money using it. Over the course of the past few years, that has changed, but not soon enough to save Envision.

On September 19, 2018, I learned that Tom Main, a long-time friend, mentor, Envision board member, and investor, had died unexpectedly of a pulmonary embolus, just hours after we had communicated about the next round of funding for Envision. While I grieved Tom's death, I realized it was the death knell for Envision, too.

Although I spent the next six months desperately seeking alternative sources of funding and used a considerable amount of Tim's and my personal savings to do so, I was unsuccessful. We closed down Envision in early 2019. I spent the next several months working in a strategy position at Kailos Genetics, an innovative company focused on pharmacogenetics, as well as doing 5,000 pre-pandemic Teladoc visits, consulting for Oliver Wyman's healthcare practice, and, continuing to see some patients at the internal medicine practice I have been part of since 1993, now part of Atrium Health.

Out of the blue, a recruiter contacted me in July 2019 for a CEO position at a North Carolina-based company called Eventus WholeHealth. When I looked at the job description, I couldn't believe it — it read like my dream job.

Eventus is a company that provides an integrated model of care to medically vulnerable adults who reside in skilled nursing facilities, assisted living facilities, or are home bound. I started the position in November 2019. Since then, the integrated primary care, mental health, and podiatry care model has expanded to more than 1,200 facilities and private homes in five states.

The 650 providers and support staff have been on the front lines during the COVID pandemic, serving the sickest, most medically vulnerable patient population with patient-centered, evidence-based models of care.

I believe the Eventus model of care is not "ahead of its time" but, in fact, just in time, as our country takes on the challenge of providing whole-person care to the 70 million baby boomers beginning to enter their senior years. Eventus is positioned to be a transformative healthcare delivery platform just when our aging population needs it the most.

In 2021, I left Eventus and am looking for my next adventure. I believe all my previous experiences, from running multimillion-dollar businesses to startups; developing deep expertise in care model design, healthcare policy and economics; and continuing to practice (very) part time in the internal medicine practice I've been a part of since 1993, positions me to continue to improve our healthcare delivery system. Stay tuned . . .

It is said that women leaders do not articulate their accomplishments as assertively as men and that is one reason we aren't as likely to rise to the top leadership positions. Maybe that is true. Here are some things I haven't talked about here.

While I have been living the life I articulated above, I've written three books, served as vice-chair of the federal Physician-Focused Technical Advisory Committee (PTAC) commission, chair of the American Medical Group Association (AMGA), a board member of the American Association for Physician Leadership, an advisor to the innovative IKS company, founding member of the Oliver Wyman Health Innovation Center, given scores of talks, earned a Master's in Medical Management, and, above all, tried to lead with authenticity.

I've taught myself Spanish and I still run 25 miles or so a week, although very slowly these days. I've built four medical buildings and have kept a fern alive for 40 years. I have certainly failed at a lot of things. Just Google me if you want the dirty details.

Today both my daughters are married to wonderful men. Katy is an attorney and pregnant with my first granddaughter. Robyn is in medical school. I doubt when she graduates there will be many other women physicians who can say that she has both a mother and grandmother who are physicians. Tim is most certainly not "a 22-year-old unfocused young man" anymore. My gorgeous gray-haired husband of 38 years continues his own successful career in health information technology and remains the love of my life.

My Message

The story I have written here is not the one I expected to write. It is deeply personal and one that speaks to many elements of my life that are not directly pertinent to my day-to-day role as a physician executive. I have not discussed in detail my 21 years of experience as chief executive officer or my more than 30 years as a practicing physician in terms of lessons learned that might help other women physicians considering a career in medical management.

Instead, I have decided to share my story within the context of my complex roles as daughter, mother, wife, and daughter-in-law because I believe it is these roles that help define how women are viewed as professionals and the special skills they bring to their leadership responsibilities.

We are at the beginning of what I expect will be the single fastest transformation of any industry in U.S. history. Physician leadership in healthcare during this transformation is crucial and the healthcare delivery system transformation will be an enormous opportunity for women. But the relative lack of women in leadership roles in healthcare currently needs to be understood and addressed.

I would suggest that one approach to addressing this discrepancy is through the language of archetypes as articulated by Carl Jung. Jung theorized that archetypes are symbolic figures hardwired into our unconsciousness. He focused upon the archetypes of hero, father, mother, temptress, witch, villain, wise old woman (or man), and innocent, ingrained in our collective unconsciousness as identified in myths across cultures and times.

Unlike men, most of the female archetypes are characterized by relationships that adhere to traditional social roles (mother, daughter, grandmother, sister). Although men are also represented in archetypes based upon traditional social roles (father, son, grandfather, brother), there are some strong male archetypes based on the relationship between man and society. These are the roles of hero and villain, both of which are external to the family. The hero is focused more upon saving the group, defending the weak and innocent, administering justice. The villain is his foil.

Our country's future success depends upon our ability to transform our healthcare delivery system to one that is equitable, affordable, and effective. That transformation will require leadership from many individuals who have neither prepared for nor expected to play these critical roles.

For women is it crucial that we understand that effective leaders learn the language of leadership and master it. Using Jung's paradigm, we need to appreciate how we are perceived in various situations in order to discern how a particular female gender archetype might impact our message. By listening to the language used by others, we can create the situational story in which our role is played. Then we can choose which voice to use in order to be most effective leaders.

The *grandmother voice* is the storytelling voice. It is particularly useful when giving a presentation, as the human mind is designed to retain information it hears from stories. For physicians, a story about a patient that teaches a lesson and evokes empathy can be a very powerful tool.

In the working world, the *mother voice* can be dangerous. It can be perceived as both loving and scolding and should be used with caution. On the other hand, the *sister voice* is powerful because it is collaborative. The connotations of sisterhood eliminate inappropriate sexual overtones and its implied equal status in the sibling relationship can positively impact team building.

Women tend to overuse the *daughter voice*. Female subordinates often find the daughter role to be a safe relationship with male bosses/mentors because it may diminish sexual tension. However, this is a problem when attempting to transition to a leadership role. Beware of language in which sexual allusion are used in descriptions of women.

The *temptress/prostitute* archetypes are universal and powerful, but not appropriate within the context of leadership. Likewise, the *domineering woman/bitch* role is dangerous. Some women avoid leadership roles because they fear being depicted within this context.

The most enigmatic role for women is that of *witch*. The witch role is powerful, but frightening because it is a role contextualized around female power that is outside of the standard male dominant cultural context. Powerful men may rely upon the language of the warrior/hero archetype as the context for their effective leadership, but being perceived as powerful using the witch archetype is generally a problem for women in leadership roles.

As women leaders, pay attention to the language you are speaking and the language in which others speak to you. Pay attention to the subtle messages of clothing, body language, and underlying archetypes in the language of colleagues. Choose the voice with which you speak and the language with which you organize your leadership roles. Think about those symbols that project power.

Leadership is an existential construct based upon social roles, language, and archetypal understandings that constitute the deep wisdom written into the human experience. We ARE tomboys, sisters, mothers, daughters, grandmothers, temptresses, bitches, and witches. To be leaders we must also be authentic. I do not believe authentic leadership for women is found within a neutered male heroic archetype. It rises out of our own experiences. Pearls are a woman's necktie.

I wrote the above message for the original *Lessons Learned: Stories from Women in Medical Management* published 10 years ago. When I reflect on those words about my life story since, I do not see anything I would change in the narrative to that point, nor my general beliefs about how women physician leaders can navigate some of the gender challenges that often bedevil us. I believe the Jungian archetypes are still pertinent and listening deeply to how one is spoken to in conversations can help one perceive gender biases.

The archetypes for me are life hacks, allowing me to judge quickly how to steer through some of the unconscious stereotypes inherent in the dialogue and alter my responses accordingly. My "pearls are a woman's necktie" is meant to distinguish gender-based equivalent signals of power and professionalism that can serve to equalize in appropriate business settings. But boy, a whole lot has happened in the world and to me since I wrote those words and used that metaphor, from the #*metoo* movement, great progress in LGBTQ+ rights that have challenged such gender binary categories altogether, to the defeat of Hillary Clinton by Donald Trump, with all the not-so-subliminal gender-hate speech the 2016 political campaign evoked. I will leave the reader to reflect on their own regarding the relevance of my original necktie metaphor within the context of the national dialogue, but I believe updating my own story has relevance, too.

Bottom line: Here's the lesson I've learned over the past 10 years: For women in leadership roles, there is always a fine line between bitch and badass in how one is perceived. Turns out that fine line is what my "strangeness" is really all about. At this point in my life, I'm good with that.

"We are at the beginning of what I expect will be the single fastest transformation of any industry in U.S. history. Physician leadership in healthcare during this transformation is crucial and the healthcare delivery system transformation will be an enormous opportunity for women. But the relative lack of women in leadership roles in healthcare currently needs to be understood and addressed."

– Grace Terrell

Managed Care:
For Profit and
Not-For-Profit

*"The career of a medical manager can begin
in many ways and take many paths."*

– Christine A. Petersen

CHAPTER SIXTEEN

A Continuing Search for Challenge

By Christine A. Petersen, MD, MBA

THE CAREER OF A MEDICAL MANAGER CAN begin in many ways and take many paths. My 40-year journey has been satisfying and challenging, both professionally and personally.

My early career was one of numerous relocations, which provided me with expansion of my medical management experience and lessons in adapting to different management styles, reporting relationships, and job responsibilities. For my young children, these moves meant adapting to new schools, new friends, and ever-changing nannies and childcare givers.

I spent 10 years as CMO and vice president of medical affairs at Sierra Health Services in Las Vegas, Nevada, before choosing retirement when the corporation was sold to United Healthcare. Instead of ending my management career, I transitioned to a new leadership role as head of my own healthcare consulting practice. Unlike working within various managed care organizations, consulting brought its own set of challenges but it has allowed me to utilize all the skills and experience I have been fortunate enough to obtain over the years and to continually expand my professional network.

I am a board certified internist and had a private practice in Grand Junction, Colorado. In 1983, I was asked to become the first full-time medical director of Rocky Mountain HMO. Although I was intrigued by the idea, I initially said no. I couldn't imagine leaving my practice and patients. Four months later, I was telling my patients that my move out of practice was only temporary and I would return to private practice in two years.

I had absolutely no experience as a medical manager other than participation in HMO committees. As I started to perform my job, I realized that I had no management or business tools other than intuitive ones. My CEO and mentor supported my decision to join the American College of Physician Executives (now American Association for Physician Leadership) and take Seminars I and II. What an eye-opener. Suddenly the lights went on and the pieces began to fall into place. I was hooked. I developed a detailed business plan for myself that focused on enhancing my medical management experience, obtaining expanded responsibilities, and positioning for advancement.

In 1985, FHP, Inc, then a primarily staff model HMO, was expanding into the IPA arena in new geographic areas. I accepted a position as medical director for the new Arizona region. The challenges were incredible and the experience invaluable. I had the opportunity to start the medical department from scratch, help create and manage 13 separate IPAs, introduce the specialists to capitation, and interface with all the other providers required for a complete network. We applied for and received a Medicare Risk contract — another set of challenges and opportunities! Two and a half years later, we had 50,000 members, started our staff model overlay, and began our Tucson expansion.

My next move was to corporate headquarters in Southern California as part of the medical affairs team. I completed my MBA to help advance my career and broaden my business training. My children and I loved living in California, but I really wanted more operational responsibility, so when an opportunity came up with FHP in Utah, we went for it. In addition to my responsibility for medical affairs I had profit and loss responsibility for our large dental, optical, and pharmacy operations.

We were also in the final architectural drawing phase for our hospital construction, and that was a fabulous challenge. There were so many time-sensitive tasks, from medical staffing to policies and procedures and everything in between.

Three years later, the hospital was opened and the first surgical procedure performed. I was then offered a position back at corporate as vice president of medical affairs, so the children and I moved back to California. During that time, I was responsible for medical informatics, medical policies and procedure, medical management education, training, and recruiting. The role was challenging, but I really wanted to get back into the direct operations. When I was recruited to Prudential Health Care to work in Southern Group Operations in Atlanta, we were on the road again.

This position came with lots of travel throughout the Southeast and opportunities to meet and work with many different and talented people. It also gave me the chance to work for a very large company with a national presence. After 14 months in Atlanta, I was asked to become the national director for utilization management with responsibility for 45 plans. I was tasked to develop the business plan for Medicare Risk contracting expansion. I lived in Atlanta, but also maintained an office in New Jersey. If I thought I was traveling before, it didn't hold a candle to this. Every week I was in either a different city or in New Jersey.

I must admit it was brutal, but worth every minute. My network was really expanded at this point and by this time I had acquired experience in almost every area in the world of medical management.

The key word was "almost." I hadn't yet been a chief medical officer. When the opportunity came up to become the CMO for Sierra Health Services in Las Vegas, of course I couldn't resist. The fact that many of my former FHP colleagues were working there made the transition relatively easy. The position brought a whole new world of very different experiences.

Although I had no direct line operational responsibility, I loved my job. I interfaced with the press and community leaders, and participated on the Leadership Council at AHIP. Together with my team, I helped to set medical policy, reviewed new technology, and interfaced with legislative issues. As we purchased operations, I participated with numerous due diligence efforts. Ten years after I arrived, we were purchased by United Health Care.

Although I " retired," I was never one to resist a challenge. While I was at Sierra, I worked with a group to start a clinic in Tanzania. After "retirement" I was able to spend more time there, hire and train staff, see lots of patients, and help with fundraising. We also started a nursing school in Dodoma which now is the largest nursing school in Tanzania and currently has 1,400 students enrolled in the various programs. We bought property in Zinga, TZ and are in the process of completing the maternal/child center and birthing center. Currently we have an operating clinic, laboratory, x-ray unit, and pharmacy.

After the sale to United Health Care, I worked with a group of physicians in Las Vegas to help set up a free clinic that would serve the needs of the uninsured. I served on the board of that clinic until I relocated to my summer home in Northern Michigan in 2019. My two sons and their families relocated to the Midwest so now, with three grandchildren and five sisters living close by, I spend lots of time with family. My consistent networking over the years has rewarded me with great friends who I often travel with and who visit regularly to enjoy the great Michigan outdoors with me.

One might ask what challenges or opportunities can be found living in a small village. The answer is many and I found plenty. I currently serve as vice president of our local, very active, environmental group, manage seven beach/shoreline clean-up teams, serve on the Grand Traverse Watershed Board, am chair of their board development committee, am chair of the ER Trail Alliance which is charged with submission of The Pure Michigan Trail Town Designation application, and was appointed to the Downtown Development Authority where I currently serve as vice chair. I am also on the advisory board of a new medical technology startup and continue on the board of IHPTZ, the Africa clinic.

My days are full, my life is rich. I am using the skills I developed as a medical manager in new ways to affect change in areas important to me such as protection of natural resources, watershed management, and economic sustainability in rural Michigan.

Lessons I have learned in my career:
- Seek challenges.
- Develop and maintain your professional network.
- Keep open to moves to new geographic areas.
- Respect your colleagues.
- Mentor your staff.
- Give back to your community.
- Have fun.

CHAPTER SEVENTEEN

A Managed Care Journey: Learning from Yourself and Others

By Susan Elizabeth Ford, MD, MBA

I PARTICIPATED IN THE 1995 VERSION of *Women in Medicine and Management*. Sixteen years later, I appreciated the opportunity to again reflect on my career and share my secrets for success. With this newest update 10 years beyond, I hope to inspire the next generation of women in medicine from the start of their careers through retirement. My life choices thus far have been sculpted by my ever-evolving visions, expectations, and experiences that have led me from clinician to medical manager.

I'd like to begin by describing those personal characteristics and propensities that have been instrumental in my decision making over the years. These will provide the reader with a framework to understand the choices I have made along my career path.

First, I am very focused. One of my most important life goals is to make positive contributions in everything I do, including my work. Second, I like process. I enjoy improving upon the status quo. Third, I love learning and intellectually challenging myself. Fourth, like many physicians, I am pragmatic and persistent, but unlike some, I also possess intuition, which drives me to think creatively and helps with planning long-term strategies and goals. From my vantage point, setting goals is fundamental to achieving a successful and rewarding career in any field.

At the age of 12, I set a rather large goal for myself. I decided to become a physician because I "liked science and working with people." This pre-teen goal turned into both my lifelong career and passion. It required discipline, hard work, and self-motivation — even when times got tough. Having unwavering faith in my abilities, I turned adversity into self-motivation. This proved to be a prescription for success in my life. I was valedictorian in high school and went off to medical school after only two years of college.

After attending evening family practice club meetings as a med student at the University of Maryland Medical School, I made the decision to become a family practitioner. It made perfect sense. I enjoyed all of my rotations in medical school equally and did not want to give up any area of medicine in order to specialize.

At that time, family practice was considered a brand new specialty requiring a rigorous, three-year residency. However, not everyone appreciated the breadth of knowledge required of those choosing that field. Many of my colleagues and professors urged me to specialize in a narrower area, telling me that I was "too smart" to be a GP. I disagreed, deciding not to take their advice.

At this point in my career, I was committed to clinical practice. I hadn't given any real thought to medical management, although I definitely had an interest in the technologic advances made in medicine and was concerned with how poorly these advances had been implemented in the general population. Whenever I was bored in class, I would find myself doodling and coming up with ways to redesign anything to do with healthcare, from reconfiguring delivery systems, to office layouts, to brainstorming better procedural methods.

In 1977, I completed my family practice residency and passed the specialty board exam. In my last year, acting as chief resident, I developed an interest in teaching and working with residents. I became involved in family medicine training programs and participated in a fellowship in the Faculty Development Program at Jefferson Medical College in Philadelphia.

The fellowship covered many areas that were useful not only for teaching, but for medical management. Topics included adult learning theory, behavioral learning, budget development, counseling skills, curriculum development, management by objectives, and broad evaluation skills. We also worked on audit and performance feedback skills.

There are many similarities between teaching and managing skills. In retrospect, I found that the fellowship was a great forum for learning generic medical management skills. After completion of the program, I remained at Jefferson as the coordinator for the Faculty Development Program.

While I was working at Jefferson Medical College, one of the residents introduced me to a book-lovers' club for single people. To make a long story short, I met my husband, who was living in the San Francisco Bay area. Because he let me choose which coast to live on when we married, we moved to San Francisco, where I joined the family practice residency program in San Jose, California.

There, I participated in the usual duties of residency faculty members, including teaching and supervision in the outpatient center. I had the opportunity to sit on several medical staff committees at the hospital. I also gave presentations to residents about the business side of practice, including explaining different medical practice settings, such as Health Maintenance Organizations (HMOs). Through the process of developing lectures and training materials for residents, I became extremely interested in HMOs. I collected copious information about managed care and set up several job interviews.

My experiences in San Jose led me to a position with CIGNA Healthplan in Dallas. My position was actually three separate roles in one: practicing physician, chairman of family practice, and chief of staff of a healthcare center. Though demanding, the job proved to be very useful in my growth as a medical manager. It was a natural fit—the organization needed a Family Practice department developed, and I wanted to learn about HMOs.

Since this HMO health plan was in its infancy, it provided an excellent opportunity to learn how all the elements of an HMO fit together into a functioning system. During this time, I also had the chance to open and develop one of the centers as chief of staff. I participated actively on quality committees, and eventually was asked to assume the position of associate medical director for quality assurance. In that role, I took my first major step into medical management.

Up to this point, my transition from clinical practice to medical management had consisted of gradually increasing administrative involvement. I always enjoyed problem solving with others to improve the big picture, but this was the first time in my career that my job became half administrative. I found that I really loved medical management, and felt that I could have a bigger impact by pursuing this career path rather than seeing individual patients. I became a member of the American Academy of Medical Directors, now the American Association for Physician Leadership, and attended two Physician in Management seminars.

Although I thoroughly enjoyed my experiences in Texas, after four years in the Lone Star State, my husband reminded me of my promise to move back to the West Coast if it provided better job opportunities for him. It was then that I realized achieving great success in life means more than having a distinguished career. It also means compromise and balance to ensure a happy, healthy relationship on the home front.

At the time we relocated to California, CIGNA had no medical director openings, so I found one with a small HMO. In addition to medical management, the position provided some exposure to various business departments within the organization. My responsibilities included medical department staffing, budgeting, utilization management, and quality assurance for a network with 29,000 patients. I also managed optometry, podiatry, mental health, medical operations, and home health.

Since the HMO was relatively small, I had plenty of opportunity to interact with the finance and business departments. I also learned, by way of the school of hard knocks, how to handle situations that conflicted with my personal ethics.

It was at this point that I learned — or re-learned if you will — a critical life lesson: It is important to be comfortable and enthusiastic about your organization's goals and ethics. Those goals and ethics should align with yours. The man or woman you report to should be someone you respect, someone of good conscience who will always do the right thing. Never work for organizations that just want to use power or that do not clearly add value to the big picture.

Remember this: Power, like information, must be used appropriately and shared to produce optimal results.

It is particularly important that the organization appreciate and support your "physician" expertise, as a physician manager, in advocating for high-quality healthcare. Healthcare advocacy is ideally a natural position for all physicians. For a health organization, it must be a key element in any well-balanced business equation. We, as medical managers, must preserve the professional principles of medicine in our work and be clear about our goals and visions and single-minded in their pursuit.

In 1989, I passed the American Board of Medical Management certifying exam. Following this accomplishment, I took a position as staff medical director for CIGNA Healthplan near Los Angeles. In that role, I had a broad range of responsibilities, including utilization management, provider network, hospital contracting, home health, and 24-hour telephone triage for 380,000 managed care patients. In addition, I had oversight for the areas that handled medical case management, medical claim review, medical social work, medical benefits interpretations, and technology assessment. While at CIGNA, I earned a Master of Business Administration (MBA) from the Executive MBA Program at the University of Southern California.

The degree, combined with my years of management experience, opened many new doors. I worked as the market medical director for Aetna Health Plans in Los Angeles; for United Health Care in Nebraska; and for provider-owned MCOs in Oklahoma and New Mexico. In each position, I gained valuable skills but chose to move on for various reasons: family, growth opportunities, and intuition that a job change would be best for my career.

My role as medical director for Amerigroup New Mexico fit me better than my past positions. The content of my job was varied and constructive and the work philosophy was well-balanced.

Amerigroup's business is Medicaid and Medicare, but in New Mexico, we also had a Coordinated Long-Term Services (CoLTS) Program dedicated to the needs of seniors and people with disabilities. CoLTS integrated medical services with home and community-based care, serving those with disabilities in a manner that promoted independent living. This position challenged and excited me. It involved a never-ending array of interesting problem-solving that resulted in improved health outcomes for our members.

Over the years, I learned that one gains credibility and competence from real experience and accomplishments, and I have been incredibly proud of the various work experiences I have had. Each experience has challenged me to learn and try new things. While continuing education is integral in our field, I firmly believe exposure to different situations and actual life experience is essential to success.

I have experienced many types of management, planning and strategy development and organizational structures, and have seen strengths and weaknesses in each situation. I have had many successes and failures and have learned from them all. I encourage you to take chances, dare to dream, set goals, and find a work-life balance that is right for you.

As far as mentoring (giving or receiving), I have been egalitarian in terms of person, gender, or professional credentials. It's important to be open-minded and always remember that one can learn from others or mentor others at any time or place.

Here are some thoughts on making career goals a reality:

Important Skills and Traits to Develop:

- Creativity and flexibility. Change is a given and essential element of life.
- Negotiation skills and conflict resolution.
- Contribution. "How do I bring something to the interaction?"
- Creating value for the whole system. Ask "Is this good for the whole or just my compartment?"
- Teamwork and collaboration.
- Enthusiasm. Be positive and don't get cynical or negative. Get people enthusiastic about work.
- Persistence.
- Prioritization. Protect your time and control perfectionistic tendencies; close your office door when it is necessary to concentrate.
- Learning to lose, risk, try, learn. welcome opportunities
- Forgetting past inequities. They just demean and slow one down.

195

Skills for Working on One's Career Development (Self-Mentoring):

- Brainstorm and write down ideas, goals, and specific steps. Then, get them organized and prioritized. Putting your ideas on paper in an organized way helps move from thoughts and ideas to reality.
- Always have a clear idea of your main goals, tasks, and time frames for both the short run and the long run.
- Mentally practice scenarios. Visualize positive and successful situations. Don't be too humble. Mentally practice how you will proceed in specific situations. Imagine certain interactions in detail or go through mock dialogues with a trusted person. View yourself positively while you do this.
- Study your own experience and observe others to improve yourself.

Retirement: A Whole New Phase

I enjoyed my role at Amerigroup so much that I never anticipated early retirement. But as happens, life intruded. In 2013, I developed a medical issue that was affecting my mobility. I switched to a medical director position, which allowed me to do case reviews from home.

Unfortunately, by 2015 my physical situation had limited my mobility to such a degree that I had to stop work altogether. This was very difficult for me. I had planned to work until 2020. It took me more than a year before I was able to use the word "retirement" as relating to why I was no longer working. I had to recognize the fact that my sense of purpose in my life had always been wrapped around the idea that I made much of my contributions through what I did at work.

What I learned at Amerigroup about caring for people with accessibility issues helped me with some of my subsequent personal adjustments. For example, my house has raised garden beds that basically follow Universal Design principles (the design of buildings, products or environments to make them accessible to all people, regardless of age, disability or other factors).

Although I am fully retired now, I still use my teaching skills. I help as a community medical faculty volunteer, teaching medical students via Zoom. In addition, I have been mentoring Master Gardener interns — also using Zoom.

When you are starting out, thinking about a career, retirement seems so far away that most of us don't really think about it and we certainly don't consider what might happen if during working life medical issues emerge requiring new plans. So here are a few of my thoughts about that:

Planning ahead:

- Even if you don't anticipate problems, it makes sense to do some "contingency planning" just as you would do risk management in the workplace. This includes planning for alternate, unexpected retirement dates; planning for alternate retirement activities and interests depending on your capability at the time. Stuff happens whether you like it or not. With aging comes physical and mental changes. Count on them happening sooner or later.

- Do you want to age in place? If so, plan to make environmental modifications:
  - —Universal House Design and other accessibility ideas are really helpful (e.g., a raised bed to help gardening).
  - —Keep your environment safe, easy, and accessible, especially the kitchen and bathroom.
  - —Choose comfort and ease over style — like wearing comfortable shoes instead of dress shoes.
  - —Consider cognitive pain management/mindfulness/ cognitive therapy methods (good tools for anyone anyway!).
  - —Engage in brain stimulation and human interaction by Zoom meetings, Zoom book clubs, online courses (edx, Coursera, Great Courses, etc.).
  - —Utilize community resources.
  - —Keep active but don't beat up yourself if you can't do everything you planned for.

My final thoughts about retirement:

- You don't have to keep up to date in medicine or in areas that you worked in. In fact, it might be helpful to put this entirely behind you if it helps you accept a new stage in your life.
- You may need new friends and activities — not necessarily the same as during peak work life.
- You don't need to follow conventional wisdom or what the media tells you.
- You can be happy in one spot. You don't need to travel. Nature's beauty is everywhere.
- Consider what you enjoyed doing as a kid. That might work again. Play and be creative.
- Eat dessert first!

Here are some links with ideas. All these ideas are related to living independently as one gets older and/or has mobility problems.

Universal Design: *https://en.wikipedia.org/wiki/Universal_design, www.washington.edu/doit/what-universal-design-0, and https://projects.ncsu.edu/ncsu/design/cud/about_ud/udprinciplestext.htm*

Accessibility: *https://en.wikipedia.org/wiki/Accessibility*

Independent Living: *https://en.wikipedia.org/wiki/Independent_living*

Chapter Eighteen

The "Other" Side

By Deborah E. Hammond, MD

In the middle of a memorable phone conversation with a surgeon in 1988 regarding the lack of approval for an elective procedure, the decibels suddenly decreased and the surgeon's tone shifted to one of open questioning: "How did you get this job? What do you have to do to get this job? I have been thinking about a change. Would you recommend this type of job?"

After a few seconds of stunned readjustment on my part, we went on to have a very pleasant conversation covering these questions. We then completed our less-than-pleasant discussion concerning the lack of approval for the surgical procedure.

I related this story in the original *Women in Medicine and Management* monograph published 17 years ago because it had reaffirmed in my mind that the role of the professional medical manager is deeply involved in the running of healthcare organizations. In 1995, the medical manager role had already changed from a predominately end-of-career position to an option as an independent career path. That's even truer today.

Doing It Over

Now with the luxury of almost two more decades of experience, I am asked if I would do it all again. The answer is an emphatic "yes." Yes, even if I were just starting out in 2012 facing the implementation of the Patient Protection and Affordable Care Act (Obamacare) rather than 1980 when I began my medical management career by volunteering to become a section leader at a group model health maintenance organization (HMO) in Suffolk County, New York.

So how does a person, especially a female physician, find or create the opportunities to take advantage of this option? An exploration of the path I took, the lessons I learned, and the skills that I believe are paramount to job satisfaction and job success may be helpful.

My present position did not evolve from a preplanned scheme. I came to this role using an ongoing process of defining and redefining my professional goals, of including the roles desired, of being open to and acting on opportunities to learn, of seeking out mentors to help guide me, of taking risks and trying new things, and, finally, of actively identifying management and leadership skills that need improvement.

Professional Beginnings

My career in management began when I agreed, at the age of 16, to be a lead counselor for a summer day camp for kids. It was my first experience in the need for teamwork. Only years later did I realize that individual efforts account for a small portion of success in management. The team determines success!

My next lessons occurred during my college years. Each summer, an anesthesiologist and close family friend hired me to fill in for vacationing support staff of an anesthesia department in a large teaching hospital in Chicago. I acted as receptionist, secretary, library research assistant, and, most important, surgery scheduling clerk. I learned that real power and control lies in the hands of associates at the front line. The ability to hold sway over who obtains the 7 a.m. start times and back-to-back slots was a heady experience.

As a dividend, I learned another lesson: Over time, nice guys (or gals) finish first. While a powerful surgeon could pull strings or, more commonly, rant and rave to get a preferred slot, it was the doctors who always went out of their way to be pleasant to the clerks (in some cases plying us with donuts) who consistently got the best times and preferred rooms. Use of position, title, or level in the organization to get people to act was at best an inconsistent and damaging tool.

My professional career in management began during Internal Medicine postgraduate training at Montefiore Hospital at the

University of Pittsburgh. I supervised a five-week general medicine inpatient training period for a group of medical students and interns. This is an experience that male and female residents share equally in their early careers.

While not formally recognized (the first formal recognition is commonly the chief resident position), this supervisory role should be used as the first step to building management skills for those interested in such a career. It is an opportunity to learn how to prioritize, distribute work, organize schedules, tutor and teach, and decide on who can be empowered to make certain decisions. (As an aside, I would suggest that graduate training leaders reading this include a formal evaluation of management skills for each resident and fellow.)

My next most valuable lesson came from my first mentor, the chief of the Department of Internal Medicine. He was an amazing person, able to deflate a pompous medical professional with a mere glance. One night, while covering the hospital, I was called to a cardiac arrest on the "gold coast" floor. A private duty nurse had been caring for the patient and in the midst of the chaos, I banished her from the room. In my mind, she had no idea what she was doing.

The next day, I was called to the chief's office. He offered me tea and then calmly asked how publicly throwing the nurse out of the room helped the patient. With that one question, my defense crumbled. I knew he was right; it didn't help the patient. Lesson learned: The end does not justify the means, and the means can significantly hinder your success.

Real Jobs

My first formal management position happened quite by accident. I was in practice with a not-for-profit multispecialty group on Long Island, New York, seeing a majority of HMO patients and a minority of indemnity fee-for-service patients.

As a woman in practice in the early '80s, I attracted many older women patients who had been "waiting for a female doctor." I immensely enjoyed the role of practicing internist, especially the aspect of continuity of care, something that was lacking in my medical school and postgraduate training. The HMO's adherence to preventive care for all members and the lack of financial barriers to obtaining high-quality healthcare for my patients fit my concept of providing accessible health care to all.

When the chief of the Department of Medicine left, I assumed that an experienced administrator would be asked to assume the role, but the medical director came to me. After a brief period of consideration, I took the position. The lesson here: Don't be afraid to take risks.

My first task (and nightmare) was to determine scheduling for Thanksgiving, Christmas, Hanukkah, and New Year's. The previous chief had left little documentation. Each person claimed they had worked all the previous holidays.

Remember, whatever the decision, you can't make everyone happy. That's a particularly difficult lesson for women to learn. I know I have an innate wish to please that cannot exist in full concert with the roles of effective manager and leader. However, it is important to be able to explain your reasons for the decision in the context of the overall vision of the organization, to demonstrate fairness, and to lack favoritism. In this case, I scheduled myself for Christmas and pointed out that care had to be provided, asking who wanted to work which holiday.

During this period, I began to work on quality assurance, utilization management, and associate training projects in the hospital and group practice setting. It is important to seek out these kinds of extracurricular opportunities. They provide opportunities to hone technical skills, to network, and to build a management résumé prior to your first formal management position.

Before starting this job, I had negotiated a year's leave of absence, unpaid, for future childbearing and rearing activities. Unless you are convinced that you will never want children, discuss and confirm maternity and childcare benefits prior to taking any position. During my leave, following the birth of my daughter, my husband and I decided to leave New York for Oklahoma.

I returned to work as a volunteer instructor in ambulatory adult medicine at the Tulsa Medical College, University of Oklahoma. This allowed me to network, learn about practice opportunities, and be in the right place at the right time. Blue Cross and Blue Shield of Oklahoma was looking for an experienced managed care doctor to help start its first IPA capitated HMO. Because of the controversial nature of the project, physician leaders living in Oklahoma had turned down the Medical Director position.

It was the early 1980s, and managed care was a controversial and undesired opportunity for the Oklahoma physician community. I decided to take a leap and move into full-time medical management. Once again, don't be afraid to take risks.

Here, I met my next mentor and my first non-physician boss. His unique approach was to demonstrate empathy and involvement to each and every associate. One particular crisis management issue exemplifies the value of his approach. Claims were behind, exacerbated by rapid membership growth. Claims associates were demoralized, and the manager position was unfilled.

When I arrived at work on a Saturday morning, my boss asked me to help pay claims. It was a great experience. The associates were astonished and energized by the sight of us pitching in. Demonstrating that you are willing to walk in another person's shoes is a powerful team-building exercise.

In addition to building management skills, I was able to link with other Blue Cross and Blue Shield medical directors. Networking provided me with invitations to visit HMOs for in-depth sharing of best practices and of lessons learned. Networking provided me with peers who had gone through the same struggles as I had and who were a sympathetic sounding board. Networking provided me with my next job.

While in this position, I was also given the opportunity to serve as a consultant to the Federal Office of HMO, reviewing and scoring applications for federal HMO qualification. This allowed me to view best practices, meet industry leaders, and learn about the diversity of the managed care industry while honing my skills in consultation, analysis, and auditing. Advice: Locate part-time consulting opportunities, such as with the National Committee on Quality Assurance and the Joint Commission on Accreditation of Healthcare Organizations.

My next position came about when a medical director mentioned me (without my knowledge) as a potential candidate for a regional medical director role with Prudential. I first turned down the position, but a subsequent interview with the new vice president of medical services convinced me that this position was a risk worth taking.

I had a new mentor in my new boss and a new role as a staff medical director supporting nine managed care operations. I was given opportunities to learn beyond the field of managed care. These included the methodology of life and health insurance underwriting, the handling of indemnity or traditional medical insurance administration, marketing to prospective national clients, running large-scale associate training programs, and the basic tenets of contract law and proactive risk management.

Once again, I let my boss and others know that I wanted to try new things. An invaluable experience was being placed on the team that transitioned 236,000 employees and dependents from an indemnity healthcare policy to a point-of-service managed care benefit plan in 14 locations.

Within a year, I was offered the position of vice president of medical services, responsible for clinical leadership and oversight of both the managed care and the indemnity businesses. This was the most complex role I had held up to that time. I had little direct power and a great deal of responsibility.

To achieve my goals, I had to refine and strengthen my skills in collaboration, persuasion, and team building. In staff positions, most of the people you depend on to carry out actions and meet objectives don't work for you. Intimidation and table pounding don't work.

This proactive approach to risk-taking and volunteering established my credibility in the organization. I was appointed to the national utilization management policy board and to the national quality improvement committee. I led projects on improving the quality of claims administration by establishing a continuous quality improvement approach to claims management. I became the business leader for Prudential's start-up mental health managed care business unit until it was turned over to a psychiatrist business leader.

The biggest growth opportunity I was given was to be the business leader in charge of improving the existing mainframe computer-based utilization management system while developing a completely new application using an integrated approach with all other managed care computer systems. Each one of these assignments allowed me to work with other business leaders in Prudential, glean best practices, locate new mentors, and test my skills. The lesson learned here is that it is important to demonstrate flexibility and a willingness to work in areas that are not directly related to clinical issues.

In October 1993, I became executive director of PruCare Operations in New York, New Jersey, and Connecticut. This was a planned action on my part. Approximately three years earlier, I had let my boss and her replacement know that for my next career move, I wanted a job leading a large multifunctional operational unit. I asked what I needed to do to achieve this. Both bosses suggested skills I should acquire, interactive training opportunities, and smaller operational assignments I should consider adding to my experience.

It is important to discuss career goals with associates and ask for frank feedback as to how to obtain those goals. People are not mind-readers. For instance, I was quite open about my willingness to move for the right opportunity.

That opportunity came unexpectedly in 1998 when Prudential Healthcare was purchased by Aetna US Healthcare. I was given the chance to lead part of the transition — particularly the integration of the data warehouse and the clinical quality and medical cost data analysis teams into the structure of USQA, the analytical arm of Aetna.

While helping 367 individuals locate their "landing' zone" within the business units of Aetna, I learned entirely new areas of the business and sharpened my political skills to locate and use leverage to assist staff find positions in or to smooth their exit out of the company. During the transition I also had to deal with five separate changes of management in eight months. Eventually I was given the position of leading the regional analytical teams for USQA. Data and its effective use became the center of my work universe.

One area of skill everyone in medicine today must possess is using and analyzing data — both clinical and financial. At the moment, Excel proficiency is critical. Physician managers should know how to do pivot tables, the basics of medical coding (service level and diagnosis level), how to read a profit and loss report and balance sheet, and how to develop a business budget. These are vital skills that are not learned in medical school.

While advanced degrees can be helpful, it is not the only way to acquire specific business skills. There are inexpensive local community college courses offered on nights and weekends. The American Association of Community Colleges (www.aacc.nche.edu) provides links to these schools.

After managing the analytical teams for USQA, the reorganization of Aetna (and USQA) led to another transition opportunity in 2001. I was given two options: take a "regular" medical management role or lead the transition of my teams into the new business structure with a severance package. I opted for the latter. This was not long after September 11th and I wanted to do something different.

With the help of an old friend, I found "different." I had been reading and hearing about managed Medicaid and a new product called Medicare Advantage. A failed experiment in the mid '90s in Medicaid at Prudential had given me a healthy regard for the complexities of taking care of the poorest of the poor. Visiting with pioneers in this line of business convinced me it would be very different.

I joined AmeriChoice, attracted by the sharp vision of the leadership team and the fact that I would need to acquire a whole new set of skills for the alternative world of government programs. I led the medical management team of care managers, case managers and utilization review professionals working in the New York and New Jersey markets.

My experience highlights the fact that as a medical manager, one needs to constantly keep up with all the latest trends in the world of healthcare. That requires using a mix of sources — newspapers (the *Wall Street Journal* is the best for the business impact point of view), email alerts from industry watchers (*Modern Healthcare* is one great source), and association bulletins. Anyone seeking an administrative role in healthcare should invest in various subscriptions to maintain their edge.

For me, my professional landscape continued to change. UnitedHealthcare purchased AmeriChoice in 2005. With the integration into UHC, I moved onto the national team, utilizing my past medical cost analysis and data processing skills to help lead the installation of claim editing software and supporting the implementation of a new claims system for the Medicaid products.

I continued to work on medical cost and other special projects while AmeriChoice went through multiple re-alignments until 2008, when I turned down the opportunity to return to a "regular" medical management role and took another severance package, starting the search again for something different.

While sitting in the sun in Ridgewood, an old friend walked up and asked if I knew anyone with Medicaid experience in managed care looking for a job. I answered, "Depending on what the job is, I may be; I want something different." He told me about a hospital-owned managed care company in New York City seeking a medical director to help start a branch in New Jersey. It was different from my past experience: provider owned and managed and a start-up. I joined the organization in 2008, working in both New Jersey and New York at Healthfirst.

Interim Words of Wisdom

It is not always easy to be a leader, but the role can be extremely rewarding. Moreover, physician leaders who are able to straddle both the clinical and business sides of medicine possess skills that are truly unique. As one of my greatest mentors, Ron C., a senior operational leader said, "Deborah, remember you (medical directors) have turf that no one else can step into, but everyone in this (healthcare) organization has turf you CAN step into. Your turf is nearly infinite, so be very careful not to 'blank' it up without a plan of entrance (and exit)." Because he was a profane Texan, I can't do justice to how he actually worded it. Dialogue right out of a Larry McMurtry novel.

For physician executives, accountability stops with you. As an administrator, that means your desk, your email, your signature (which is now digital), your attestation. If you are the top clinical leader in your organization and a medical decision is needed, there is no other place or person to delegate the task. Even when the decision concerns some operational aspect of your business, if that operation involves patient care, you will likely be involved. What makes this so rewarding is the fact that you can have great influence over the eventual decision and steps taken for the good of the organization while serving patient care needs.

In addition to acquiring hard skills, I would advise learning to be an extrovert. Most physicians test as introverts on the Myers-Briggs personality test. Take the test, learn about your "type" and learn how to move out of type to connect with people, including gaining experience in public speaking (said to be the most dreaded voluntary activity in the world). Toastmasters International (www.toastmasters.org) is an international leader in communication and leadership development. There are chapters in every part of America. Over the years many of my "new" recruits to administration have joined and gained the skills needed to stand out in a crowd.

Even if you are just recently out of medical school and residency, consider some aspect of administration as a future option — whether you think you might want to be a senior medical leader or not. Volunteer. In my experience, most organizations will appreciate your offer to help. They are especially interested in younger women physicians who are usually "too busy" to do such work or worry their offer would be rejected.

Networking is key to discovering options open in medical management. Find those you hope to emulate and simply ask: "How did you get your job? Why do you like it? What would you change if you could? How can I get a job like yours?" In most cases, you will find people willing to provide guidance and share their expertise. Not only will information pour out, but the person you've asked will likely remember you!

Impact of 2021

In 2014, I had the opportunity to sell and then close the New Jersey operations of our health plan. I was able to draw on my past experiences of selling a health plan and learn the nuances of selling only a small portion of a much larger organization.

After completing all the regulatory required components, I moved to the New York operations and became the "inside" lead medical director for clinical operations. My additional role was to stand-up, with financial leaders, the company-wide medical cost management operations for all lines of business.

This greatly enhanced my financial abilities to be able to understand all aspects of utilization and cost data. Our team proposed initiatives for changes to programs in medical management, reimbursement, and contracting with providers including value-based arrangements supporting implementation for any approved actions.

Then in early 2020, COVID appeared. Organizing a team of subject matter experts, as the clinical leader and overall coach for all aspects of COVID, I led the team in addressing many challenges, from access to care to reimbursement to standing up telehealth capabilities to promotion of vaccination. This crisis improved the skills of many in my view— especially doctors and nurses. Physician leaders should ask to be included in any (crisis) problem-solving leadership team.

The Future of This Work

Approaching the end of my career in healthcare management has led to several musings. What do I do next? What did I learn? Who will I hang with in the future? What did I leave as a legacy?

After examining these questions, the most valuable thing I gained was the experience of working with and growing with others. My world has been filled with highly committed healthcare professionals — people from many cultures with clinical, health policy, financial, contracting, legal, business, and/or other expert training or experience— something I never could have imaged in medical school or post-graduate training.

As compared to 1980 when I was chief of medicine and my peers were mostly male leaders, I am now surrounded by an equal mix of genders, with peers from over 50 cultures/backgrounds.

Shifting more of my time now to mentoring others, while continuing to lead a handful of key processes, I am focused on the hard task of effective delegation and consultation to many but boss to few. Twice, I worked my way into no direct reports while retaining cross-collaboration with others, focusing on leading the identification, funding, and implementation of business projects to impact healthcare costs while also supporting the outcomes for members of the health plan.

From this experience, I share with you these *constant* tenets of clinical leadership, especially for women. The kernel of each has been set even as the style for each has changed through the decades. Observing other leaders, their importance has been reconfirmed for me and, to my chagrin, if I do see a failure on my part, it is because I did not hold to them with my own plans, actions, and/or interactions.

Determine the prize. Adapted from the hymn "Keep Your Hand on the Plow," by civil rights activist Alice Wine in 1956, "Keep Your Eyes on the Prize" should be your watch song. First, determine what the prize is. You will take many twisting paths to get there in your complex role as a clinical leader in management. So, pin down the prize. Make it simple for others to participate in the attainment. Create a vision of that prize for others. Andrew Carton identifies four "sense-giving" actions: narrow the focus, be concrete, set milestones, and give it life. Spend the time to hone your messaging with these steps and you will boost your chances of success greatly.

Develop poise along with your own personal image, your "persona." There will be disputes in business and many will be about power. Don't let your emotions take over a thoughtfully planned set of resolution actions. When you do respond, stay focused of the core issue; act and speak professionally, avoid any distraction by the other party or by you. You will have sent a message of strength and power and reset the relationship for the future as you resolve the current issue.

Use your turf wisely. Other than attorney, actuary, or CPA, there is almost no role in healthcare that a clinician, especially a doctor, cannot move into. Your turf is nearly infinite, and others know it and may likely fear or resent it. Acknowledge their space and power-base explicitly

Express appreciation of others with precision and clearly give credit. "Appreciation is a wonderful thing: it is what is excellent in others belong to us as well" Voltaire said in the 18th century. In business, too many words/notes of appreciation miss the mark. This is especially the case with today's remote work and use of social media and electronics. Be very specific and at times unexpected. Intermittent *precise* positive appreciation is so valued. Follow-up with crisp clear specific credit naming a person or group for a specific action or outcome.

Don't expose the public to your sausage-making too soon. Transparency is good but only when the reveal is ready for the audience it is meant for. A complex business problem requires a diverse group of subject-matter experts (SME) who must thresh out all the possible solutions prior to focusing on one or a few options to present to executive decision makers. This does not mean avoiding diversity of opinion/SMEs; it does mean getting diverse voices into the room, even if virtual, to discuss, debate, and create the solutions for final decision making.

Seek out others to participate in a two-way mentoring program. As a clinical leader and automatic executive, you will have missed the opportunity to grow as a business leader. Formal mentoring programs in large healthcare organizations are oftentimes structured for middle management participants. They are not set up to mentor a newly minted clinical executive who is hired at the associate vice president or vice president level.

We have the advantages of rank without the depth of experience. Therefore, create your own opportunities for (informal) mentoring. Find others to study how they operate, then seek out a few to collaborate with you. Seek other SMEs to develop two-way relationships; actuaries, lawyers, and operating officers will share arcane but critical business requirements with you. As you gain experience, continue to seek out others to mentor as well as be mentored by. Always make it a two-way street.

Continue to follow the money. Make sure you understand all aspects of how the organization takes in revenue, distributes such revenue, utilizes such revenue, and demonstrates financial success (depending on the type of financial armature). Learn value-based financial management methods. Learn to read and interpret all the financial reporting you can access. Whether for-profit or non-profit, money is the most central tool to understanding the aim of the organization and how it works. Are your books red, black or something in-between? How did you contribute, as a clinical leader to the result? And as a woman it is very satisfying to have an equal seat at any financial discussion.

Learn the key operational workflows of the organization. Any healthcare organization has three to five critical workflows making up their backbone. A managed care plan has sales, medical management, and claim processing at its core. A health system has patient acquisition, medical care, and securing revenue. The time spent to understand the mechanics of each of these areas allows you to better plan and collaborate with your peers. Know what they experience each day. The insight you gain is invaluable. Understand a HFCA 1500 (professional) or UB-04 (institutional) claim form and health service coding such as ICD-10 and CPT/HCPCs. Understand how the data elements are used to process claims and in quality and other key reporting.

To conclude, I can state categorically that healthcare administration is not boring. It can be stressful, exciting, and fun all at the same time. It is an ever-changing critical area of need and focus for any (successful) healthcare organization. As you read/experience the ups and downs of this industry you can observe/visualize the role played by expert clinical leaders working with other expert leaders and learn much.

The role is not for faint of heart. You must hone your skills to persuade, communicate, collaborate, and act with a wide range of individuals outside your comfort zone of medicine. But it is worth it. You can create a career and advance to the highest level of leadership with the right experience and exposure. So, jump in when you are ready and there will be many other women leaders waiting now in 2021 to greet you!

Plan for your career goals and update it frequently aligning with your family and community aspirations. This is especially important for women. Today, young women have that knowledge; use this information in your life plan calculation.

CHAPTER NINETEEN

From Great Mentorship to Finding My True Purpose — The Greatest Lesson of All

By Traci Thompson MD, MBA, CPE

MY MOTHER, A NURSING ASSISTANT, EXPOSED me early to the healthcare profession. When I had a day off from elementary school, she would bring me to work and I would pass out graham crackers and juice to the nursing home residents.

My decision to become a doctor was not solidified until I was almost 12 years old. While in middle school, I got my first job babysitting for Peggy Sugar, a semi-retired nurse. After almost 20 years as a registered nurse, Mrs. Sugar decided to quit her job and stay at home with her son.

One day I shared my thoughts for a future career in medical technology. Aware of my recent acceptance into the International Baccalaureate program, she asked why I didn't want to be a doctor. She told me that even at my age, I was smarter than some of physicians she knew and said that I should become a doctor. That did it for me! From that moment on, becoming a doctor became my goal.

When I tell people about the origins of my career decision, they are uniformly amazed at how that one simple statement changed the course of my life. That one episode in time illustrates the power of positive belief. Mrs. Sugar believed that I could become a doctor. As a result of her belief in me, I believed that I could achieve that goal and so much more.

My subsequent undergraduate and medical school choices of Georgetown University and Johns Hopkins University School of

Medicine, respectively, were firmly grounded in the belief that I could achieve great things if I aligned my thoughts and actions with my desired end. Therefore, it is so important to carefully choose mentors who want the best for you, who want you to succeed, who believe that you can achieve and encourage you to dream big.

To better foster a relationship between medical students and faculty, all medical students at Hopkins were assigned an advisor. The four-year advisor program encouraged an active exchange between student and faculty. My advisor and mentor was Dr. Fred Brancati, an internist with a strong research interest.

While still a medical student I worked on his clinical trial as part of the Diabetes Prevention Program. I really enjoyed interviewing and following patients during their visits. My desire for bedside interaction with patients was one of the reasons I chose to pursue a residency in internal medicine.

My work with Dr. Brancati allowed me to interact with other members of the general internal medicine faculty including Dr. Lisa Cooper who became my role model and second mentor. Her research on racial disparities within healthcare and her work to bring greater attention to the needs of women and minorities at Hopkins inspired me to always strive to do more.

I initially contemplated fellowship training in general internal medicine, which included completion of a master in public health. However, the paucity of women in tenured positions in academic medicine in the mid-1990s made me reevaluate my initial decision to enter academic medicine early in my career.

Another less-spoken reason was the lack of timely and successful advancement of purely clinical physicians in academia during that time. The research track was well established, but the clinical track was largely unchartered. I clearly saw the gender disparity between the advancement of men and women in academic medicine.

Not to say that such disparity in position and pay did not also exist outside of academics. However, in hospital medicine I saw greater equality and growth potential. I also could capitalize on the flexibility and transferability of skills if I ever chose to return to academic medicine.

At that phase in my life, I turned to colleagues and other professionals in the field to help navigate my transition from residency to clinical practice. After talking with fellow female residents in medicine and other primary care specialties, about 30% of my third-year class of internal medicine residents decided to enter general practice and not sub-specialize, which was a significant break from the Hopkins tradition. I chose to go into hospital medicine because of work-life balance. With a more predictable schedule I would have more time for my future family, which came five years later with the birth of my first child.

During my tenure in hospital medicine, I continued to explore my interest in academics by teaching medical students and working with administration on quality improvement projects. I collaborated with case management and other hospital ancillary departments to ensure timely patient disposition and transitions of care.

This experience exposed me to the world of administrative medicine. As medical director of a hospital medicine program I was responsible for tracking and reporting the physicians' adherence to core quality measures and developed a pay-for-performance program to achieve 100% compliance with these metrics.

With more than 11 years of practicing medicine at the bedside, I acquired first-hand experience in caring for a forgotten portion of society: the uninsured and underinsured. I observed numerous people turning to the emergency room as their last, and often their only resort for healthcare. Many individuals who had state-sponsored health plans still frequented the emergency department; their assigned physicians were often too busy with routine office visits to squeeze in urgent same-day appointments.

All too often, I witnessed the difficulties patients experience in navigating through a complex system like government-sponsored healthcare. I would often personally call to schedule follow-up appointments for patients before they left the hospital, especially if I knew the task would be onerous. When a young woman finally confessed to me "it's hard to be on Medicaid because no one wants to take your insurance," I realized I needed to do more.

Coinciding with my desire to address the increasing social demands on my patients, I had reached a point in my career where I needed to recalibrate the work-life balance. After returning to work following the birth of my second child, the reality of 14-hour shifts began to take its toll. So, I turned to physician executive recruiter, Dr. Deborah Shlian.

Dr. Shlian possessed an invaluable breath of experience and perspective given her expansive background in managed care. She helped me realize that all my prior experience managing physicians' behavior and practice patterns could easily translate into the arena of managed care. Armed with this timely advice, I welcomed the opportunity to join WellCare Health Plans, Inc., as a medical director of utilization and care management.

I transitioned from clinical practice to managed care because I wanted to focus on improving access to quality care for an entire population, not just for individuals. For several years, I worked full-time as a managed care medical director while continuing as a hospital-based physician some weekends a month so I could still help the most vulnerable individuals negotiate the healthcare system. I believed my continued practice of clinical medicine gave me increased credibility when discussing care management issues with providers.

I was also able to voice member, provider, and hospital concerns when it came to my company's managed care policies. In my dual role as practicing physician and health plan administrator, I could make decisions that reflected my own high standards of care. I took immense pride in knowing that countless members and providers benefited from my accumulated clinical experience.

People, especially other physicians, often ask me how I entered administrative medicine. After I describe the events of my journey, they come to realize the importance of knowing and connecting with the right people at the right time. This statement is certainly true of my relationship with Dr. Vincent Kunz, my first supervisor at WellCare.

As a general surgeon who had spent over 17 years in practice before assuming the role as medical director over a multi-specialty group, Dr. Kunz openly admitted that he entered administrative medicine late in his career. He became an ideal mentor for me because he freely provided me with advice and encouragement and took it upon himself to expose me to all aspects of managed care. He had an open-door policy and urged me to attend various committees and interdepartmental meetings to expand my knowledge base.

I believe the best mentors are the people who do not see the mentee's ambition as a threat to their own professional success. I have found the best advisors among my colleagues who are well-anchored in their career or on the tail end of their career. They do not have anything to fear from my questioning and frequently welcome the opportunity to cultivate my interest.

During one of our weekly one-on-one sessions, Dr. Kunz advised me to obtain an advanced management degree since I was early in my career in administrative medicine. Never one to second-guess sage advice, I began researching executive MBA programs. As I often do, I consulted my husband who wholeheartedly agreed that now was the time to pursue my MBA. Being in a very business-minded environment, I knew an MBA would be more easily recognized and accepted than other advanced management degrees.

I sought to find the best program that would provide an expansive breadth of knowledge and the flexibility I needed with two small children at home. I chose Howard University's online Executive MBA program to achieve my professional goal of becoming an effective physician leader while allowing me to continue my administrative responsibilities without disruption.

During a mock interview session with my medical school mentor, I told him that my goal in life is "to run something big." Although that statement shocked him and even caught me off guard for a moment, it appears fitting when I look at my career trajectory. I graduated with honors from a top ranked medical school, completed my internal medicine residency training at a world-renowned medical institution, and accumulated more than six years of managerial experience leading up my decision to pursue an advanced management degree at Howard University.

Increased advancement opportunities are now available for female physician executives in both the private and academic sectors.

Academic medicine has made significant strides during the past 10 years in solidifying the succession process of several well-deserving women who are now full professors, department chairs, and hospital executives.

I am proud to say that one of my medical school mentors, Dr. Cooper, who was an assistant professor some 10 years ago, is now a full professor and the recipient of the prestigious "genius award" — the MacArthur Fellowship — for her groundbreaking work on health disparities.

Both academic institutions and private healthcare companies now realize the imperative to address the needs of the female physician executive. For me, family and personal commitments ultimately weigh heavy on my career choices. Many of my female colleagues agree that maintaining flexibility in their schedule to attend school and professional conferences, fair remuneration for their skills and talent, and timely promotions are important considerations for job selection and loyalty.

With the rising costs of healthcare and increasing demands on our human and financial capital, physicians across all sectors face ever-changing priorities to deliver high quality, efficient and effective care for all stakeholders involved. My transition from purely clinical practice to administrative medicine was a natural progression for me. I witnessed the challenges of a hospital system as it realigned physician incentives to reflect quality performance and patient out-comes. Working in a managed care organization I witnessed a similar paradigm shift linking fiscal growth to quality measures.

I knew that I needed to expand my business acumen to be a suc-cessful physician executive in the healthcare industry. The business strategies and skills that I would learn in the executive MBA pro-gram would allow me to critically analyze current business processes to identify and eliminate areas of excess and waste and develop a more efficient workflow of evidence-based standards in care delivery.

In 2012, my journey as a physician executive was just beginning. One of the keys to my early entrance into administrative medicine was finding the right mentor at the right time. In my life and career, I found that mentors are for a time and come in many different forms.

Little did I realize that one conversation with a semi-retired nurse at the age of 12 would translate into a blossoming career in medicine and now as a physician executive. The full effect of an individual's influence on your life is usually not evident until many years later. Additionally, the far-reaching effects of personal decisions made years and decades ago often meld together seamlessly to form your present career trajectory.

An End and a Beginning

At the beginning of 2013, I was running the infamous rat race — working an 8 am to 6 pm administrative medicine job, still moonlighting at local hospitals as an evening and weekend hospitalist, completing my last semester in my Executive MBA program at Howard University, and being a wife and mother with two children under the age of six! No wonder I had lost so much weight and my hair was thinning.

Over Mother's Day weekend, I was celebrating the completion of my Executive MBA program with all my family. We had gathered in D.C. for a weekend of festivities to celebrate the momentous occasion. I finally felt relieved to be graduating from school . . . again! When I received that fateful call on July 17, 2013, at 4:30 am, several days into my younger brother's hospital stay for uncontrolled diabetes and worsening kidney function following a trans metatarsal amputation of his great toe, I knew instinctively that my life as I knew it would be changed forever.

Finding my true purpose in life took internal reflection, an honest assessment of my present situation, and acceptance of what I wanted to leave as a legacy for my children and family. I faced this daunting task in the hours and days following the unexpected death of Billy. Losing Billy felt more like losing a child than losing a brother. My sister and I always looked out for Billy. We felt responsible for him and were so excited that he finally decided to pursue his artistic talents on the collegiate level. But all that came to an end. It was an end for him and a beginning for me.

Losing my brother helped me find something that I had lost sight of: my true, authentic, and genuine self! In the race to be everything for everyone, I fell into the common trap that can plague professional and ambitious women in a male-dominated profession. I was so busy taking care of others that I failed to take care of myself. Looking at my life from the outside, I looked like Superwoman, handling a multitude of responsibilities and ready to take on the next challenge. I had essentially forgotten to put on my oxygen mask before helping others.

For me, the process of internal reflection started with my brother's untimely death at the age of 35. Fortunately, I was not alone in experiencing that loss and together helped my older sister and mother grieve. I was so blessed to reconnect with my older sister, Jackie, during this life wake-up call. She was my non-judgmental sounding board that helped me identify the areas in my life that I had neglected and needed work. It was at her suggestion that I speak with someone professionally to help me best deal with the loss and to help me find my true voice. It took time and courage, but that process of internal reflection is something that is an ongoing whenever I experience a major life event . . . such as an impending divorce, an unforeseen job termination, or an unexpected job offer.

Sowing the Seeds

I can do more . . . I need to do more. In the years following my brother's death, I worked to build a dynamic and diverse team of clinical and non-clinical professionals in my former role as chief medical director for medical management and external relationships at WellCare Health Plans, Inc. I participated in various panel discussions and presentations on disparities on the local and national level. I actively engaged with the National Quality Forum through work on committees and as part of technical expert panels to share the experience as a physician executive in a managed care organization solely focused on government-sponsored health plans.

My mantra in onboarding new physicians was to make the same decision that you would make if you were at the bedside. Meaning, don't hide behind a computer when making utilization review decisions.

I was proud to create a strong succession plan for my physician leaders and for the non-clinical team. I often held "office hours" where doctors, nurses and other staff would drop in and we would discuss work, family, school, or whatever topic they wanted advice on from Dr. Traci. As a woman, a physician, and a mother, I am constantly sowing seeds for the next generation. As my mother took me to work with her at the nursing home as I handed out graham crackers and jelly to the residents, I routinely brought my daughter to work with me as I attended conference calls and video meetings. My goal is to intentionally expose her to the many facets of my day-to-day life, from being on work calls to even helping me prepare for webinars by listening and critiquing my presentations.

When I came face to face with an unexpected sabbatical following the acquisition of WellCare, I finally had a moment to breathe and ultimately found my true purpose. I had time to contemplate my next career move and what I really wanted to do. I reflected upon my prior work on disparities and how many community-based organizations exist to help a wide variety of communities.

However, the burning question that I wanted to directly address was: "What happens when an organization brings all the resources into that particular zip code, effectively addressing the social determinants of health that adversely impact residents' health outcomes, morbidity and mortality?" Dr. Traci's House was born as an answer to that very question.

I founded the non-profit organization affectionately called Dr. Traci's House to be that organization that brings together early childhood development and education; after hours and sick childcare; adult educational support; career development and arts education; holistic health and wellness with medical, behavioral health, pharmaceutical and dental care; nutritional support with a community garden and access to freshly prepared meals in a commercial grade kitchen; a resource center for childcare; living expense stipends for community residents seeking career certifications or job training; and most importantly, subsidized housing. (Yes, I know that is a lofty vision but my theme for 2020 was "Dream Big and Execute and Live Mindfully"!)

By implementing the Dr. Traci's House community development model, a zip code once identified on a community needs assessment as showing the worst health outcomes and health disparities will no longer be on that list. Dr. Traci's House provides the blueprint and building blocks to revitalize an under-resourced community and provide its residents with the tools and resources to live and thrive in their neighborhood. Dr. Traci's House is a community-inspired approach to building a healthier community from infants to older adults with key resources in their very own community to create a sustainable model for generational health and wellness.

Dr. Traci's House, Inc., as a 501c3 organization, wants to break that vicious cycle by placing the disconnected social needs together with the healthcare services in one comprehensive ecosystem of community care that is high touch, engaging care providers, residents, caregivers, and institutions in a deliberate manner to optimize health outcomes for the community. By focusing on the needs of a community utilizing published community needs assessment data, Dr. Traci's House, Inc., will bring early childhood development, comprehensive health, and nutritional programming to the community where it is needed the most.

Serving the community takes time and collaboration. I have enlisted the assistance and support of several key stakeholders that will bring my true purpose—service to the community to life. I did not get this far in my medical career alone and so I have learned an invaluable skill as a healthcare executive and that is the skill of delegation. I can honestly say it took YEARS for me to truthfully admit that I was able to delegate important tasks and duties to others. Thankfully, I have nurtured a phenomenal group of women (yes, they are all women!) who will usher my dream of Dr. Traci's House into reality.

At the writing of this new book chapter, I am embarking on a new chapter myself. I recently accepted a position as regional vice president for health services for Humana Florida Medicaid — coming full circle in my medical management journey. I started my career as a hospitalist caring for predominantly Medicaid and uninsured patients and now I will be the chief medical officer for a growing number of Medicaid beneficiaries. This role will bring together my passion for community engagement and my purpose to serve the most vulnerable members of society.

In addition, Dr. Traci's House is set to open its doors to the community in the upcoming months. My life has taken many turns over the years but at each turn, I have taken time to pause, reflect and assess. Even when things didn't appear to go as planned or expected, the ability to reframe an experience or event, has brought me peace and purpose. My hope is that my life and my service to the community will be the legacy shared by my children and others for generations to come.

CHAPTER TWENTY

Medicine and Leadership: An Unplanned Journey

By Eugenie Komives, MD

I WAS BORN WITH MULTIPLE VASCULAR ANOM-ALIES that led the doctors to tell my parents I might not survive to leave the hospital after birth. Obviously, I did. . . . but I spent more time in hospitals and doctor offices by the time I graduated from high school than most folks probably do in a lifetime.

I do not remember much about any of those experiences except that I grew up feeling different from my classmates and tried to hide my "different-ness" much of the time.

I was not able to participate in physical education, and that gave me more time for academic classes in which I always excelled and found pretty easy for the most part. I also played the flute and for a while thought I'd be a flautist when I grew up. That changed when I went off to a band camp at UW Madison and was 30th chair out of 60 flute players. I realized I'd likely end up a high school band director if I continued to focus only on music as a career. Nothing against band directors, but I could not envision a life dealing with surly teenagers.

My best friend's father was a radiation oncologist and cancer researcher, and after a brief period of thinking about veterinary medicine (I was allergic to cats!) I entertained biochemistry and research. After graduating as valedictorian of my high school, I started at UW Madison to study chemistry and biology.

My father was a small-business consultant (his focus was the study of the psychology of entrepreneurs) and my mother was a frustrated math and science major who did her master's degree in home economics because in her day "if you went to graduate school in science or math, you would never marry." She drilled into her daughters the importance of having our own careers (but did make sure we also knew how to type!)

Both of my parents were very demanding of their daughters' education and expected that we would be straight "A" students. They never said that we could not accomplish something because of our gender.

None of my family members was a physician, however. My parents were not wealthy. My mom made all our clothes. I remember the first time she let us buy a pair of Levi's late in high school – it was such a splurge. However, my parents scrimped and saved so that we were all able to go to college.

While in college, I was often asked why I was not a "pre-med," since I excelled in science and math there as well. It was just not on my radar screen. However, I had the misfortune of suffering a retroperitoneal hemorrhage (related to my vascular birth defects) while on a family vacation in Quebec, Canada. I was left in horrible pain and during that hospitalization, I clearly remember having some "interesting" physicians.

One was a neurologist who barely spoke to me and inflicted pain on every visit (and was seemingly unconcerned about this). The other was a hematologist (the first woman I ever had as a physician!) who was caring, kind, and took the time to talk with me about what was happening. I remember thinking at the time that the world needed more physicians like her and fewer like him, and that maybe I should be one of the empathetic ones.

I returned to Wisconsin and, after a long recovery, got back on my feet and continued my junior year of college. Though I did not immediately change career paths, after a stint in a research lab, I realized that I needed more people around me to be happy. That was the point when I realized that I should go to medical school.

Fortunately, my courses prepared me well so I was able to graduate on time with my classmates. I applied to several medical schools. Some had me interview with only men, some of whom were less than supportive of filling medical schools with women. Others clearly made an effort to demonstrate that women were welcome, using women faculty as interviewers. At that time (1980), women comprised roughly 25% of medical students in the United States.

My younger sister was enrolled at MIT and encouraged (read: FORCED) me to apply to Harvard Medical School. Much to my surprise, I was accepted. We planned to live together while she was still there, so I moved to Boston (I had never lived in a true city.)

I met my future husband on my first day of medical school. We began dating a few months later, and moved in together after completing our first year of med school. He is a wonderful, supportive, grounded fellow and I love him as much now as I did when we first met. Once asked what the secret to a long relationship with a "Komives" woman was, he remarked (after a moment's thought), "If she says she's going to do something, get out of the way." I think that response typifies the sort of support he provides – he's there when I need him (which I often do), but does not get in the way.

My husband had taken a year off from medical school to do some research, so while waiting for him to graduate, I did a one-year internship in internal medicine at Beth Israel in Boston. I was never so miserable as I watched way too many young people die. I felt my inability to "fix" them was a failing on my part.

Originally I had planned to do a residency in Ob-Gyn once my husband finished medical school. However, he had done a one-month clerkship in family medicine in rural Maine and reminded me that family medicine had once been my goal.

The support for primary care at Harvard at the time was minimal to none so I'd given up the idea. However, after some thought and reading, I decided my husband was a very wise man, and I applied for family medicine residencies while he applied in pathology.

We matched together at Duke, where the director of the family medicine residency was a woman whom I will always think of as one of my main mentors. She was strong, ethical, patient-oriented, tough, and kind. She was also a wife (of another family physician), and a parent. She believed that women could "do it all" if we just put our minds to it. While in residency, I worked with many other wise, wonderful women as residents and faculty. Many of them remain close friends and colleagues today.

I also learned that behaviors that were acceptable from male residents were frequently not tolerated from the women. For example, while men could "tell" staff what they needed, we were expected to politely ask, or we would be labeled as "difficult" or "bitchy." While I believe this gender differentiation is unfair and unreasonable, perhaps medicine would be better served if ALL providers had to politely ask for what we needed in the care of our patients. Needless to say, I was pragmatic enough to temper my "bull in a china shop" attitude and work collaboratively with my colleagues.

After finishing my residency, I contemplated a career in public health. My husband still had several years more of residency and research before he would be ready to settle on a job. Realizing that for at least a while I really just wanted to be a primary care physician, I finally took a position with Kaiser Permanente in Durham for what I assumed would be a few years' stint before we would both move on.

Little did I know that the Kaiser Permanente pre-paid integrated model was the perfect clinical fit for me. I truly believed then, as I do now, that we do best for our patients when we provide them with ALL of the healthcare they need, and yet ONLY the healthcare that they will benefit from, using the evidence as well as the art to guide our decisions.

I had never planned a career in management, but when the chief of family medicine role became available, I asked to take that on. I think this was born of my desire to "fix things" and a need to feel like I had some influence on how care was delivered.

Despite the fact that our area medical director, probably rightfully, felt I was not ready for the role (only three years into my career as practicing physician), he let me assume the position on condition that I agree to mentor with one of our senior female physician leaders. Though she and I were as different as night and day, she took her responsibility seriously, providing me timely and helpful advice as I moved into the management role.

Kaiser also had a management training program that taught me the basics of management (e.g., how to run a meeting, how to influence others, the difference between leadership and management, how to provide performance evaluations and have "difficult" conversations). It also gave me the opportunity to meet other physician leaders, including many women.

After only two years, I applied for an associate medical director position (a 70% administrative role). I was so excited and proud that our executive medical director had the confidence to offer me the job. However, immediately after our first "senior" staff meeting during which I had remained silent, trying to take it all in and figure out my role, he criticized my lack of participation. "I did not hire you to sit there quietly," he said. "I want to hear your thoughts and opinions as a part of this team. They are critical to me, and to our success."

This was a real eye-opener. I have since learned that this was the type of leader I need to seek out. I need to be comfortable being me – to share what I'm thinking and my opinions openly and without concern, in order to be both satisfied in my role and also to be the best leader I can in my organization.

Unfortunately, unlike other parts of the country where Kaiser Permanente is a stable force in the market (e.g., California), that was not the case in the North Carolina market. Prepaid healthcare in a restricted network was a foreign concept in our market, and we attracted "adverse risk" from an underwriting perspective, while our largest client (the NC State Health Plan) charged us an extra fee because our members were slightly younger than the average (though I believe we took on every hemophiliac in their member population, for example.)

Ultimately, we were simply too expensive for our parent company in California to continue to support, so they made a decision to divest themselves of the North Carolina market. (For a more detailed analysis of this, see Daniel P. Gitterman *et al.*, "The Rise and Fall of a Kaiser Permanente Expansion Region," *The Millbank Quarterly*. 2003;81(4):567-601.)

After an 11-year run with Kaiser, and a 10-month period back in full-time clinical practice, the remaining physician group went out of business. Luckily, just in time, I was offered a position with Blue Cross and Blue Shield of North Carolina by the same physician who had hired me out of residency for Kaiser.

I had a wonderful opportunity to work with an outspoken, strong, open-minded man who took over the leadership of our state health plan and worked himself (and the rest of us) as hard as possible to make changes needed to bring it back to fiscal solvency. He trusted my judgment in all things clinical, and I learned a tremendous amount from him about the finances and business of running a health plan.

When he retired, I took a position as a senior medical director and soon vice president, managing BCBSNC's healthcare quality programs. In that role, I had to deliver many difficult messages to my fellow physicians, all in the interest of improving the quality and the evidence-base of care delivered to our members — their patients.

I spent countless hours meeting with representatives of the medical society, various specialty academies, hospital leaders, and others to help them understand how we could better partner together to achieve our shared vision of improved healthcare in North Carolina.

After almost 12 years working at BCBSNC, I was able to look back at what I had accomplished and see that being a physician leader allowed me to make just as important contributions to the care of patients as I had as a clinician.

For example, my colleagues and I reinvented payment for primary care physicians in smaller independent practices, focusing on achieving "patient centered medical homes" and rewarding doctors financially according to that effort. We implemented programs with partner organizations such as the North Carolina Academy of Family Physicians to increase the numbers of medical students going into primary care in the state. We stimulated improvement in the care patients receive during hospitalization as well as at the time of discharge. We reduced the number of patients who inappropriately underwent imaging procedures and some surgical procedures.

While proud of all of those accomplishments, I am most proud of the fact that we did that while creating collaborative and friendly working relationships with physicians across the state who shared our goals of improving care for patients. In honor of that collaboration, I was awarded a "President's Award" from the NCAFP, and was asked to take over the leadership of the North Carolina Medical Society Foundation's Kanof Institute for Physician Leadership, which develops physician leaders for North Carolina.

The use of "we" above is very intentional – I had a wonderful team of nurses and other staff who took my crazy ideas and made them reality through their hard work and commitment to our goals.

All that said, I did miss the care of patients, and had always envisioned returning to the clinical world. That opportunity came when a practice affiliated with Duke Primary Care in my small town decided to add another physician. I joined the group and was able to practice with physicians I had known for many years, including a close colleague from Kaiser Permanente. Though that was another big "leap" and was not an easy transition, those doctors were committed to helping me be successful. My part-time clinical role also created a bit of space in my life.

But, as things turned out, that hiatus from administrative work was short-lived. After 18 months in the practice, I was asked to take on the role of senior medical director for a new population health organization at Duke, to assist in implementing an accountable care organization.

We successfully participated in the Medicare Shared Savings Program and multiple other value-based payment arrangements with other payers, and were preparing to expand our care management program in preparation for North Carolina's Medicaid Managed Care implementation. The vision for NC's Medicaid program was unique, blending the existing medical home care management program into a multi-payer pre-paid health plan implementation.

One of the health plans offered me the role of chief medical officer, and once again, I made a career transition. After several delays, our Medicaid program is now up and running, and in the process, I have learned a lot very quickly about how Medicaid programs work and am enjoying working with another great team of colleagues fully committed to the work.

Lessons Learned

My professional success has not come without a price. My husband and I adopted twins from Vietnam in 1996, who at one time thought their mommy lived in California (due to travel for Kaiser Permanente work.) Fortunately, my husband and I have been able to share the family duties roughly 50-50. I missed many soccer games, track meets, cross country meets, basketball games, and parent-teacher conferences, but so did my husband – and at least one of us was at almost all of them.

That said, I think my now 25 year-olds have come to understand that in terms of career options, the world is wide open to them and they just need to decide what role they want to play. They understand that sometimes we must work harder than we want to, and that we all make choices and need to be accountable for them.

I do not think I would have been a better parent if I had stayed at home with my children, though that does not stop me from feeling guilty when I talk with moms who made different decisions.

Along the way, I have enjoyed the opportunity to mentor other younger leaders who are just starting their careers. It is truly exciting to see that there are new, developing leaders who will take what we've put in place, improve it or throw it away, and continue the commitment to improving healthcare that each prior generation has fostered.

It should be clear from my story that my career has been less than intentional. I have wandered into many roles that have been interesting and exciting without ever having had a "plan" or what felt like true "ambition." I did not set my sights on being a leader in a medical practice or in a health plan. However, I did take advantage of opportunities as they came along, and at my core have followed my desire to serve and to lead.

My advice to other women physician leaders is to do your best to keep some balance in your life. Too often, women who attempt to do it all have a difficult time asking for help. We don't allot enough time to take care of ourselves, which includes spending time with our family and friends. It is too easy to let the career take control of our lives, at the risk of losing other things of greater value in the long run.

Let's collectively seek balance not just for us, but for our husbands, sons, and daughters, by insisting on the changes needed in our workplaces to ensure that they will be sustainable into the future.

CHAPTER TWENTY-ONE

Enduring Leadership

By Barbara Le Tourneau, MD, MBA

MY EARLY CAREER WAS A PROGRESSION FROM an emergency room clinician to physician executive via an MBA. As opportunities for more and varied leadership responsibilities presented themselves, I moved from part-time into full-time administrative roles — starting in private practice group management, then health plan administrative leadership, and back to delivery system executive positions. Within these organizations I was able to learn the healthcare system from the administrative perspective of physicians, health plan, and hospital.

Participation in several national organizations, including the American College of Physician Executives (now American Association for Physician Leadership), The American College of Healthcare Executives, and the National Association of Managed Care Physicians, augmented my administrative work. I received a number of awards and certifications.

Mentors were key to my development as a manager. I had several important mentors, some male and some female, who gave me advice and opened doors for further education and experience. My early management career advancement was covered in the 1995 *Women in Medicine and Management: A Mentoring Guide*. In the 2012 updated version, I dealt with new leadership opportunities. Now in this newest update, I have focused on my evolving view of leadership, including my decision to finally retire

Soul Searching 1

In the late 1990s, while working as the vice president of medical affairs (VPMA) of a region of a Twin Cities integrated delivery system, I went through a divorce. Like so many women with full-time jobs, I had depended on my husband for support at home. Suddenly I had two young children and no partner. Losing that relationship and unwinding a marriage forced me to rethink my life, including my goals and priorities for the future.

Many of us face similar turning points: the loss of a spouse or partner, as mine was, the death of a parent, children leaving home, or a personal health crisis. What I learned from my own experience is that stopping to take stock of one's life and career is important — even without a significant life crisis. As we age and mature, our life paths and views of life change. If we don't reassess with openness and flexibility, we may end up locked into unsatisfactory paths.

So when is the right time to take stock? In my experience, it takes at least five to 10 years — first in clinical practice and then in management — to acquire a good sense of the joys and tribulations of each. It also takes that long to appreciate what is important in life and career. When this happened to me I had been in clinical practice for almost twenty years and in full-time management for six years.

In the late 1990s, during the time of my reassessment, I was working as vice president of medical affairs of the north region of an integrated delivery system in Minnesota. The system resulted from a merger between an HMO with over a million members and delivery systems with several large hospitals and a large multispecialty clinic. At the time of the merger I was the interim medical director of the health plan. After the merger, I took the VPMA job on the delivery side, working primarily with the two large community hospitals in the northern suburbs of the Twin Cities.

An interesting opportunity presented itself in 1998. I hired a consultant named Hugh Greeley to help with education as I reorganized the medical staff leaders of my hospitals. He liked my approach and invited me to work with him with other medical staffs. So once a month I was on the road, helping other hospitals do what I had done at my own hospital. It was fun and interesting to see how different hospital medical staffs functioned and what kinds of reorganizations they developed. I learned a lot from these other organizations while bringing my own experiences to them.

Consulting was a new form of leadership for me. One of the roles I enjoyed most was that of change agent. As a consultant, I could work with other medical staffs and help them design and implement change. This occurred at about the time I was completing my term as president of the American College of Physician Executives (now American Association for Physician Leadership). National work as consultant and president of the ACPE introduced me to a new kind of leadership role. Rather than being immersed in the politics and struggles of designing and implementing change in just my own organization, I could work as a change agent and advisor, or coach, to many different organizations.

As I thought about it, this incorporated some of the reasons I had always liked emergency medicine. It was episodic and short term. Like an ER doctor, a consultant does not need to be immersed in the day-to-day change issues to provide a fresh eye and new ideas when a crisis occurs or when a different approach is needed. This role helped me maintain my enthusiasm and expand my perspective. As I assessed my life and career in the late 1990s, new ways to provide leadership became clearer to me.

By 1999, I had been in full-time executive positions for nearly seven years. Before that, I had been in a half-time executive position in my private practice emergency medicine group for five years. As I spent more and more time in a corporate structure, I found myself tiring of corporate life. There were several issues that made working in a corporate setting frustrating for me.

First, I did not see many physicians move into the highest senior leadership ranks of corporations, and women physician executives were certainly not going there. Those physicians I did see in corporate senior leadership, while capable, tended to be part of the male bonding system. Nationally, I was not seeing corporate senior leadership ranks populated by individuals with diverse views, such as women and non-Caucasian men. There were many opportunities in hospitals and group practices, but few if any at the corporate senior leadership level.

Second, while physician executives were asked to engage physicians in their organizations, a majority of senior management did not take them seriously when they actually presented these physician needs. As a physician executive, hospital or corporate leaders often expected me to bring physicians into line with hospital or corporate goals. My suggestions as to how to accomplish this were often minimized or ignored. When someone on the management team made a misstep, ignoring my advice to avoid an activity or strategy, I was expected to manage and appease the unhappy physicians.

While I had many opportunities to implement what were very innovative ideas in 1999, the practice and frustrations of leaving physicians out of decision-making enhanced my dissatisfaction with physician executive work. I was never sure if the differences in philosophy were due to old-fashioned thinking on my part or too much business centeredness in high-level management thinking. I suspect that many of my partners in management found it equally frustrating to work with me since I did not share their goals and principles in dealing with physicians.

In 1999 I decided to leave my full-time executive work and start a consulting company. I planned to work half time as a clinician in the ED and half time as a consultant, both in my own company as well as for Hugh Greeley at The Greeley Company. Because I was marrying again in 2000, I knew I could rely on my fiancé's full-time job for health insurance benefits for my children and me once my COBRA benefits expired.

Throughout my executive career I had always maintained some clinical practice. My specialty of emergency medicine allowed me to pick up a few ED shifts here and there. I realized that I still thought of myself as an ED doc and that I still enjoyed touching the lives of patients and their families. In the late 1990s, I recertified my Emergency Medicine Boards and worked very occasionally in the ED. I still had clinical skills and drive to help patients more directly.

As a result of self-examination I decided that it was time to make a leap from full-time executive practice into my own business as a consultant. Although I am not entrepreneurial by nature, I came to see myself as a bit of a risk-taker. I happily left my full-time job and regular paycheck with full benefits for two part-time careers as a consultant and a clinician.

A Little Variety Please

During this time of my life, I found many leadership opportunities — both professionally and personally.

Consulting allowed me to be a change agent, coach, and mentor. As I returned to part-time clinical practice, I suddenly realized that to take care of patients at times of crisis requires definite leadership skills. The ED physician advises and coaches patients and their families, helping them deal with many problems of acute and chronic illness. In addition, I continued some national work for ACPE and began serving on several non-profit boards of directors. These activities provided a variety of leadership opportunities I had not yet experienced.

Outside of my professional life, I discovered personal ways to provide leadership through volunteer activities. I developed new skills, including becoming a master gardener and teaching others to be successful gardeners, composters, and environmental stewards.

It wasn't until late 2000, as I wrote for national publications, spoke on national platforms, and held national positions as a way to build my consulting practice, that I finally realized I am neither a marketer nor an entrepreneur. At first a surprise, I began to acknowledge the obvious: I have never been good at selling things. I don't have the instinct for setting up and closing a deal. I certainly am not good at selling myself and I do not have the drive to build my own business. However, as is true for many physicians, I don't act like a 9 to 5 employee either. Because of this, more and more of my consulting work has been from my independent contractor relationship with the Greeley Company and not through building my own personal practice.

One downside of leaving a full-time management position was the loss of certain perks. For example, my organization had always paid for me to attend several meetings a year. Now I had to pay my own way. However, building a consulting practice requires high visibility at these national meetings. It is expensive to market oneself and requires a special kind of savvy or even pushiness. I learned that my strength was in leadership presence, not in drumming up business or marketing myself.

Settle into Something

At the end of 2001, a recruiter contacted me about a VPMA position for a local hospital. I knew that outside recruiting for a hospital VPMA job in the Twin Cities was rare, as most hospitals that are part of large systems tend to recruit internally. As it turned out, this was a hospital where I had often worked as a medical student. Suddenly, the idea of finishing my career in a familiar place was appealing even though I had not been considering taking another full-time executive position.

It had been two years since I had worked in a corporate setting, but I had been in many hospitals as a consultant. I was happy with my half-time consultant, half-time clinician work, but the paychecks were variable and I was interested in being home every night. So I interviewed for the position and felt that the hospital president shared my philosophy about the roles of physicians. I became the new VPMA in early 2002. As a bonus, clinical work in the ED was part of my contract. I was also able to maintain a small consulting practice as long as I used my own vacation time when I had to travel during business hours.

I was excited to be in a more concrete leadership role again, eager to bring lessons learned and ideas discovered in my consultant role, to lead a hospital and medical staff of my own. Although it took time to learn the medical staff systems and culture, I was eventually able to introduce a stronger medical staff leadership system, bring a new method of physician peer review, and work with nursing and various specialties to design systems introducing evidence-based practice into the hospital.

Having strong medical staff leadership has always been one of my core beliefs. Strong physician leaders are needed to come to the table with the management team to advocate for the needs of their patients as well as the needs of physician colleagues practicing in the hospital. If physicians can learn to speak with one voice, whether employed or independent, they are more likely to be heard. This became a primary goal for me as VPMA. It was also an important principle in my consulting practice.

I was very happy in this role, despite the inevitable corporate bureaucracy that delayed many of the programs I hoped to initiate. Once again, as a hospital executive, I was working not only within a hospital, but also with a large medical group and a health plan system, trying to manage their disparate interests. I particularly enjoyed the influence I could bring to system level projects.

In late 2003, the hospital president who hired me retired and within a few months a new hospital president came on board. Unfortunately, he and I did not have the same vision of physician involvement that I had shared with his predecessor.

In 2004, I sensed the focus shifting to a stronger corporate identity with more emphasis on corporate needs and less on the needs and involvement of practicing physicians. It seemed that corporate quality initiatives were decided at an executive level, with assistance from executive physicians, but without the involvement of medical staff leaders. After the decision was made, the practicing physicians were expected to follow the program and I was expected to make them do so at the hospital level.

I learned more about my nature as a leader in this VPMA role. I realized that I am unable to lead in a direction I don't believe in—something I should have understood in 1999 when I left my last full-time management position. Now I saw more clearly that I couldn't set aside my personal beliefs for the good of the job. Perhaps if I had been more skilled at expressing those beliefs to the corporate leaders, I may have succeeded in shifting their thinking. However, I believe my personal values and ideals versus those of the corporate leaders were too different to reconcile.

In late 2004, I left the corporation and returned to consulting and clinical practice. I remained on the hospital staff and continued to practice in the ED. I still had my clinical skills and the desire to help people as a clinician. My departure from my VPMA position was amicable and there were no issues with my clinical ability. I had maintained a consulting practice with the Greeley Company and also with my own small company. Luckily, my husband's work covered my health insurance.

Within a few months of leaving any job, it is important to do some self-analysis to discover patterns and lessons. When I did that, in my own "aha" moment I realized that I had left each full-time executive job after three to five years. That seemed to be how long it took for me to understand the particular organization and become successful as a leader there before I found the work to be too routine. At that point, I stopped growing as a manager and became frustrated and even negative about the job. Whenever my dissatisfactions outweighed the benefits, I became less effective and either had to leave the position or put aside my principles and needs.

Soul Searching 2

In 2005, my life once again took an unexpected turn. My husband, who was in the army reserve, was activated in the spring and deployed to Iraq. During his deployment I had my own two teenage children and my teenage stepson living with me. A younger stepson lived with his mother. The children living with me were old enough to pitch in and help with household activities, but not old enough to stay at home alone when I traveled or worked overnight.

Once again I had to prioritize. Since my income was larger than my husband's, I had to continue working. Luckily, we had the resources to hire help for cleaning, shopping, errands, and driving. In addition, my mother stayed at my house when I traveled. I had to develop a new set of leadership skills — helping my husband's children cope with his absence while coping with it myself.

Things changed dramatically again in 2006 when my husband was killed. Once again a life trauma led me to seriously reassess what was important. Because the army took good care of the children and me after my husband's death, I was able to take three months off to adjust to the changes in my life.

I was nearing the final five to 10 years of my career. How and when did I want to end my career, and how did I want to live the rest of my life? I began to realize that, for better or worse, leadership and influence are engrained in me. I also recognized that I am unable to sacrifice my principles for the good of a job. Moreover, I now understood how important clinical practice was to me.

Enduring Leadership

Because my husband died in the line of duty, the children receive military health insurance coverage through college. I am covered for the rest of my life. This freed me from having to take a full-time job for health insurance benefits. Although I could have retired at this point, I still wanted to work and felt I had something to offer both as a leader and change agent and clinician.

As I prepared to return to work in late 2006, an opportunity presented itself — a recurrent theme in my life. The Greeley Company needed more full-time consultants. They asked me to consider a leadership position in the company. I was not ready for that level of commitment or another full-time corporate position, but agreed to the role of senior consultant as a half-time employee. I was also able to continue my clinical practice, moonlighting at several hospitals.

In my consultant role, I worked with many large and small hospitals as advisor, confidant, coach, and change agent. I focused on helping medical staff develop into stronger leaders. Sometimes this was accomplished through education and sometimes by modeling leadership behavior. My best role was that of change agent, as it was when I had full-time executive positions.

I was not involved in the leadership of The Greeley Company. This worked for me since I had learned that corporate politics and influence at that level was personally frustrating. It brought out a tendency for me to resist change rather than shape it. Also, as a consultant I did not have to work in a corporate office, giving me more freedom and control. I was much happier being an employee under these circumstances.

The same was true in my role as clinician. I worked at only one hospital. Working part-time helped me better tolerate my frustrations when dealing with both the healthcare system in general and the individual difficult patient.

Next Phase: Retirement

I retired from the clinical practice of emergency medicine in May 2012 at the age of 62 when my medical staff appointment expired. It wasn't the electronic medical record that stymied me nor was it the requirements of checklists and protocols. It was the nature of emergency medicine practice, the constant interruptions, which began to make it hard for me to maintain focus and concentration in the ED.

I still enjoyed taking care of patients, so I joined the Minnesota Disaster Medical Assistance Team (DMAT). These state teams are deployed to assist in times of disasters such as hurricanes and earthquakes. I still enjoyed my work as a consultant and I continued to train physicians in leadership, peer review, and credentialing.

As I adjusted to semi-retirement, I found a slower pace of life. I traveled to the Oneness Temple in India to deepen my spirituality. I made many trips to a healing center in Brazil for meditation. I began to deepen my relationship with the Divine and eventually was ordained in a healing ministry in 2018, finding a spiritual community that matched my own beliefs.

While working on my spiritual development, I volunteered at the hospital where I had worked prior to retiring from clinical practice. I also volunteered at animal rescue organizations, sometimes cleaning kennels and feeding animals and sometimes acting as a caregiver to sick or injured animals.

I traveled all over the world and have been to every continent. I have hiked in Africa, New Zealand, Nepal, Europe, Indonesia, and many other places, including the US and Canada. My consulting work, spiritual activities, travel, and volunteer work have kept me very busy. They have deepened my understanding of myself, the world, and what it means to be a leader. I'm a better listener, a more compassionate teacher, more focused in my choices, and more empathetic to those looking for help. At 70 years old, I felt as much joy and fulfillment as ever. Then came COVID.

With the lockdown in March 2020, everything changed. After finding my way from busy clinical and consulting practices in 2012, to consulting, volunteering, and personal development, COVID-19 brought a hard stop to all of it as animal rescues closed, hospitals told volunteers to stay away, and travel and consulting ended. Homebound, except for shopping for necessities, I searched for new opportunities. I meditated more, read more, hiked regularly with a friend close to home, connected with people on Zoom, Google Hangout and Face Time, and learned to work out virtually.

As often happens, when one door closes another opens. A new opportunity became available. DMAT teams were being deployed to help COVID-overloaded hospitals and healthcare systems. I volunteered in April 2020 to do COVID relief at an ED in Georgia. For two weeks, I worked as an extra physician while the full-time physicians provided critical care. In July, my own DMAT team was deployed to Arizona to provide similar assistance to an ICU and ED for two weeks. I also found opportunities to provide food and other assistance to organizations helping those who lost their jobs.

When the consulting work began again in early 2021, I finally opted for full retirement. I want to spend more time with my first grandchild, so while I will continue to work on the DMAT team, I won't return to regularly scheduled volunteer work.

Bottom line: As I consider this next phase of my life, I think a lot about enduring leadership and how I have kept it alive throughout my long career: clinician, senior management, consultant, non-profit board member, volunteer. It's been truly interesting. I hope my story offers some lessons for younger women physician whose time has come to move into leadership roles within the healthcare system.

"I hope my story offers some lessons for younger women physician whose time has come to move into leadership roles within the healthcare system."

– BARBARA LE TOURNEAU

Pharmaceutical Industry

*"Life is a great journey ... I still believe
the best is yet to come, for medicine,
for our patients, and for our world.
Our grandchildren are counting on it."*

– ELLEN STRAHLMAN

Chapter Twenty-Two

Doing Well by Doing Good

By Ellen Strahlman, MD, MHSc

"Life can only be understood backwards,
but it must be lived forwards."
— Soren Kierkekaard

I can't remember a time I didn't want to become a doctor. My childhood pediatrician was the soul of kindness, eyes twinkling through thick, slightly smudged glasses at the curly-haired girl who didn't stop talking. I asked so many questions that day he told my parents to send me to medical school to find the answers!

During my childhood, my mother suffered from manic-depressive illness. It is difficult to remember a breakfast with Mom and we never knew what awaited us coming home from school in the afternoon. As the eldest, I spent many weekends with Dad shopping, cooking, and doing household chores. I have many poignant and affectionate memories of our Sunday afternoons together; especially folding laundry for our family of 6, while he explained football play action, basketball tactics, and scoring on the baseball field. I became a devoted a sports fan, a pleasure I enjoy to this day. Watching my mother's suffering, I wanted to become smart enough, skillful enough, to help her. By becoming a doctor I could help her and others who were sick and this would be the work of my life.

Born in 1957, I grew up in the late 1960s and 1970s, a time of civil unrest in the United States. Tensions in my mixed-race schools on Long Island often kept us out of the classroom. Black friends who played with me in elementary school became distant, militant, and sometimes violent adolescents, and many never finished high school. I had some frightening close encounters with my classmates during those years and fortunately talked my way out of most of them. These experiences taught me lessons of tolerance. The terrible consequences of inequality cemented my values of fairness and social justice. No person should be deprived of essential human rights. Governments should take care of the basic needs of all their people, especially healthcare.

My desire to understand the world through medicine grew stronger during adolescence. Although Dad worked two jobs for most of his life, our family still struggled financially, especially considering my mother's illness. My dream of becoming a doctor would not have been materialized without scholarships that enabled me to attend Harvard as an undergraduate and Johns Hopkins for medical school.

None of this would have been possible without the intervention of a gifted teacher, Joe Holbrook, and the persistence of my high school guidance counselor, Dan Froelich. Joe grew up on an army base in Japan where his father was deployed after WWII. While there, he developed a profound respect for the country's educational system. He returned to the US in the early '70s with a passionate belief that ALL kids could benefit from concentrated and accelerated learning in mathematics and science. The experiment was simple: give me 20 8th graders with good grades in math and let me teach them twice a week after school.

The guidance counselors selected only boys at first. Although I'd "hit the ceiling" on the mandatory statewide IQ tests in math, I was bored in class and not making good grades. Knowing my family circumstances, Dan petitioned Joe to include me, and he agreed. That opportunity changed my life.

The experiment proved successful and Joe went on to apply his approach in all the school districts throughout his career. For me, the principles of mathematics unlocked the reasoning power of my mind. I sailed through four years of high school mathematics that year, then studied college-level mathematics. I attained a Top Ten ranking in the annual nationwide Mathematics Association of America examination three years in a row (the only girl to do so) and participated in the National Olympiad for Mathematics. I became similarly motivated to excel in my other subjects, and because of these efforts, was admitted to Harvard.

As an undergrad, I was fascinated by biochemistry and the emerging fields of molecular biology and genetics. My work in applied mathematics bolstered my problem-solving abilities. The application of mathematics to any problem taught me how to represent issues, frame problems, establish boundary conditions, and develop iterative lines of attack. All would prove valuable skills throughout my career.

I treasured my medical school years at Johns Hopkins. I loved the study and practice of medicine. The school has a long tradition of patient-centered care and research. As students, we interacted with patients from the very first year. We were also encouraged to apply our minds to research in the laboratory or in the clinic. I met (and later married) my "medical school sweetheart" and entered my formal training with optimism and excitement.

Patients, Public Health, and the Path to Industry

As an ophthalmology resident at the Wilmer Eye Institute, I did clinical research at the Dana Center for Preventive Ophthalmology and met the founder, Dr. Al Sommer. Al and his team discovered the link between vitamin A deficiency, blindness, and diarrheal death — a finding that saved the lives of millions of children. Applying epidemiology in this manner was a complete paradigm shift for me, having done lab work or patient case series in my previous research.

At the same time, another paradigm shift: the birth of my daughter Stephanie in 1985. Once she arrived, I knew, with sudden, certain, and joyful clarity, that my priorities were forever changed. Of course, she was the most beautiful baby ever. I realized I never wanted to choose between my child and the urgent needs of a patient.

By the time I was pregnant with my second child, I needed a different plan from the usual clinical fellowship. With Al's support, Johns Hopkins sponsored me for an Andrew Carnegie-Mellon Public Health Fellowship in 1987. Each year, two physicians are selected and provided tuition for a master's degree, a living stipend, a book allowance, and a modest research grant.

I was the first ophthalmologist and the first surgeon to receive this award. A bouncing baby boy (my son Mike) arrived in June, and I started my work in September, completing a master's degree in epidemiology and biostatistics at the Johns Hopkins School of Public Health (1989) and completing clinical research that was published in the *Archives of Internal Medicine* (1990).

After my fellowship, I accepted a position as Senior Medical Officer at the National Eye Institute (NEI) in Bethesda, Maryland. My responsibilities included the design and conduct of epidemiologic research and clinical trials for ophthalmic diseases, particularly age-related macular degeneration, and myopia.

It was an exciting time to be at NIH, where nearly everyone was caught up in the furor of the AIDS epidemic. I was invited to join Tony Fauci's Special Task Force for advancing new discovery and treatments for AIDS, which included colleagues from NIH, FDA, and academia. Our work became the foundation for the "expedited pathways" for drug development at the FDA. It was a salient experience for me to realize the powerful impact such a collaboration could have on the world.

It was not easy to balance the needs of family and career. My marriage suffered, even as work and the children were flourishing. These pressures led to a divorce, leaving me uncertain how to continue my career. As I was contemplating what to do, a call came in from a headhunter – my first experience with recruitment—about a role at a pharmaceutical company, Merck.

I'd never considered working in industry, but went for the interview anyway. I started thinking that discovering new drugs could save the lives of patients, millions at a time. Meeting the people at Merck "sealed the deal"; these were the brightest, most passionate and dedicated people I'd ever met. The role nearly doubled my government-based salary and allowed me to work at home in the evenings with no on-call schedule. It seemed an excellent solution for my mind, my heart, and the balance of my life.

Industry, Part 1: From Expert to Manager to the C-Suite

Joining industry was NOT a popular career path of choice for physicians in the 1990s. My family worried it meant turning away from patients and my academic colleagues thought I'd be trading scientific objectivity for business interests. They were wrong, not only about me, but about the thousands of people who work in industry. I felt sure that I need not, and would not, give up my ideals of helping patients and staying true to medical science.

Joining Merck in 1991, my initial responsibilities were for drugs in development for ophthalmology. After only nine months, I was asked to lead the languishing flagship program (dorzolamide for glaucoma), becoming the youngest program director in the history of the company. We were successful. The global dossier for dorzolamide was filed in 1992 and approved worldwide in 1993. With this accomplishment, I was promoted to director, and within a year had expanded responsibilities for launching the ophthalmology programs.

I became intellectually restless, wanting an opportunity to apply my epidemiology skills to other areas, and in 1993 was promoted to senior director in epidemiology. I was responsible for all outcomes research programs in ophthalmology, neurology, infectious disease and endocrinology.

By early 1995, our team developed pharmaco-economic models for a "break-even" price for Crixivan for HIV, a drug that eventually saved hundreds of thousands of lives. We also developed a financial model for free distribution of ivermectin for onchocerciasis ("River Blindness") in Africa. It was the best of all worlds in this role: ophthalmology drug development, outcomes research for HIV, and a philanthropic global health program — "doing well by doing good" to be sure!

Later that year, another headhunter called. Bausch & Lomb (B&L) was searching for an ophthalmologist with pharma experience for chief medical officer (CMO). The chance for a role with greater challenges was compelling. Our family's financial circumstances were also a factor since a C-suite role at a multibillion-dollar company paid well. I accepted the job in February 1995 and left Merck on good terms.

My responsibilities were typical of a CMO of a pharmaceutical and medical device company: all medical ethical and safety queries, final sign-off and review for all development programs and first-in-human protocols., occasional interactions with the media. In those days, B&L also had dermatology, hearing, sunglasses, and animal health businesses, my first experiences with medical devices and consumer products. I also led the integration of the research, development, regulatory, and process scale-up operations from three contact lens businesses and was rewarded by being promoted to corporate vice president of medical and scientific affairs. At 38 years old, I was the youngest corporate VP in the history of the company.

In this new role, I led the technical due diligence for two major acquisitions: Storz Ophthalmics and Chiron Vision. My first experience with large-scale M&A work was exciting, and after the deal closed, I was responsible for the integration of the scientific, medical, and regulatory affairs groups. By early 1998, I was promoted to senior vice president and global head of research and development (R&D) for the Pharmaceutical Division.

This new role included oversight of all research, development, regulatory, process scale-up, and medical marketing activities for B&L Pharma. The Tampa site, a state-of-the-art liquid generic manufacturing operation, produced more than 200 products for the US market in ophthalmics, otics, inhalants, nasal sprays, and IV medicines. Dr Mann Pharma in Berlin, Germany, was the leading provider of ophthalmics and nutraceuticals in Germany.

Our teams brought more than 30 generics and three new medicines. We also launched the first-ever drug-device combination therapeutic for the eye, Retisert, an intravitreal drug delivery system for the treatment of uveitis. And in Germany, 12 new nutraceutical programs were launched.

Despite these successes, the company decided to re-structure and downsize in 2000. During my six years at B&L, we'd re-structured eight times and I was weary of the disruption. We'd always wanted our children to study abroad, so we moved to England in 2001 so Stephanie and Mike could study there. I left B&L on good terms for a promising new role in London.

Industry Part 2: International Experience and Biotech

In January 2002, I was invited to join Virogen, Ltd., as its chief executive officer. After 10 years at big companies, leading a small, energetic group of people with brilliant ideas seemed a refreshing change. Virogen specialized in virology, notably Hepatitis C, Hepatitis B, RSV, and HIV. A spin-off from the UK Medical Research Council for Technology, the nascent company had seed money but now needed venture capital (VC) funding to advance its programs.

As CEO, I had responsibility for all business operations, including fund-raising and investor management, medical, scientific, commercial, manufacturing, and contractual obligations. Fund-raising was most important, by far, the quintessential lesson from my experience in biotech. After three months of intensive VC shopping (24 firms in 12 weeks) we received two initial term sheet offers for capital, but at a substantial premium. A financial analysis determined that selling the company would provide a greater return on investment and a more secure route for the employees' future, so the board voted to accept an acquisition offer from Arrow Therapeutics in London.

It was exhausting work. I'd spent more time raising money than thinking about new medicines, and I hadn't particularly enjoyed it. Bringing a new drug to market often takes more than 10 years, so the VC funding model was far from ideal. My sentiments were shared with Martin Murphy of MVM Capital, one of our funding partners. Over several beers one evening, we agreed that longer-term funding for early-stage life science companies would be a better alternative. This proved to be a prescient moment for both of us.

By the time the deal closed in May 2003, I had a job offer from Novartis. After working in biotech, I was ready to return to a big company. Combining my R&D and commercial skills, I became senior VP, head of global development for the Ophthalmology Business Unit based in Basel, Switzerland. This role was perfect for staying in Europe, since the kids had two years to complete their high school education in the UK.

Novartis Ophthalmology had groups in Switzerland, Japan, and New Jersey, as well as joint ventures with several other companies. The cultural differences between countries and companies gave me a tremendous appreciation for the perspectives and needs of other businesses. The teams successfully developed and commercialized many useful products during these years, particularly therapies for "wet" (neovascular) age-related macular degeneration, the most important cause of blindness among the elderly populations of the developed world.

By 2005, Stephanie and Mike completed high school studies and were ready to start college. Mike was admitted to Oxford and planned to stay in the UK. Steph was accepted to NYU and had unfortunately developed some health challenges. Fortuitously, I was offered a position at Pfizer in New York City as the worldwide therapeutic area head for ophthalmology in 2005 and returned to the US to take up that role and be close to Steph.

This decision would turn out to be a turning point in my life – although I wouldn't realize the full impact of it until nearly 10 years later.

I joined Pfizer in March 2005 as worldwide therapeutic area head for ophthalmology, with responsibilities for R&D, medical, and business development programs. In two years, we completed three external licensing deals, three drug delivery platform technology deals, and advanced 12 programs in the pipeline. Pfizer ophthalmology now had more than 500 colleagues worldwide (excluding manufacturing) and became an established, productive, and profitable business.

I'd greatly enjoyed and was recognized for our licensing work, so I was invited to become vice president for worldwide business development in 2007, with responsibilities for both in-licensing and out-licensing. The latter was new for Pfizer, so I set up the department which eventually externalized de-prioritized portfolio assets. My search teams completed a dozen deals in a variety of therapeutic areas from oncology to inflammatory diseases during this period.

Turning 50: A Time for Reflection

Toward the end of 2007, I turned 50. This became a salient moment for me as there seemed to be a "convergence of change" in my life.

Both kids were doing well in college, Mike thriving at Oxford and Steph now healthy and well. They'd been my priority for many years, but as young adults, their needs changed, all for the good. This was also a big change for me. Now there was more time for friends and fun. I started playing piano again. The kids and I learned how to scuba dive (not an obvious choice for a confirmed claustrophobic!) and had some fabulous adventures together in the Caribbean.

I'd also become keenly aware of the reputational and environmental challenges our industry was facing and wanted to be part of solving these problems on a larger scale. I was once again restless for change, craving an opportunity to bring a more expansive, holistic, patient-centered approach to my work, and hoping my diverse portfolio of experiences would allow me to serve in a role that would be meaningful and impactful.

GSK: Return to the C-Suite and Inspiring Change through Authenticity

In the spring of 2008, GlaxoSmithKline (GSK) offered me the role of CMO. At the time, GSK was the largest and most diverse pharmaceutical company in the world. However, the company was facing significant challenges in the areas of medical governance and product defense. Andrew Witty, the newly appointed CEO, wanted a physician with industry experience to oversee three broad areas: medical risk management, organizational change, and an interest in matters of global health. There was a great "meeting of the minds" during the interview process and I joined the company in the summer of 2008.

I was the first woman to be appointed CMO for a large pharmaceutical company – a significant milestone in the healthcare industry. Thanks to Andrew's support, I felt very comfortable among the notable, accomplished, and talented men and women in GSK's senior ranks.

As CMO, I had oversight for all global medical, regulatory, safety, compliance, quality, medical advocacy, and access policy functions for the company. The work included the pharmaceutical, vaccines, and consumer health businesses for the company. I was accountable to the chairman of the board for all matters of patient safety, general medical governance, ethics and integrity, medical information, and investigation involving human subjects relating to any GSK products in development or on the market.

I was also accountable to the chairman of R&D for all pipeline governance safety matters. In this role, I chaired the Global Safety

Board and served as a C-suite member of all major company committees, including the board of directors' Audit & Risk Committee.

A particular pleasure was joining the board of directors of ViiV
Healthcare, plc, in 2009. ViiV is a joint-venture company between
GSK and Pfizer, designed and dedicated as a business to serve the
present and future needs of HIV patients all over the world.

My teams were responsible for strengthening, codifying, and
embedding the Medical Governance Framework across GSK. With
senior leaders from all over the company, we gained the alignment
and cooperation of all business units to this effort, leading and
delivering the successful close-out of many regulatory inspections
(including FDA, MHRA, and others). In 2010, Global Quality and
Compliance organizations was added to my responsibilities, and
our teams extended the work of codifying governance activities to
these areas.

Along with these responsibilities, my attendance on the Board
Audit & Risk Committee made me appreciate the vast array of risk
management issues facing a company the size of GSK.

Although I had always valued teamwork, communication, and
collaboration, my skills in these areas grew exponentially in this role.
To inspire change in thousands of people required communicating
with colleagues at scale, for we had colleagues all over the world
engaged in this work. This took hours communicating in small and
large settings, in-person and using advanced video technology, and
in-house social media. We even had a blog (!) to the amazement of
my children and their friends!

It seemed to work. The changes were made, continuous improvement measures instilled, and the company moved forward with the
energy and dedication needed to advance the pipeline in other areas.

GSK: Including the Whole World in Our Work

With the medical governance and product defense challenges behind
us, a decision was made to re-structure the role of CMO in 2011. At
the same time, discussions were underway to significantly expand the
scope of GSK's contributions to global health. Given my background
and passion for this area, Andrew offered me the role of senior vice

president for neglected tropical diseases and global health. Reporting directly to him, I could use the leverage and resources of a multibillion-dollar company to expand GSK's programs and start new ones. I remained on the ViiV Board and became the executive sponsor of the vaccines public health forum. This role was the deepest expression yet of my personal journey to positively impact the lives of patients, millions at a time.

GSK already had a long-standing well-regarded donation program for albendazole, for treatment of lymphatic filariasis (LF). The program began in 1999 and a decade later, GSK dedicated a new albendazole production facility in India. My job was to accelerate this contribution. At the time of this writing, GSK has donated more than 10 billion tablets in 92 countries, improving the lives of hundreds of millions of people, especially children. In 2021, 17 countries announced elimination of LF, and the number of people at risk for infection has almost halved. GSK remains committed to continuing to donate albendazole tablets until LF is eliminated as a public health issue.

I travelled the world representing GSK on numerous committees and commissions, such as the United Nations' Commission on Life-Saving Commodities for Women & Children and the WHO Partnership for Disease Control Initiatives, and became a Fellow of the Salzburg Global Seminar. Our contributions included product donations, sending teams of people into underserved areas during health crises, providing infrastructure support for vaccine deployment, and leveraging expertise within the company in the service of global health challenges.

A highlight of the year was a visit to the Carter Center in Atlanta where I had the honor of meeting President Carter to discuss our programs. Meeting a man whose passion for service makes him one of my heroes was truly an inspirational moment.

Representing Industry at the FDA

In 2008, I began my service at the FDA as the industry representative to the Dermatologic and Ophthalmic Drugs Advisory Committee (DODAC).

FDA's Advisory Committees provide independent advice from outside experts on issues related to human and veterinary drugs, biological products, medical devices, and food. The Center for Drug Evaluation and Research (CDER) has such committees for every therapeutic area in drug development. In addition to the relevant experts on scientific, technical, and policy matters, an industry representative is included as a non-voting member. Members serve a five-year term and FDA seeks highly experienced individuals who have gained the agency's trust during their career.

When purpose-driven colleagues in industry and FDA work well together, breakthroughs occur that greatly accelerate getting new medicines to patients – as we've seen during the COVID pandemic and as I first experienced on Dr. Fauci's Task Force for HIV. That experience was my template for leading constructive industry interactions FDA over the years, so it was a great honor for me to be chosen as the industry representative for DODAC.

DODAC reviews and evaluates data concerning the safety and effectiveness of marketed and new medicines for ophthalmic and dermatologic disorders and makes recommendations to the FDA Commissioner. We reviewed several dozen new products during my tenure, and I was often asked about items in the company dossiers. I sought to use my knowledge to provide objective, critical, and constructive advice. It was fascinating and rewarding work and I gained valuable insight into the workings of the FDA.

Board Service: Viiv Healthcare and Syncona Limited Partners

During the GSK years I joined my first board of directors. The legal responsibilities of boards and board members vary with the nature of the organization and between jurisdictions. For companies with publicly trading stock, directors are appointed based on their C-suite experience, their specific expertise, and their ability to contribute to the company's mission and direction. While the CEO, senior executives, and management run an organization, the ultimate responsibility for the company's performance, governance, and direction rests with its board of directors.

Simply speaking: "The buck stops here."

At GSK, I was a director for ViiV Healthcare. My role was to supervise the company's drug development and donation programs. It was a very rewarding five years. This was the first time I could utilize my experience and knowledge without the back-breaking work of day-to-day management. It's incredibly freeing and mind-expanding to contribute in this way, and I truly enjoyed the challenges.

In late 2012, I received a call from Nigel Keen, chairman of Oxford University Innovation, with an offer to join the board of Syncona, a newly created company. To my surprise and delight, its CEO was Martin Murphy. They'd acquired a seed investment of £100 million from the Wellcome Trust and set up Syncona to take a long-term view to building globally competitive life science businesses. It seemed that Martin had created a company with the right investment model for biopharma companies after all.

Between 2012 and 2016, Syncona created eight new companies focused on novel treatments in areas of high-level unmet need. In 2016, Syncona merged with the Battle Against Cancer Investment Trust (BACIT), becoming a FTSE 250 healthcare company and expanding its permanent capital base. As of 2021, Syncona has added 17 companies to its portfolio, investing over £780 million in areas such as cell and gene therapy. Four companies have been listed on the NASDAQ and two companies acquired by larger entities sold at an aggregate multiple of 6.2X. I had the privilege of serving on the board from 2012 to 2020 and look forward to the company's continued success.

In the Meanwhile . . .

During these years, Stephanie and Mike graduated college, began their post-graduate work and careers, and met and married their respective spouses. My son married a young woman from Finland, and I was asked to travel there to help with wedding plans. However, my future daughter-in-law's parents weren't comfortable speaking English, and I certainly didn't know any Finnish! Luckily, I'd mentored the daughter of a former colleague from Pfizer, Dr. Reijo Salonen, also from Finland. Reijo is a neurologist and viral immunologist (MD-PhD) from the University of Turku in Finland. He'd had a similar career to mine: from academia to industry, working in executive roles in the US for more than 10 years at both GSK and Pfizer. In 2006, he was recruited to the C-suite of Orion Pharma, a European pharmaceutical company as senior vice president of R&D and CMO. And he was the only person I knew in Finland.

Reijo and I had worked together well at Pfizer and could readily relate to each other's work and life experiences. We met often in Finland that year, first to help the plan the wedding, but soon thereafter for our own fun. By the time the kids married in August 2014, Reijo and I knew we'd be together for the rest of our lives. I never expected the joy of romance and the depth of compatibility in a relationship at this time in my life – neither of us did. But it was something to treasure, and we were willing to make it work.

Becton Dickinson: Saving the Best for Last

My experiences in the global health role at GSK made me realize that improving the lives of people takes more than any single medicine or treatment. Access to treatments by strengthening systems of care and enabling innovation at scale is necessary to meet these needs. I wanted to address these challenges in a new way, hopefully combining drugs, medical devices, and logistical support to deliver the goods.

I also knew that whatever I did next would be my last job in corporate life – and I wanted it to be my best job, ever. And that's exactly what I got when I met Vince Forlenza in 2012, the newly appointed CEO for Becton Dickinson & Company (BD).

BD is one of the most famous medical device companies you've probably never heard of. But if you've drawn blood with a Vacutainer, administered a dose of insulin, deployed a vaccination, counted T-cells for HIV or cancer patients, then a BD medical device has touched your life (or laboratory). BD was in the business of "innovation at scale," deploying high-quality medical devices, billions at a time or, alternatively, developing sophisticated cell counters and sorters that could identify more than 100 surface markers to enable research into breakthrough therapies. In 2012, BD was known as a purpose-driven company with a mission to "help all people live healthy lives."

Vince believed the company could do more and was determined to make it happen, knowing the benefit for patients and for shareholders. "Doing well by doing good" had always been a theme of his career. Vince also had the rare combination of a vision for transformation and a long tenure with the company; he knew what needed to be done and how to make it happen. He and close colleague Bill Kozy (BD's chief operating officer) designed an innovation system for BD meant to capture the magic combination of innovation at scale and enabling access to care. Now he wanted someone to lead it, uniting R&D and medical groups that had traditionally operated independently and working with the chief marketing officer to unite similarly disparate commercial teams.

We "clicked" over a three-hour dinner. I was representing GSK at a UN Commission Meeting the next day, a meeting Vince was also attending on behalf of BD. We kept the conversation going, and after meeting Bill and the rest of the senior executive team, I joined Becton Dickinson in April 2013 as senior vice president for research and development and CMO. Another first: I was the first woman to lead R&D and serve as CMO for one of the largest medical device companies in the world.

It was an exciting and wonderful time to be at BD; my responsibilities included overseeing the innovation system, delivering the new product pipeline, improving R&D productivity, working with Vince and others on engaging external stakeholders and partnerships, and all the responsibilities of a CMO. BD operated its business units separately, so we established the Office of Science, Medicine & Technology (OSMT) to unite these efforts across the company. By 2015, the OSMT included nearly 5000 associates worldwide, there were more products in the pipeline than ever before, with the promise of more on-time launches than at any time previously in the company.

These results did not go unnoticed, and in 2015, BD was honored by the Product Development and Management Association with its prestigious Outstanding Corporate Innovator Award. This was a profound and significant external recognition of the success of our innovation system and organizational transformation – and it is the professional accomplishment I am most proud of. Working with my colleagues and teams at BD was the finest and most rewarding experience I had in my career.

2015 also brought a great sadness: the passing of my father after a long battle with cancer. I was very close to Dad, especially given our tumultuous and difficult childhood. He'd been the source of strength and light that kept the family together, was always there to support us. My colleagues at BD, many of whom were aware of my love for my father, sent hundreds of emails and/or called with expressions of sympathy. My mother's home was full of flowers and gifts and thousands of dollars were donated to the American Cancer Society in Dad's memory. Vince prided himself on the constructive and caring culture at BD, and I'd experienced this environment from my very first day. It was a tremendous source of comfort to me during this sad time.

When I joined the company in 2013, there were 30,000 associates in 50 countries, with revenues of about $8 billion. The company undertook two significant mergers during my tenure, acquiring CareFusion in 2015 and CR Bard in 2017.

I was promoted to executive vice president with expanded responsibilities for integrating the new companies into our existing systems. Product development and delivery needed to be maintained with high quality and on schedule. It was a busy and productive time, with the launches of dozens of new products that have and continue to improve the lives of patients all over the world. At the same time, we developed partnerships with organizations across the spectrum that enable innovation at scale and provide access to care.

After completion of the Bard acquisition in 2017, it was time to consider retirement. As if on cue, my granddaughter Sini arrived in March, and Reijo had long planned to leave his role at Orion that year. Happily, he'd moved to the US permanently in September, so we were together in one place, at last!

Becton Dickinson was now larger than ever, with more than 65,000 associates serving 190 countries with revenues of $16 billion, and with the need restructure for efficiency, it seemed the perfect time to "pass the baton" to the next generation of leaders. Vince accepted my decision gracefully (if not enthusiastically), and I left BD with heartfelt thanks and appreciation in January 2018.

Retirement, Part 1: Making up for Lost Time!

I'm sure many of my work colleagues thought I'd never retire – I truly enjoyed and treasured my career, and worked hard at it! However, I always had a sense that I'd know when it was time to leave formal working life behind, and then leave it gladly. Which I did.

Our goals for retirement are quite simple: Enjoy time with those we love, only eat and drink what we like, do our best to age gracefully, and try to avoid needless suffering. For me, spending time in nature every day is a priority. As for Reijo, he never wants to wear socks.

In early 2018, we made plans to travel for pleasure, especially to more remote places. Our first trip was to Antarctica, surely the most unique, exotic, and starkly beautiful place on earth. In 2018 and 2019, we continued our globe-trotting adventures, travelling to Asia, Australia, and New Zealand, the Galapagos and Machu Pichu, and two cruises in the Mediterranean. It was exciting and rewarding to travel the world without the pressure of work or deadlines. We also invested time setting up our homes in Marco Island, Florida, and Naantali, Finland. Both overlook the water with ready access to nature – an essential requirement for me.

We were looking forward to a life as "international snow-birds": overlooking the Gulf of Mexico in Florida in the winter and the Baltic Sea in Finland in the summer. This plan assured the relentless pursuit of Reijo's socklessness as well as my daily desire to be out-doors. The effort in getting ready for stay-at-home life turned out to be more prescient than we could know.

In early 2020, we embarked on a glorious two-week Safari in Kenya and Tanzania, then flew to Cape Town to board a cruise ship with plans for numerous stops in Africa and Asia before arriving in Singapore six weeks later.

We never made it.

As the scourge of COVID-19 swept the globe, port after port closed and we were quarantined for 17 days on the ship until it docked in Western Australia. Once in Perth, we again quarantined in a hotel room on a dedicated COVID floor, where silent gowned and gloved staff left food on a tray outside our door, scurrying away before we opened it. Flights home were not easy to find. We eventually flew from Perth through Doha to Miami on sparsely populated planes, returning to home to Florida in mid-March.

Circle of Life: The COVID-19 Pandemic

The global pandemic struck the world with a ferocity not seen in 100 years, often likened to The Great Influenza of 1917-1918. In our lifetime, as terrifying HIV/AIDS epidemic was, it paled in comparison to COVID-19. As global society came to a screeching halt, we settled into pandemic life.

I was, and still am, grateful every day for living on Marco Island, where we felt safe and could enjoy a good quality of life. Introverts by nature, we didn't miss socializing that much. We transformed our evenings into "dinner and a movie date nights" interspersed with sports events. Like many people during the confinement period, we upgraded our eating and drinking skills – I am a better chef and Reijo is more knowledgeable than ever about wine. Luckily, our proximity to outside venues have kept us in good shape. However, we were deeply vexed by the inability to see our far-flung family in person.

Between us, we have five children, ages 31–41, living in Helsinki, London, Boston, New York, and Florida. Both of us have aging parents in Helsinki and Florida. Our four grandchildren obviously live with their parents, with Sini, Levi, and Ari in London and Lily in Boston.

For the adults, excepting those in Florida, we could cope with FaceTime. But we've sorely missed time with the little ones, where a physical presence is so important at their young ages (2 months to 4 ½ years). For a while, I was convinced that Lily and Levi thought we lived in the computer screen!

We did our best during the pre-vaccination phase, with FaceTime calls once or twice a week with everyone. Our entertainment skills improved enormously, and we expanded our repertoire to singing (in English and Finnish, of course!), puppeteering, and play-acting. We bought Tyrannosaurus Rex pajama-suits for the dinosaur phase, I've refreshed my abilities on a variety of musical instruments, and Reijo has been spotted wearing a Princess Anna tiara from "Frozen." When we were finally able to see them in person, Sini, Lily, and Levi remembered us well, and we are grateful to our children who made sure we kept up regular communications.

On a psychological level, I was greatly troubled by the loss of my long-held assumption that I could always go anywhere I needed to be, at any time. I'd emotionally coped with the distance of loved ones by telling myself I could get to them within 24 hours. Not being able to do so rocked me to the core. It was not easy to cope with these restrictions.

As for both the government response and the reaction of people during this pandemic, it's felt, sadly, like (in the words of the great Yogi Berra) "Déjà vu, all over again." The destructive stances and ant-establishment rhetoric reminded me of the HIV/AIDS epidemic: I remember watching as gay men in San Francisco protested closing the bathhouses, horrified that it had come to this.

Seeing again the most vulnerable populations taking anti-pandemic positions has been disheartening. The drama of the 2020 election and events leading to the insurrection at the Capitol in January 2021 compounded my distress. Many nights last winter I woke with flashback nightmares of violent experiences in my youth during the Civil Rights movement and tragic disease and death among my HIV patients. Fortunately, the sun arose each morning, and a long walk on the beach of Marco Island enabled me to shake off nights' terrors.

After Joe Biden was installed in office and vaccinations deployed, my personal unrest subsided. But the experiences gave me pause for deep reflection and a fundamental shift in considering retired life. I was struck by Barack Obama's reminders that democracy is not a given, and participation by all is needed to keep it stable, effective, and safe. We will not agree on everything, but we must agree to abide by the rule of law and work constructively for society's needs to survive and thrive.

In the previous 10 years, without realizing it, I found myself surrounded by like-minded people. It's not hard to do, with a busy work and family life. I told myself that if we came out of this period physically and emotionally intact, I would personally commit to participate in society more than before, with a specific intention to engage with people who are NOT like me, and in venues outside my comfort zone.

Retirement, Part 2: Treasuring Life with Intention

I didn't expect to experience a strong sense of purpose during retirement, but now that it's happened, there's no going back. I've taken on several roles that hopefully allow me to live up to this idea. No solo acts or on-stage performances (unless for teaching purposes). No outside recognition needed. And not too time-consuming. Now that we are vaccinated and can travel again, being with family, especially grandchildren, and treasuring life and our good health are still our biggest priorities. But now there are a few other things.

Closest to home is serving on the board of directors for our condominium's homeowner's association. In the summer of 2020, I was asked by the board for advice about pandemic safety procedures for the building. Since the great state of Florida is not always aligned with mainstream public health guidance, my resolve was tested in convincing fellow residents to accept precautions needed before widespread vaccinations became available. Despite our differences, I was pleased to be invited to "run for office" and joined the board in 2021.

The most fascinating, challenging, and potentially impactful role is my service on the board of directors of Altria, starting in November 2020. While it seems contradictory for a physician to join the board of a Big Tobacco company, under the leadership of Altria's new CEO, Billy Gifford, the company has a stated vision to responsibly lead the transition of adult smokers to a smoke-free future by 2030. Can you imagine the potential impact to human health if the company is successful?

It is a mission Altria is deeply committed to, with heavy investment. The potential for real progress has manifested in the convergence of FDA oversight and active review of reduced-harm products, the increase in public policy support for such products, and the decline in youth smoking and vaping.

The challenges are equally substantial, however. Despite decades of efforts to improve and rebuild trust, there is still a long way to go. While nicotine is not benign, it is not the primary cause of disease and death from smoking, it's the combustion of tobacco. However, recent surveys indicate that more than 70% of people and more than 80% of physicians "strongly agree" that nicotine directly contributes to cancer, COPD, and cardiovascular disease associated with smoking.

Nowadays, the concept of moving smokers to less harmful products is supported by many public health advocates, regulators, and the scientific community. Altria is therefore focused on responsibly transitioning adult tobacco smokers who can't or won't quit from cigarettes to less-risky alternatives. Billy speaks openly of the time when cigarettes are no longer sold or marketed by Altria in the US, and "moving beyond smoking" is a company mantra. Altria is not the only Big Tobacco company embarked on the organizational transformation to reduced harm; the entire industry is heading in this direction.

Nevertheless, I approached the offer with trepidation. When I met Billy, the board, and members of the senior executive team of Altria, hard questions were asked and answered on both sides. But the intent and passion for this dramatic transformation are strong, relentless, and realistic. It will take years of investment and resolve to make it happen, and the company is up for the challenge. I believe my career experience and equal passion for transformational change will be valuable in these efforts, and I will do my best to contribute in a highly impactful way to support it.

Finally, in the spirit of nurturing international relationships both at home and for society, Reijo and I were appointed as visiting professors for a flagship program of the University of Turku (Reijo's alma mater). The InFLAMES (Innovation Ecosystem based on the

Immune System) is the brainchild of Professor and Academician Sirpa Jalkanen, MD, PhD, who developed, designed, and acquired funding for the program in 2020. Sirpa is a force to be reckoned with, internationally renowned for her work in immunology and drug development, a winner of several international prizes, and the co-founder of two listed biotech companies. She's one of the nicest people on the face of the earth – and impossible to refuse.

InFLAMES is designed to transform the immunology research efforts within the University of Turku into collaborations with industry to enhance entrepreneurship and the translation of new inventions into commercial products. We began our visiting professor duties in September 2021, which include giving lectures (which we do jointly – great fun!), mentoring colleagues for career advice, and advising groups seeking to develop and commercialize new medicines. So far, so good, and we're enjoying working together.

Putting the finishing touches on this piece, I am watching the roiling waves on the Gulf of Mexico, a distant effect of the weather from the North. I am reminded that any good effort, no matter how far away, has the potential to make a difference. I am again filled with gratitude for my life and the privilege I have in living here, and hope there are still many good years ahead for us.

Life is a great journey and I think of myself as a "realistic optimist." Despite the incredible challenges before us, when I consider all that science, technology, communications, and globalization could offer every single person on the planet — with my head in the clouds and feet firmly on the ground— I still believe the best is yet to come, for medicine, for our patients, and for our world. Our grandchildren are counting on it.

CHAPTER TWENTY-THREE

Led by Passion

By Elizabeth Garner, MD, MPH

I AM A WOMEN'S HEALTH PHYSICIAN DRIVEN BY a passion for improving the lives of women so they may discover a path to a better life for themselves and their families.

As a pharmaceutical executive, I spend every day working on new treatments aimed at addressing serious conditions that affect women and their families. Many would say I have made great contributions to women's health, but I am far from satisfied with what I have achieved so far. The field of women's health has long been neglected, and I want to play a key role in changing this landscape and bringing the issues women deal with every day to the forefront of investment, science, and development.

For me, understanding the *"back story"* is always extremely informative when learning how people become who they are from both a personal and career perspective. So here's mine. . . .

I Was a War Refugee

My identity as a physician who works toward leading change comes directly from the foundation of my formative years. My mother is a white American, born in Huntington, Long Island. As a fresh graduate of Mount Holyoke College, she started immediately on her way to life as a change maker by joining the Peace Corps. She was dispatched to teach German in Nigeria, a fledgling country that had just won independence from Great Britain two years earlier. My father was born in rural eastern Nigeria to proud Igbo parents and worked his way up to a degree in electrical engineering and economics from Leeds University in England.

My parents met shortly after my mother's arrival in Lagos, the capital city of Nigeria. After a whirlwind romance, they married in 1964, at a time when interracial marriage was still illegal in the United States. In the months after they married, a time of civil unrest began between the north/south of the country and the east, commonly known as Igboland, where my father was from. As the unrest grew to violence, my parents ultimately left Lagos and moved to the town of Enugu in the eastern part of Nigeria, where I was born.

Eleven days after my birth, the civil war, known in history books as the Biafran war, broke out. We were eventually forced to flee from bombings in Enugu, leaving everything behind. We lived in my father's village of Nanka during the first year of the war. With my dad being away most of the time supporting the Biafran war effort and struggling to keep us fed and safe, my mother managed with two young children, no electricity, and no running water, surrounded by my dad's family whom she barely knew. With no English speakers around her she used her natural language skills to learn Igbo.

Ultimately, as it became clear that Biafra was heading toward losing the war, my mother, my older brother, and I were flown out of the country as refugees in the dark of night, leaving my father behind to oversee Biafra's electricity grid and the Biafran airports.

We landed in Lisbon, Portugal's capital city, and made our way to Madeira, where my maternal grandparents were living. After a year in Madeira, we moved to Cincinnati, Ohio, where my Aunt Beth (for whom I was named) lived. As a "single" white woman with two mixed-race kids, my mother had difficulty finding a landlord who would rent her an apartment. We lived in Cincinnati until the end of the war in 1970, after which we returned to Nigeria to be reunited with my dad.

A Magical Childhood

My childhood in Nigeria is full of wonderful memories and richness. My mother had developed an unbreakable bond with the country and transmitted that to her children, but I truly owe it to my father for having ensured that we understood and appreciated our Nigerian culture. We visited Nanka at least once a year and developed strong ties to our village family and to our Igbo heritage.

Until Nanka became electrified in the 1990s, we lived each Christmas visit using kerosene lamps, or "tilly lamps." We finally installed a generator in the 1980s and what a thrill that was! Until the mid-1980s, we used an outhouse, but now have an enormous water tank behind the house that gets filled before we arrive in the village. Sadly, there is still no potable water supply in the village.

I was educated largely by missionaries. My elementary school in Lagos was run by the Anglican church. The principal was the wife of the minister who married my parents, and they were central to our lives. After one year attending a government boarding school — a sometimes-terrifying experience I will never forget — I transferred to a multidenominational missionary high school in the northern, mostly Muslim part of the country.

The mix of students from all around the world was simply unmatched. We loved each other dearly and we learned to accept each other regardless of our differences. I am extremely fortunate that high school was one of the best times of my life.

While my dad taught me the importance of culture, my mother taught me idealism, curiosity about the world, and adaptability. Where she saw that something important was missing, she filled the gap by starting things. As a notable example of her initiative, she co-founded Nigerwives, an organization to support foreign women married to Nigerian men.

My mother recognized in me a young girl who loved responsibility, achievement, and service, and enrolled me in the Brownies, an organization that was a perfect fit and foundation for me until I left for boarding school in northern Nigeria at the age of 11. I still have my first brownie uniform and treasure it as a memento of my childhood.

The Benefits of Code Switching

Growing up, I was privileged to travel far and wide with my family. We regularly traveled to London where my father frequently worked, and visited Las Palmas, Spain, almost every summer on the way to visiting my grandparents in Madeira. I grew up living with extraordinary cultural, ethnic, and geographic contrasts.

It was fascinating to realize as a young girl that I was different from most of my friends. I had relatives all around the world, black Africans, black Americans, white Americans including fair skinned redheads, white German relatives, and mixed-race aunts, uncles, and cousins. Our two sets of grandparents lived in vastly different worlds, from a rural village in eastern Nigeria to the island of Madeira, Portugal.

My mother also ensured I was exposed to other cultures beyond those in my family. In fact, my Egyptian woman pediatrician was the first person to spark my interest in medicine as a career; clearly from the get-go, the concept of women in medicine was obvious to me.

With these varied experiences, my brothers and I learned as children to navigate seamlessly from one world to another, changing even our accents and mannerisms depending on the location and situation. For us as adults, this ability to code-switch has been invaluable, and we frequently talk about how comfortable we are with people of any culture, color, or walk of life.

Recognizing Gender and Social Inequities/Unnecessary Loss

As I matured into my late teenage and early adult years, I observed parts of my Nigerian culture that were disturbing. I realized that women and men were not treated equally, and as I witnessed in my father's village, the burden of raising children, cooking, cleaning, fetching water, selling goods at the market, and tending livestock fell to women and their daughters.

At the same time, I have fond memories of and enormous respect for my female relatives in the village, in particular the older women, who were well ahead of their time. These women were not afraid to speak up to their husbands, even at the risk of backlash often in the form of physical beating.

The strength of individual women in my village community was astounding, but nothing compares to the power of the village sisterhood. In an Igbo village, in an extended family or clan, each

271

person is responsible for everyone else. Women have each other's backs like no-one else, with a bond far stronger than the bonds to their husbands.

Women who are daughters of the same family are known as the Umu-Ada of the family, and when they get together, men, be afraid. One woman alone is powerless, but when surrounded by her trusted sisters, even the quietest of women will demand justice from an abusive husband or an overbearing brother.

In parallel with witnessing the amazing strength of women, I have also witnessed terrible suffering and loss among female family members in Nigeria. My cousin Georgina died at early age due to undiagnosed cancer. I attribute her late diagnosis to poverty and stigma around abnormal bleeding. My cousin Atu's wife died following the delivery of her first child, who also died shortly after birth; as best as I can put the story together, she had an intrauterine infection and could not access basic antibiotics that could have saved her life and that of her baby.

My aunt Grace and my cousin Rosa both died following years of untreated mental illness, and my cousin Rhoda who likely had severe autism, never diagnosed, has disappeared and I have been unable to find out from her family where she is. The list goes on, but these are the most painful as I reflect on the massive and serious unmet needs of women in the developing world.

Discovering My Passion for Women and Women's Health

Following high school, I chose to attend my mother's alma mater, as I was excited at the prospect of attending a women's college that had as its mission to teach young women never to fear change. During my years at Mount Holyoke, I learned the extraordinary power of women united for a cause and the need for women to challenge the status quo.

I was fascinated by the extraordinary legacy of alumnae such as Frances Perkins, the first woman cabinet member, U.S. Secretary of Labor, and creator of Social Security; Virginia Apgar, who invented the Apgar Score that I used every day during my residency training; and many others.

I remember vividly my first experience with activism as I watched students protest apartheid by pushing against the college's investment in South African stocks. These protests ultimately led to the board of trustees' decision to divest in 1985. Seeing the direct impact of the protests was a powerful lesson as I learned the importance and the impact of speaking out with one voice against wrongdoing in the world.

Following college, I went straight to medical school, planning to be a primary care doctor. One of my earliest clinical memories is that of an elderly man who presented to the emergency room with an acute exacerbation of congestive heart failure. This is a dramatic event to witness and extremely frightening for patients, who without immediate treatment can literally drown in fluid that gets pushed into the air spaces in the lungs due to a weakened heart and back up of blood in the veins that transport blood through the lungs. Within minutes of receiving intravenous diuretic medicine, the situation was reversed, and his life was saved.

I also took care of a 60-some year-old woman who came to the hospital agitated and delirious. Two days later following surgery to drain a massive deep neck abscess I was shocked to walk into her room to find her calmly reading a newspaper.

There were so many lessons learned in just these two cases, never mind the hundreds of others along the way. The biggest takeaway for me was that access or not to medical care is the difference between life and death. Had either of these patients' treatment been delayed or substandard, they would not have survived.

I added a year to my medical studies and pursued a Master of Public Health as I wanted to better understand the social and cultural aspects of health and the basics of epidemiology and global health.

Following graduation, I started my residency at Massachusetts General Hospital in Boston and realized within months of starting my primary care training that 1) I did not enjoy taking care of generally healthy people in the outpatient setting, 2) I enjoyed managing very sick patients with acute medical issues, and 3) I was skilled at learning and doing procedures.

I knew a change in residency programs was going to be necessary and considered several potential options that would better align with my interests. I decided that obstetrics and gynecology with a subspecialty in gynecologic oncology would not only align with my desire to treat complicated patients and my natural dexterity, but would also fit with my longstanding interest in women's public and global health that had developed over the years as I witnessed the experiences of my relatives at home in Nigeria.

The Leap to Industry

I loved clinical practice. As a gynecologic oncologist, I was also a trusted expert and worked hard to be available for my fellow ob/gyn colleagues when they had a patient who needed an urgent consult for potential malignancy or a complicated surgical procedure. I was often called away from my laboratory to the operating room to help with a difficult surgery, and I began to feel limited by the fact that clinical work only allowed me to impact one patient — and perhaps her family — at a time.

I also recognized that the research I was doing on identifying biomarkers for early detection and treatment of ovarian cancer would not have any real impact and was highly unlikely to change treatment paradigms without greater focus and investment of time and energy.

I began to consider other avenues to addressing unmet needs in women's health. As I was mulling all of this over, I received an invitation from a recruiter to apply for a position on the Gardasil HPV vaccine team at Merck. I jumped at the opportunity.

Using the word "jumped" here makes it sound like leaving clinical practice was an easy decision — it was not. In fact it was THE most difficult professional decision I have ever made. But I knew deep down that working on the development of new prevention measures and treatments would be the most efficient way for me to lead change and help improve the lives of women around the globe.

From Merck, I moved on to Abbott Laboratories, now AbbVie, to work on elagolix, a drug for endometriosis, a common condition afflicting millions of women in the US who suffer from terrible, often debilitating pelvic pain and painful periods, and related infertility.

I played a key role in designing the Phase 3 trials for elagolix, which I am proud to say was ultimately approved by the FDA. This was the first oral treatment specifically for endometriosis ever developed, and the first new treatment in decades. I then spent two years at Myriad Genetics, the first company to create the BRCA test for hereditary breast and ovarian cancer.

The Need for More Women Decision-Makers

In 2014, I joined Agile Therapeutics, a women's health pharmaceutical company in Princeton, New Jersey, as its chief medical officer (CMO). This was my first C-suite role. During my time at Agile, the employee count ranged from 11 to about 20 individuals. When I left, there were just a few women on staff, no other women in senior management, no women on the board, and no other people of color. Fortunately, that has changed substantially since my tenure there, a testament to the efforts of the CEO to support women's careers.

Since July 2019, I have been the CMO of ObsEva, a Swiss-based pharmaceutical company focused on addressing unmet needs in women's health. The company is focused on uterine fibroids, endometriosis, infertility, and preterm labor, and we are currently at an exciting time in the company's history as we anticipate our first regulatory approval for our uterine fibroids medication.

Being in the C-suite has been and continues to be an enormous privilege. I use my platform to do what I can to amplify the issues around gender inequity, including the ongoing gender pay gap. For me professionally, however, the gender promotion gap is a bigger issue, and one that also needs attention.

I have been fortunate to be regularly promoted, both while in academia and in industry, and attained a C-suite role within only seven years of leaving academic medicine by being willing to move from company to company. The promotions from associate director up to CMO were not overly difficult to achieve; however, further advancement, potentially to CEO, feels like a much bigger hurdle.

According to McKinsey's 2020 women in healthcare report, although on several measures healthcare is one of the best industries for women and women have made substantial progress, we continue to encounter persistent obstacles to advancement, particularly for senior positions, where we remain underrepresented.

Furthermore, the number and proportion of women at the very top, i.e., in CEO roles, remains low, and the proportion of CEOs who are women of color is even smaller. Sadly, part of the battle is simply not "looking the part," which is particularly challenging for me as a petite mixed-race woman. When people meet me, CEO is the last role that crosses their minds. This means I must work many times harder to prove my leadership potential.

The increasing numbers of women in leadership positions is to be celebrated. However, until far more women are truly *at the top*, in the role of final decision-maker on investments, strategy and direction, mission, and so on, we will not see sufficient change.

In addition to my professional roles, my volunteer work on the board of the American Medical Women's Association is deeply gratifying. AMWA's mission is to advance women in medicine, advocate for equity, and ensure excellence in healthcare. Collaborating with like-minded physicians, trainees, and students is exciting, and as the organization continues to grow, I look forward to seeing even greater impact on women's leadership.

Calls to Action

The COVID pandemic forced us to acknowledge and address the terrible health disparities that have continued unchanged and unchecked for years and years. As described in Evans and colleagues in their 2020 *New England Journal of Medicine* article, systemic racism is "one of the most dangerous toxicants."

The evidence is beyond dispute: discrimination and racism "act through biologic pathways to promote cerebrovascular disease, accelerate aging, and impede vascular and renal function, producing disproportionate burdens of disease on black Americans and other minority populations." The even greater impact on black American women and other women of color is also profound.

The question for me as a biotech executive who strongly believes that industry, broadly defined, has a responsibility to do our part to create change, is "now what?" What do we really mean when we talk about diversity, equity, and inclusion in healthcare? And for those of us working in various aspects of the health industry including pharma, biotech, and so on, how do we think about our contributions to improving the situation?

For me, as a women's health physician executive, I am focused on improving the health of women around the world, in particular women from underserved populations whose health has largely been neglected.

Women's health needs true innovation, not incremental improvement. As I described in my *Harvard Medicine* article "Cri de Coeur" (*https://hms.harvard.edu/magazine/womens-health/cri-de-coeur*), we continue to lack understanding of many common and serious conditions in women's health, including preeclampsia, preterm birth, and some forms of infertility.

In the 14 years since I left clinical practice, there have been myriad major breakthroughs in biomedicine and disease treatment and yet the landscape has not changed much for women, and many of our most prevalent and serious problems remain unaddressed.

To change the status quo, investment will be needed. To state the obvious, women comprise 50% of the global population yet only 11% of NIH funding is focused on women's health; 4% of research and development dollars go to women's health; and only 1% of venture capital funding supports women's health. With the current FemTech movement, these numbers are changing, but not fast enough.

With these facts in mind:

- I call on all of us to insist on more women in leadership throughout healthcare, particularly in decision-making roles. Investors focus on what they know, so in many ways it shouldn't be surprising to us that there has been a lack of investment in women's health, nor (on a lighter note) should it be a surprise that Viagra was a blockbuster!

- I call on all of us to insist on more research and investment in women's health, which I define broadly as conditions that affect biological females only, mainly, or differently. To achieve greater investment, we must make the case that women's health is relevant to everyone.

  Certainly when we look at the massive potential positive societal and economic impact of addressing under-studied and under-supported health issues, this should be obvious. We need to show why, for example, access to contraception should matter to everyone and why treatment of pain from various conditions benefits not only individual patients but also their partners, their children, and even their employers.

- I also encourage all of us to combat continued stigma and silence associated with so many conditions and experiences that women deal with every day. Let's talk openly about our hot flushes, our heavy bleeding, our painful periods, and even our grief due to infertility and miscarriage. I am optimistic that the more we speak out, the more attention will come as investors begin to realize the potential return on investment from funding research and development of new treatments and solutions.

Closing Remarks

As a women's health physician, I am deeply passionate about the physical, mental, and emotion well-being of women throughout our lifespan. I am often overwhelmed when I think about all the important work that needs to be done in this space. It helps me to focus instead on the small, even tiny, but significant ways in which women have told me I have impacted their lives, and I am reminded that we can change the world, one individual at a time.

As an executive leader, I am aware of my responsibilities to represent women and women's health in all aspects of my work, and to use my platform to push for and insist upon change.

As a parent, I have worked as my parents did to teach my children by example and by my words — my older son to respect women and my daughter to demand respect. As the mother of a child (my youngest) with severe autism, I also imagine a day in which every parent leads change by instilling love and respect for all individuals regardless of gender, race, ethnicity, religion or creed, country of origin, socioeconomic status, and level of ability.

As a Nigerian, I look forward to a day when all women and their precious babies and children have access to equitable education, work opportunity, and adequate preventive and interventional health care.

I cannot end without sharing a few words about my life partner, my husband Kelvin. We are in our 30th year of marriage and without him there is not a chance I would not be where I am today. I thank God for him every day.

Advice

Envision the kind of future you desire for the world, and then focus your energy into helping to realize that vision.

Network, network, network. Men have advanced their careers by showing up on the golf course and asking favors of other men; women need to learn this skill and use it to their advantage and to help other women advance. A prior CEO with whom I worked had every position through networking and getting friends, fellow board members, etc., to recommend him. Take some time every day to network and develop professional relationships.

Believe in yourself. This is another thing men do very well. Data show that men apply for (and get) positions for which they are not fully qualified, whereas women focus on the experience and job description and want to be 100% certain they meet all the criteria and feel totally ready for the position before they apply.

Keep an open mind and take (calculated) risks. Two of my major career moves — switching residency programs and leaving clinical practice — took tremendous courage, as neither were common events in medicine. Both decisions required soul searching and risk taking. These opportunities also came my way during periods of reflection and openness to change.

ALWAYS treat others with respect and positivity. Be aware of the effect that you have on others, especially from a subjective perspective. How do people feel when they are around you? If you make people tense or if you are difficult to work with, it will be challenging to be successful no matter how brilliant you are.

ALWAYS be your authentic self.

"Realize that vision."

– ELIZABETH GARNER

ENTREPRENEURS
AND
CONSULTANTS

*"I used to think that being one
of the few female cardiothoracic
surgeons in the world was
my most unique quality."*

– KATHY E. MAGLIATO

CHAPTER TWENTY-FOUR

Cardiothoracic Surgeon to Entrepreneur

By Kathy E. Magliato, MD, MBA, FACS

I USED TO THINK THAT BEING ONE OF THE FEW female cardiothoracic surgeons in the world was my most unique quality. Since the inception of the American Board of Thoracic Surgery in 1948, approximately 200 women have achieved board certification in cardiothoracic surgery. In fact, it wasn't until 1961 that the first woman was able to attain board certification is this very male-dominated field. In the year I took my board exam, there were only 100 women in the field.

It is, however, even more unique for me to be a female practicing cardiothoracic surgeon with an MBA, as I have yet to meet even one. I am confident they exist, especially in light of the fact that undergraduate schools are now offering dual MD-MBA degrees. In fact, my own alma mater, Union College, in Schenectady, New York, offers a Leadership in Medicine program in which students can obtain a BS, MD, and MBA in an eight-year academic track. With hindsight being 20/20, I cannot imagine why a physician would not embark upon an academic path that ultimately leads to degree in business.

Having said this, my very own path to an MBA was a bit circuitous, and yet there was a certain convergence between getting an MD and getting an MBA. In the most simplistic terms, my motivation to become a doctor was so that I could heal people and my motivation to get a degree in business was so that I could heal more people.

At the time I applied to the UCLA Anderson School of Management, I was the director of the Mechanical Assist Device

Program at Cedars-Sinai Medical Center in Los Angeles, where I was enjoying my practice as a heart transplant surgeon. I had, in fact, founded and built the Mechanical Assist Device Program using little more than my clinical skill set from my fellowship in mechanical assist devices at the University of Pittsburgh Medical Center.

While building this clinical program and working with various artificial heart manufacturing companies, it became apparent to me that something was missing in my life as a heart surgeon and program director. In fact, that "something" was a language barrier that I simply couldn't cross — it was the language of business.

While I was fluent in the language of medicine — a complex language grounded in science, theory, and case study — I was completely ignorant of the language of business, a language also grounded in science, theory, and case study. While one language was used to save lives, the other was used to change lives, and I found them both extraordinary and necessary to my evolution as a physician and surgeon.

And that is how I found myself, at the age of 40, going back to school to take exams, write essays, and spend 40-plus hours per week "hitting the books." Unlike medical school, which was rote memorization, business school was taught by the Socratic method, and you'd best come to class prepared to lead a discussion of the latest economic debacle or Harvard Business case study or risk personal humiliation.

I found business school to be a great intellectual challenge. It was like a springboard for my mind. I found myself in a new territory of learning and exercising "muscles" in my brain that I never knew existed (and, anatomically speaking, do not exist). I also found myself surrounded by some of the greatest minds I have ever met: my fellow Executive MBA classmates. I learned as much from them as I did from my highly proficient professors and it was all very stimulating, especially coming from a field of medicine that revolved more around a technical skill set.

All of this hard work and study certainly paid off. I finished my MBA in 2006 with a new cadre of assets, the two greatest of which were:

- The ability to build and leverage myself as a brand (and recognize the importance of doing this); and
- The network of UCLA staff and alumni with whom I can collaborate and look to for advice and support in any endeavor I choose.

Also, as a result of getting an MBA, I now address problems differently. I think differently. I act on my instincts differently. And most importantly, I am now constantly scanning my life for opportunity—especially opportunities that utilize both my business and clinical skills.

In terms of building myself a brand, upon graduating from UCLA Anderson I developed a marketing plan for myself as a physician and a platform that positioned me as a national expert in heart disease in women and women's health. To this end, I wrote a memoir, *Heart Matters*, which was published by Random House. It received a 4-out-of-4-star review from *People Magazine* and went on to be a *New York Times* Bestseller for both the print and eBook versions.

At its core, *Heart Matters* is a book that educates women about heart disease. Around that core of information, I added the stories of patients whom I have taken care of throughout my career. The stories are both poignant and tragic and send the message to women that heart disease is our #1 killer and is an epidemic among women.

Heart Matters is also a memoir of my life as a female heart surgeon who is juggling a career, two young children, and a husband who is a liver transplant and hepatobiliary surgeon. In other words, a story about a woman who is trying to find balance while trying to have it all and make a difference — isn't that what we are all trying to do?

My book was optioned by Universal Studios and made into a scripted medical drama that NBC picked up to series for the 2016 television season. In the TV show, "Heartbeat" (now streaming on NBC's Peacock streaming service), Melissa George played me, and my husband was played by actor Dave Annabel. I served as a co-executive producer and worked on nearly every aspect of the show.

I found it truly fascinating to see how a television series is produced. Similar to an operating room, everyone on set has a specific job — from the writers, to the directors, to the camera operators, to the props manager, to the set designers and lighting staff. Each person must do their job to the highest standard for the whole production to come together in a unified way. Each person has a common goal: to make that episode and ultimately the entire show a success. We function like that in the OR. Everyone from the surgeons to the nurses, to the anesthesiologists, to the perfusionists who run the heart-lung machine brings their "A" game for the singular goal of a safe, successful operation.

I have also leveraged my brand to build an extensive list of speaking engagements, radio, TV, newspaper, and magazine appearances, and I have used my platform to educate women about heart disease. I have been on NBC, ABC, CBS, and FOX news, the "Martha Stewart Show," "The Doctors," "The Doctor Oz Show," "The John Oliver Show," and the Oprah Winfrey Network, and have been interviewed by Barbara Walters on "20/20." I've worked with wonderful celebrities like Queen Latifah and Joe Montana who are dedicated to building awareness about heart disease.

I would never have known how to navigate these marketing waters nor understood the power of brand-building and positioning had it not been for my business degree and my hope is that this work has impacted people's lives.

And yet, the most potentially rewarding project I am working on utilizes the second of the two greatest assets I received from my MBA: the ability to collaborate with and engage the UCLA Anderson community.

On the very first day of class, I met a fellow Executive MBA student with a PhD in bioengineering who was in the earliest stages of developing a cardiac diagnostic medical device. From that very first day onward, we collaborated on the development of that device with what little time we had outside of the classroom and MBA workload. We utilized the expertise of other classmates and professors to help us with things such as patent application, design development, and funding opportunities.

Upon graduating from Anderson, we had built our business plan, patented the device, and built an initial working prototype.

We have since completed the third and final phase of the prototype, performed safety and efficacy testing in humans, and incorporated ourselves with the addition of a third C-suite member to our company who serves as president and COO.

We initially bootstrapped the financing of the company and then secured more than $500,000 in funding through US government grants. We then created a C-corporation, Cordex Systems Inc., and funded the company with three oversubscribed rounds of angel-tiered investing and are currently raising a Series A round that specifically targets institutional investors.

Traditional blood pressure cuffs measure one metric: pressure in the blood vessels. However, this only scratches the surface of the critical cardiovascular information available. The device that we have developed, known as the SmartCuff™, uses a proprietary mathematical algorithm that can take an ordinary blood pressure cuff and turn it into a sensor that can bio-hack a human pulse at 200 data points/second to yield information regarding vascular health.

Today, there are no non-invasive medical devices capable of monitoring changes to the vascular health of the endothelium (the protective lining of your blood vessels) in routine clinical practice. Yet all of the risk factors for cardiovascular disease – obesity, smoking, diabetes, high blood pressure, sedentary lifestyle, poor diet, elevated lipids – destroy that lining by causing inflammation in the endothelium. Quite strikingly, healthcare providers are not directly measuring vascular health despite the fact that they are deploying measures (both medications and lifestyle modifications) to improve it.

To date we have tested nearly 700 patients with our clinical partners at Johns Hopkins Medical Center and are working toward the FDA clearance of the device. We are also exploring applications of the SmartCuff in patients with long haul COVID-19 as the coronavirus has been shown in both autopsy studies and clinical presentation to be attacking the endothelium as a key driver of disease manifestations.

Building a company from product ideation to prototyping to performance and clinical testing to regulatory approval and commercialization is hard work. It's like getting out of bed every morning and pushing a rock up a hill. It's also very much like approaching a tough surgical case every day. Most people think that surgeons enter an operating room thinking about how we're going to succeed. We don't. We enter an OR thinking about how we're going to fail. And then we find a way to mitigate that failure. It's failure that drives us, not success. Being the CEO of a startup means that I begin every day by thinking about how the company will fail today. And I do this while pushing that rock up the hill.

My COO and I both lost our dads recently. They died within a year of one another, but they left us each with a gift. They instilled in us the principles that have allowed us to persevere through some pretty difficult times. His dad, an extremely talented and compassionate surgeon, told him to always "play the ball where it lies." This has been our mantra as we navigate the pandemic which has been both a company stressor as well as a catalyst. I can't help but feel sometimes, though, as if we are playing the ball in a COVID fairway bunker.

My dad, the kind of guy who did business on a handshake, told me that "if you work hard, you can achieve anything." I can assure you that at our company, Cordex Systems Inc., we work hard every day. Whether the company thrives or fails it won't be for lack of working hard or playing the ball where it lies.

All of the things that I have accomplished through building and leveraging my brand and through founding Cordex Systems Inc. was made possible by networking with the UCLA community and beyond. I urge you, as prospective MBA students, to make the effort to really get to know your fellow classmates. Find out what they do for a living, what their passion is, and how they envision themselves in the future. You may be amazed by the synergy you have with them and by what a collaboration can yield.

Also, stay connected with your business school. The alumni network will be an endless resource, teeming with opportunity and only too happy to work with you. In other words, the bricks and mortar of your next company are likely sitting right beside you in class.

From my vantage point, I see an MBA creating a new breed of what I call the "entrepreneurial physician" — a physician who either creates new enterprises or uses their newly honed business skills to improve and build upon their existing medical practice. I fear, however, that doctors seek an MBA only to use it as a stepping stone to a position within health care/hospital administration and I think this could be potentially myopic. Once you get an MBA, change is in the wind, so keep your options open!

For me, the entrepreneurial route fit like a surgical glove. The high risk/reward ratio, the necessity of both speed and accuracy and the ability to exact more rapid change are the very "surgical" qualities of entrepreneurship that drew me to this field of business. And yet, I continue to stay in the "trenches" of healthcare in order to keep my finger on the pulse of what is evolving in the field of medicine. In this way, I am able to leverage real-time data for our company and our investors .

And so, for me, I will continue to use my MD to save lives one patient at a time, one day at a time and use my MBA to create technology that will change the lives of thousands. Either way, my hope is that I create a modicum of positive change in the world at large. Actor Melissa George said it best in one pivotal scene in "Heartbeat": "It's lives. High risk, high reward. And a chance to change the world."

CHAPTER TWENTY-FIVE

Creating Your Own Version of Success

By Kelly Z. Sennholz, MD

BEFORE I BECAME A SUCCESSFUL MEDICAL entrepreneur, before I was a medical manager and leader in various healthcare organizations, before I was an Emergency Department physician, I was a Registered Nurse.

I still possess the tiny handprint of the first micro preemie I cared for, long before the word "micro preemie" was coined. The positive impact I was able to have on that baby's family is forever etched on my heart. I don't know if they remember, but I do.

Working in the healthcare field as an RN, I was fascinated by the science of medicine. I found the ability to use science and complicated decision-making in order to improve the lives of others to be supremely interesting. As I moved into critical care and flight nursing, when those fields were quite new, it was truly breathtaking to be a part of the development of medicine as we now know it.

I worked in a hospital alongside some of the top nurses in the country, including the author of a major nursing textbook who was one of the few nurses with PhDs at the time. Working with her, I realized that as you progressed in nursing, you moved away from the clinical bedside and closer to research and writing. As I compared the jobs of the physicians I worked with to the PhD nurses, it seemed evident that being a physician was a better way to remain at the bedside. I took the chance and applied to medical school, receiving admission letters from two on my very first try. It was a new path for me, but one that held great excitement and opportunity.

The same day I began medical school, my son was starting kindergarten. I clearly remember standing there, he with his red and yellow briefcase schoolbag with large A, B, C's on it and me with my heavy backpack, wishing each "Good Luck" on our new path. We were both ready for a new adventure. I was a single mother with a very supportive ex-husband and later, "wife-in-law," who made my life much easier. Still, it was quickly apparent that being a single working mother and going to medical school was something of an aberration in Oklahoma, even in the late 1980s.

I accomplished medical school in two parts: I finished the first two years of didactic material commuting to Oklahoma City, while I completed the two years of clinical immersion in Tulsa, where I lived. The needs of my growing son were my first priority and affected every decision I made regarding my career. While I juggled mothering duties and worked to sustain my son and me along with my medical studies, it never occurred to me that those without obligations like mine found simply being a medical student so onerous. Although at the time it actually seemed exciting and fun, I couldn't even tell you now how I did it all. The story of the oil that lasted for eight days comes to mind!

After medical school, I chose a residency in Tulsa in order to stay near my ex-husband. The medical school was just starting a Med-Peds program and since I loved pediatrics and had received the "Outstanding Student in Pediatrics" award, this seemed perfect. However, one year into the program the pediatrics department unexpectedly increased their on-call requirements. As a single mother, I felt I couldn't handle the increased call responsibilities and ultimately decided to leave the pediatrics portion of my training behind. An outstanding Emergency Medicine group in our city invited me to begin moonlighting with them. It was exciting and interesting. Moreover, it provided additional experience that helped advance my career.

At the end of my residency, I joined that group as an attending and clinical instructor. By the time I was 30, I had worked in a range of medical areas: pediatrics, neonatology, internal medicine, and emergency medicine. Because of the changes in residency programs today with earlier specialization, few physicians have the opportunity to work in as many areas as I did — a change I believe is not good for medicine. For me, the ability to experience a real breadth of medicine has made for quite an unusual career.

Despite the outstanding on-the-job training I received from some of the best ER docs, I had come "of age" too late to be grandfathered into Emergency Medicine boards, which limited my working in some of the larger academic institutions. So I moved to North Carolina where I found opportunities in trauma centers and ERs at smaller hospitals.

I was eventually offered the director position for emergency services of a small county hospital. During those years, I joined a number of professional organizations in which I held several leadership roles. I became a representative for the medical society, president of a medical society, board member for state emergency physician group, medical examiner, regional EMS director during seven hurricanes, state child fatality task force member, and more. I was responsible for creating five full years of funding for a clinic for the working poor. I also created legislative successes in the medical genre in two states.

As I look back on these experiences, I realize that in my family of origin, we were taught that every citizen has a responsibility not only to forward their life, but also to give back generously. I considered these activities my way of "giving back"— not necessarily a career-enhancing move. Nevertheless, they did help my career —if not directly — in subtle ways. I made lots of great friends and interacted with some exceptionally bright and talented people. From administrative positions to medical society leadership, from grant acquisitions to community activities, I was able to see medicine from all sides in these settings.

Ultimately, several things happened to cause me to move away from the clinical aspects of medicine to a more business approach to my career. The first occurred as a result of my work with the state medical society. I thoroughly enjoyed the camaraderie of fellow physicians. However, as the years passed, I realized the society was doing little to combat what I felt to be the negative influences of medicine: namely, the loss of an independent physician–patient relationship.

The second was the recognition that the care we (physicians) were providing was not necessarily optimal. I had begun learning about wellness medicine, which suddenly made me view medical care in an entirely new light. One example that illustrates this was a patient who came in each month for a "pain shot" for osteoarthritis. Normally, I just gave him the injection and discharged him. But this day, I asked him what his doctor was doing to cure the problem. Exercise? Weight loss and nutritional guidance? Supplementation? Physical therapy? He looked bewildered and said, "Vioxx." Unfortunately, symptomatic treatment is often the rule rather than the exception. For so many patients we are not addressing their core problems.

The third was the recognition that emergency medicine is a young person's game. Looking down the road, I didn't want to be like the gray haired doctor I knew who was still working night shifts at age 65, taking abuse from drunk and belligerent patients.

As a result of these insights, I re-examined my personal and professional goals, trying to understand what had made me choose medicine initially and what parts of my career brought me real happiness. For many physicians, it is the exactness of science, the need to be "perfect" that drew them to the field. But for me, the most rewarding aspects of medicine involved making a difference and bringing joy and health to patients. On those days when I was actually able to change the outcome of someone's life, I went home full of energy and enthusiasm.

Once I had completed this self-assessment, I was able to determine the direction I wanted to go next. I decided to leave clinical practice and study business — not formally through a degree program, but "on the job" — much as I had in the emergency room.

Determined to start my own business and focused on improving the lives of physicians and patients, I started a small aesthetics facility. Although the learning curve was steep and not always easy, ultimately I developed a successful wellness program, then expanded it to a program to teach physicians about wellness. This success led me to start a technology company, eMedical Mall, an ancillary services management system that physicians could use in their offices to save them time and increase their reimbursements.

The experience of starting and managing my own company not only broadened my understanding of the business side of medicine and non-medical endeavors, but allowed me to work with experienced, high-level entrepreneurs who taught me the in's and out's of stocks, options, management, fundraising and many other core skills of the entrepreneur. My new venture, OSL Medical, also provides in-house clinic programs. It allows the office manager to significantly improve clinic revenues, patient satisfaction, and overall results without disrupting normal clinic flow.

In order to hone my leadership skills as I developed these companies, I took lots of classes. I also read numerous books on business, entrepreneurialism, and finance. I studied hard as I was learning. I asked a million questions of my co-developers. I was a sponge. I love to learn and because this was a whole new arena for me, I was primed to learn the old-fashioned way: through trial and error.

My progress was made much easier by the many mentors I found along my path. Receiving and giving support, friendship, advice, and feedback are a major necessity for those venturing out into this interesting but challenging world.

My first real mentor was a powerful woman who was named one of the top 50 women of the millennium, was awarded the Presidential Medal of Freedom, and honored upon her death by the president for creating a brighter future for all Americans. Wilma Mankiller taught me many of the first lessons I needed to have the confidence to try anything.

Yes, I got lucky on my first mentor. However, wherever you live, there are literally thousands of talented, successful, generous, and educated leaders who are more than willing to give of their time and talent to assist you in your transition. The only thing they will expect in return is that you take the relationship as seriously as they do. As my career has moved forward, I have been privileged to become the mentor for others coming after me.

I personally do not think that physicians who want to be entrepreneurs need to go back to school to get an MBA. Having the degree may be more helpful if you are interested in entering the corporate world. It will definitely help you understand the concepts and verbiage of the business world. But it is not necessary for most ventures you may choose to start on your own. Instead, consider taking classes for bio-entrepreneurialism, which are not degree programs. These can teach all the skills needed to get started in a shorter timeframe. In my area, the University of Colorado offers an excellent series on bio-entrepreneurialism. There may be similar offerings in other areas of the country.

Another good way to develop as an entrepreneur is to start attending networking events for business people. In almost every city, high-level entrepreneurs have groups that meet to share ideas and receive input. These offer terrific opportunities to begin learning the behaviors and talents required for a successful business. Listen, listen, listen. Take notes. Ask questions. We have a group in Colorado called SOPE (Society of Physician Entrepreneurs) that also has an interactive online presence on LinkedIn. Find a group in your city, jump in, and start swimming.

Probably the best advice I can give to any physician starting down the entrepreneurial path is to choose a small project first, set aside time to work on it, and just begin. When you reach challenges, identify quality people who can assist you. I am constantly amazed at how generous all the more-experienced business people have been on my journey. I, likewise, give back in any way I can.

As I have traveled down my career path, my personal and social life has varied a lot. Sometimes, working a regular job and starting a business required my full attention. Other times, I have found streams of income that allowed me more freedom in my personal choices. It is okay to forego personal activities for a time while starting a business, but it is also helpful to get feedback from friends and family if this time away from socialization has become too long or too hard.

Each individual is different, but creating an ongoing balance is important. That is the holy grail in entrepreneurialism. There is this mysterious "perfect amount" of family/private time which I doubt anyone ever achieves for more than a week! But getting regular exercise, carving out time for relaxation and spending time with those you love are all key to making life worthwhile. Make sure you put these things on your calendar every week. Schedule them in just as you would schedule in an appointment with someone else. Remember, you are a someone, too.

In general, growing a career now is much easier for women than it was decades ago. Certainly, younger men are much more accustomed to dealing with women in the workplace. When I began my career, people commonly questioned whether women should work outside of the home. Such a query would bring an incredulous look from most young women today. Not only do a majority of women now work, but they are starting businesses at a record rate.

As more than half of the classes of many upper-level educational systems such as law and medicine are female, women need to take on the challenge of learning leadership. Some leadership skills will not always come naturally for the feminine energy. Enhancing natural abilities of communication, empathy and dedication with the skills of guidance, leadership and power are going to be critical not only for the women and participants involved, but for our country and our world.

For the younger women still on their educational path, I would recommend stopping every month or so and formally reviewing what you have learned, where you are going, and what areas you can improve upon. By making personal development a regular part of your life, you will avoid some of the plateaus and disappointments that can arise when living life on autopilot. By making this a habit, you will be developing the habits of champions, thereby improving your odds of having a championship life and a championship career.

Find someone whose career represents where you want to go and ask them for mentorship and advice. Finding two or three mentors is even better. By having guidance and putting your time toward the growth and development of your own life, you can achieve anything. By creating a positive framework for your business career, you will then be free to express your innate intelligence and caring.

Part of what made my success in business was the same thing that made my medical career successful. Although I had little understanding or experience when I went into medicine, my intention was to do it and I simply figured it out as I went along. Likewise, in my business career, I envisioned my dream of what my life would look like and what my career would look like. I just jumped in and started swimming. I utilized my mentors, my learning skills, and my excitement and the end result was success.

Part of my desire to share this story is to provide some of the insights into the tools available to assist you with creating a new career. Keep your innocence and excitement, but use the abundant resources of people and knowledge that are available to make it easier and to avoid time and money-consuming pitfalls.

Since the original publication of *Lessons Learned: Stories from Women in Medical Management* in 2012, my life has held many new adventures. With financial success achieved, I wanted to really give back and improve the world in creative ways.

I had been a co-founder of a political action committee, a co-founder of an international art colony, a founder of multiple charitable endeavors, board member of elite charities, and other interesting side projects. I decided to expand upon my previous experience and use my time and talents to focus on some urgent community issues.

My life as a physician, a mother, an entrepreneur, a political activist, and a philanthropist has had a common vision. I think that Ellen DeGeneres recently said it very well: "I stand for honesty, equality, kindness, compassion, treating people the way you'd want to be treated, and helping those in need. To me, those are traditional values. That's what I stand for. I also believe in dance." Well said, Ms. DeGeneres.

My newest project is Legacy. I am currently setting up a charity called The Dobberke-Sennholz Billion Dollar fund. Marie Dobberke was my grandmother, a humble Native American woman who taught me love. Her religion was the moon, and nearly every single night I gaze at Mr. Moon, feeling her love still powerful, putting everything into perspective. The soft, daily power of love is like water on rocks, shaping and determining everything.

The remainder of my estate, along with any contributions, will be set up to grow until it reaches a billion dollars, at which time a portion of the yearly proceeds will be distributed to women, children, the environment, Our Earth. I share this with you as one of the greatest joys of creating wealth and abundance is to own the power to change our world to a better place. If you are interested in contributing to this goal, you are most welcome to contact me.

To everyone (in particular the women) reading this book with the goal to be inspired in your leadership journey, my wish for you is to establish your "Why" and your vision early and to never forget your destination. Thank you for being a part of our leadership community.

I warmly wish each of you the best of luck in your travels within and outside the medical world. Life is a journey to be enjoyed and you are still the best and brightest women on the planet. The world needs your input. The world needs your excellence. Don't be afraid to make a mistake; that is all a part of the journey. Laugh a lot, live fully, and create your own version of success, not someone else's.

CHAPTER TWENTY-SIX

A Road Less Traveled

by Deborah M. Shlian, MD, MBA

"Two roads diverged in a wood, and I— I took the one less traveled by, And that has made all the difference."
— ROBERT FROST: THE ROAD NOT TAKEN

 I WAS FORTUNATE ENOUGH TO HEAR ROBERT Frost himself speak those words when my mother took me to a literary seminar at Johns Hopkins University. Although it was long ago (I was in grade school), I remember very clearly the message I took from that brilliant poet: it was okay to be different, to explore possibilities and options others might not, to "do your own thing."

Growing up in the late 1950s and early 1960s, a time when family and career roles were still fairly rigidly differentiated by gender, this view required adjustments from parents, friends, and particularly school counselors who regarded nursing or teaching as much more acceptable careers for women than medicine. Indeed, the idea of career itself was "something to fall back on," to be dusted off should a husband die or family economics really get tight. Full-time wife and mother was the generally accepted proper role for a woman of that era.

Needless to say, I took Frost's words to heart, starting with aiming for a medical career early in life, and then by taking various forks in the path as opportunities presented themselves. And that, for me, has made all the difference.

The first fork came at the end of medical school when I had to make a decision about specialty. In 1972, although there had been some brief mention of family practice as a new specialty, there were very few residencies in the country and even less guidance as to where to find them — particularly on the East Coast. So, despite my fascination with the concept of a "new, complete physician," I chose the road of least resistance and matched with a Hopkins radiology training program.

Changing Courses

It was a chance vacation to Los Angeles during my internship year that changed the course of my clinical career. My husband (we married in my junior year and his senior year of med school) arranged for a meeting with the head of family medicine at Kaiser Permanente. Our preventive medicine curriculum in medical school had included a comprehensive study of what was considered by many traditionalists to be a renegade operation (or worse, socialized medicine) i.e., a group model, health maintenance organization (HMO).

The notion of salaried doctors working in a prepaid multispecialty group that functioned as a partnership was different if not heretical in the 1970s, when the vast majority of doctors were in solo private practice. But my husband and I had found the concept more than intellectually interesting. It seemed to make a lot of sense and we were anxious to see the system up close.

Dr. Irv Rasgon was my first real role model and mentor. Chief of family medicine at the Sunset facility, he charmed us from the moment we met him. Irv was the quintessential Marcus Welby — he even looked the part. A great clinician, outstanding teacher, and natural leader, he was passionate about family practice and Kaiser. "Why specialize and become so narrowly focused when you can be a family practitioner and take care of the whole patient?" he asked us.

Irv took us on hospital rounds and his patients, from the very young to the very old, obviously adored him. Moreover, it was clear that his peers in other specialties respected him. When he offered us the opportunity to come to Los Angeles, finish our training as FPs and become Kaiser staff physicians, we readily accepted. I left radiology, my husband left ophthalmology, and together we headed out to Southern California where we completed our training, took and passed Family Practice boards and joined the Southern California Permanente Group as partners.

Looking back, the 10 years I spent as a clinician in the Kaiser group provided the kind of education in medicine and management that no didactic program in either medical or business school could ever provide. We were at the forefront of what has been nothing short of a revolution in healthcare — working in a fully integrated system that allowed us to deliver quality care (as much of the full spectrum of pediatric and adult medicine that was feasible in an urban hospital/clinic setting) without the stress of wondering whether our patients could pay for the care they required (what we know today as "managed care").

We had the advantage of being hospital-based, making our in-patients easily accessible during the day while we saw our scheduled outpatients in our offices, which were located in the same building. Similarly, we could often grab "sidewalk" consults from specialists who worked down the hall or just upstairs, thus avoiding long appointment delays for our patients. Lab, X-ray and other ancillary services were a floor below — another efficiency.

We were given a half day a week of "paid education time," which my husband and I used to teach residents at UCLA. Medical students from both UCLA and USC spent one month electives at our Kaiser offices and I was even able to satisfy my clinical research interests with such projects as a study of "Screening and Immunization of Rubella Susceptible Women" published in *JAMA*.

My department held regular quality assurance and peer review sessions; we developed clinical guidelines long before it was fashionable. From a quality standpoint, I believed then and still believe today, that the group model is an ideal way to practice medicine. Unfortunately, it is also extremely capital-intensive and in the kind of highly competitive market that characterized California even in the 1980's, some of the original idealism began giving way to market pressures.

As a primary care clinician, I became increasingly frustrated at my inability to influence policy. I felt that front-line physicians had the best perspective for identifying and correcting problems within the system. Yet despite the fact that legally the group was a partnership, in reality it was governed no differently than most corporate entities, i.e., top-down, and the top physician leaders were almost exclusively specialists.

For example, the chief of my hospital was a surgeon who often stated that patients did not care about having their own physician, that they were primarily motivated by easy access to the system, and that any clinician — doctor, NP, PA — would do just fine. It didn't matter. Needless to say, this undercut the fundamental principles of family medicine: taking care of the whole patient and being able to provide continuity of care by the same physician.

In fact, this chief refused to accept the validity of our early studies (later, a group out of Vermont published the same findings) showing that patients with their own primary care doctor had fewer emergent visits and less inappropriate hospital admissions — both a significant cost savings and quality improvement.

Again with hindsight, I now realize that his intransigence on this and other healthcare policy-related issues created an opportunity for me to take my next fork in the road: my husband and I both decided to leave Kaiser.

With no one to provide career guidance, we began investigating how we could use our skills and understanding of healthcare to have a greater impact on the system. I wrote several articles as well as a consumer health guide for a national HMO and we both spoke at various venues around the country about problems involved with the delivery of care in the managed care environment.

During the first few months of my "retirement," we were persuaded to start part-time law school at Whittier School of Law in Los Angeles with the intention of developing an expertise in health policy and health law. However, not long after starting my first semester, I was recruited to a management position at the UCLA Student Health Service (SHS).

I became director of the primary care unit of SHS, which serves all 33,000 undergraduate and graduate students on the university campus. As many as 400 patients per day were being seen in our clinic — most of whom used Student Health as their only source of medical care.

What attracted me to the position was the opportunity to take many of the lessons learned from the Kaiser system and adapt them to this setting. In particular, I wanted to change the orientation of primary care from essentially a triage area to a comprehensive ambulatory care facility staffed by clinicians competent enough to have admitting privileges at UCLA Medical Center. That meant letting non-board certified physicians go and hiring only well-credentialed family practitioners, pediatricians, and internists — a process fraught with legal/risk management/personnel issues that I had to quickly research and understand.

In addition, I wanted to integrate our service with the outstanding teaching programs in the medical school. That required developing a new level of diplomatic skill, delicately balancing the egos and agendas of various departments within the school. But happily, within a relatively short time we had created an impressive educational and research program that helped to attract medical students and graduate students as well as superior clinical staff. Our quality of care and patient and personnel satisfaction all measurably improved.

Another Fork in the Road

As my administrative duties expanded, two significant issues surfaced that ultimately led to yet another fork in my career path. First, was the question of whether I could be a successful manager and maintain a clinical practice without compromising both. Increasingly, I felt caught between what I perceived as two equally important and demanding responsibilities.

In the past there seemed to be consensus that despite the difficulties, one could not be an effective and credible leader of clinicians without concurrently having an active clinical practice. In fact, with the exception of the few full-time regional medical directors, that is still the model Kaiser uses today for most of its physician administrators. On the other hand, in many other healthcare organizations, the role of physician executive has expanded so that those who wish to assume broad management responsibilities within these companies realize they must relinquish the clinical role, instead bringing the strong patient care background as a resource to a new, more comprehensive job description.

Still, I must admit, for me it was not an easy decision, although looking back, it was one that has made all the difference in my success as a manager. As an executive who was also a physician, I was in the unique position of developing and enhancing collaboration and integration of the medical and administrative staffs in the daily management and operations of the organization.

The other issue had to do specifically with my expanding operational responsibilities. Up to that point, everything I had accomplished as a manager was achieved without the benefit of a formal educational foundation. For example, I was asked to develop a budget, but had never taken a finance or accounting course. I was asked to make staffing projections, but had never learned the kind of operations research tools needed to create a truly robust model.

Without a working knowledge of the language and concepts of business, one becomes totally reliant on non-medical administrative personnel whose orientation to the bottom line may at least sometimes run counter to quality. This revelation convinced me to switch from law school to business school, and in 1988, I completed an Executive MBA program at UCLA's Anderson School of Management (with my husband, by the way).

Two things occurred as a result of the MBA program. First, my job description expanded to include policy formulation, strategic planning, broader budgeting responsibilities, contracting for outside specialty care, risk management, and helping to develop and implement a computerized patient record to capture data for outcomes measurement. I became part of the senior management team, attending meetings heretofore open only to the non-physician administrators.

Second, I began receiving telephone calls and letters from recruiters alerting me to other opportunities in medical management. Suddenly, I was advised that my experiences as both a clinician and manager in two managed care settings, coupled with my MBA degree, made me a strong potential candidate for many organizations looking to import that kind of expertise. Both flattered and curious, I decided to explore a few of these possibilities.

I had never worked with recruiters before, and so had no idea what to expect. Someone would call my office, identify themselves as representing a particular job opportunity, then inquire as to whether I wanted to be considered as a candidate and if not, did I know someone else who might. Surprisingly, the recruiter often had minimal information about the organization, asked few relevant questions about my management experience and none about my interests and career goals.

Moreover, when I did interview, I often found the opportunity quite different from that described to me — from the nature of the job to the organization itself. It seemed clear that these recruiters were not serving their clients optimally; sending inappropriate or disinterested candidates is a waste of time and money. However, as I've come to learn, even negative situations can become potential opportunities.

As a result of these disappointing searches, I suddenly realized that an unfilled niche existed: full-service, comprehensive search consulting in the managed care market. True, there were plenty of people out there calling themselves recruiters, but no other firm dealing in that specific market had someone with my credentials.

As a respected physician manager continually interfacing with the national medical community, I felt I could bring a unique perspective to searches. My credibility could further enhance a client company's reputation as I discussed available opportunities with prospective professional candidates.

The other value-added component would be my willingness to develop long-term relationships with fellow physicians, guiding them through the search process — even putting some on the management career path initially, then mentoring them along the way. As I had personally experienced, no one in the search industry seemed interested in investing the kind of time (and thus capital) it takes to develop an individual executive's career, nor does anyone (as far as I know) have the kind of hands-on understanding of the talent pool to give appropriate advice.

Despite the sense that I could do it better, it took many months of soul searching before I actually took the next fork in the road, eventually making the career transition from physician manager to medical management search consultant. My position at UCLA was vested, I had spent almost a decade developing staff and programs I believed in, including collaborations with both UCLA's Anderson School of Management and the School of Public Health, I loved working with the students, and I had been told by my professors in the management school that more new businesses fail than succeed — especially consulting firms. According to an article in *Fortune* magazine at the time, only one new consultancy in five actually thrived. If I really wanted to be an entrepreneur, I had to be willing to take that risk.

Becoming a Consultant

Armed with a business plan, including a mission statement, I finally decided to take the plunge. Starting in 1993, I began to slowly build a firm that initially concentrated only on physician executive searches. As a career counselor to potential candidates, I often spent untold hours evaluating career goals and life priorities, reworking resumes, developing better interview techniques, and assisting with contract negotiations. The best payback has been the satisfaction of having launched many successful management careers, watching these individuals make significant contributions to a variety of healthcare organizations.

Over time, my clients began to request broader services, so I expanded my focus, becoming a consultant for various enterprises, including established as well as start-up health plans, academic institutions, utilization review companies, research organizations, even other healthcare consulting firms. I have helped these organizations build high-performance management teams by identifying appropriate entry, middle, and senior-level non-physician as well as physician management personnel vital for their success. That means fully understanding the organization, from governance to culture, evaluating specific personnel needs, conducting local and national salary surveys as the market changes, keeping close tabs on the interview process from start to finish including contract negotiations and following-up regularly with both the client company and new employee for at least a year after a placement is made to be sure an optimal transition has been achieved.

In 1994, my husband Joel joined me as president of the company. In 1998, we incorporated as Shlian and Associates, Inc., moving our main base of operations to Florida where we could help care for our aging parents.

Both Joel and I stayed active in professional healthcare organizations such as the American College of Physician Executives (now American Association for Physician Leadership) and the Group Health Association of America, always keeping abreast of changes in medicine and in particular, managed care. We also regularly contributed articles and chapters for various textbooks on current management issues. Additionally, we developed affiliations with over a dozen associates with offices across the country, all with strong healthcare backgrounds, whom we could call upon to assist with specific searches. In this way, we were able to service our clients effectively while still maintaining the boutique nature of the company.

Many small business owners feel compelled to expand in order to demonstrate success. However, according to Douglas Handler, an economist at Dun & Bradstreet, longevity rather than growth is the real measure of achievement. "Companies that last three years will usually make it," he claims. "Indeed, if you begin a company to capitalize on the wisdom and personal service of a key individual — namely *you* — big is bad. Adding staff and projects can spread the core value of your firm so thinly that customers are dissatisfied." David Birch, founder of Cognetics, an economic analysis company noted for its studies of small firms, has said: "In the knowledge-based service firm, there are no economies of scale."

After more than 17 successful years, this worked well for us. We continued to enjoy repeat business from clients who hired S&A knowing we were much more involved in the details, we personally knew prospective candidates, and we could do the job more efficiently and less expensively than larger firms with high-rise offices and huge overhead. While a large firm might be able to coast on its reputation, Joel and I never could. If we performed poorly for clients, our business would fail.

Bottom line: Being your own boss is definitely not for the faint of heart, but if your vision triumphs, the success is yours alone and therefore all the sweeter. For me, the shift from a management position in a highly bureaucratic and hierarchical organization to CEO of my own company has been the most exciting and positive experience of my professional life.

In 2009, with responsibilities for parents' care accelerating, we made a conscious effort to slow down our consulting and recruiting business, traveling less and taking on fewer clients. At the same time, we renewed our interest in creative writing.

Joel and I had collaborated on two published medical mysteries while still living in Los Angeles (*Wednesday's Child* with Simon & Schuster and *Nursery* with Berkeley Books), but much to our agent's chagrin, never wanted to give up medicine or medical management to write fiction full time. Now we decided to finish a novel about China that we had been plotting off and on for years. That became *Rabbit in the Moon* and was published by Oceanview Publishing, a small hardback publishing firm that focuses on mysteries and thrillers. *Rabbit in the Moon* has won a number of literary awards, including the Gold Medal for the Florida Book Award (we got to meet the governor); First Place, Royal Palm Literary Award (Florida Writers Association); and the Silver Medal for Best Mystery, *ForeWord Magazine*. The audiobook version even won an Honorable Mention at the Hollywood Book Festival.

In 2019, in honor of the 30th anniversary of the Tiananmen massacre and the short-lived Student Democracy Movement in China, the book was re-published with an updated Foreword. Encouraged by this success, I have written three new medical mystery thrillers in a series starring a feisty young female radio talk show host: *Dead Air*, *Devil Wind*, and *Deep Waters*. All of these were co-written with a former UCLA colleague, Dr. Linda Reid, and have also won a number of literary awards.

In 2019, I completed *Silent Survivor*, the first medical thriller written entirely by me. It won First Place, Royal Palm Literary award. This year, during the COVID lockdown, I co-wrote a children's book about a young rescue pup who decides to run for president on a kindness platform.

Joel in the meantime has developed a new interest in photography, which he finds equally creative, but with more immediate gratification (a novel takes years to write, then about 18 months from the time it is sold until the publisher releases the print version; a photograph can be seen and appreciated right away). The most important lesson these endeavors have taught us is that physicians should develop interests outside of medicine so that the transition to retirement is not a loss of identity. Sadly, a number of our colleagues have sunk into depression the moment they are no longer called "Dr."

Finally, today, as I continue to mentor young physicians, I am always asked about the value of an MBA, particularly by those contemplating switching from clinical medicine to management. I can say with great confidence that for me, the MBA education and the degree itself have made all the difference in my career. As a manager, I was able to directly apply the classroom knowledge to my work, enabling me to expand my role to include much more of the business/operations side of the organization.

As a search consultant, I regularly work directly with CEOs, CFOs, and COOs who appreciate the fact that I can speak their language. Often intimidated by physicians, they feel comfortable talking to a "fellow MBA." As the CEO of my own business, the training in accounting, finance, and marketing has been particularly useful.

Notwithstanding the value of a management education for me, I would advise any physician considering going back to school that an MBA will not provide the same kind of ticket that the MD did. By that I mean, having a business degree on your resume, even from one of the elite schools, is not sufficient to land you a job as a manager, nor is it still generally required for most positions. What really counts is management experience and the ability to show that you have produced tangible results for an organization, often identified by such measures as greater market-share, larger profits, decreased costs, reduced utilization, better outcomes and increased patient satisfaction.

An MBA should never be viewed as the means to "get out of medical practice." In fact, I would submit that if you really hate clinical medicine, medical management is not for you; it can be every bit as demanding and frustrating as clinical practice. Moreover, as the rate of change sweeping America's healthcare delivery system has accelerated, healthcare companies are reinventing themselves, developing competitive strategies that mean greater risk and more uncertainty than ever.

Medical managers entering this brave new world, particularly those at the middle level, need to understand the landscape and be prepared to deal with it. Rather than one by default, the decision to be a manager should be a positive career choice. As the traditional separation of administrative and clinical matters is becoming obsolete, the modern physician manager must be a manager first and a clinician second. Bringing a clinical background to the new role of manager can certainly enrich the job, but does not substitute for specific management skills and training.

Whether medical management as such will ever become a recognized specialty is less important than the fact that only those who understand both the language of business and of medicine will be able to straddle the various camps that now control the practice of medicine in this country.

For me, the career path from clinician to medical manager to CEO of a management search firm has been anything but a straight one. With each opportunity came a choice and a certain risk. But in the end, it has been those forks in the road that have made all the difference.

CHAPTER TWENTY-SEVEN

Six Lessons I Wish I Had Learned Earlier

By Kathleen Goonan, MD

ONE OF THE TEDIOUS THINGS YOU DO WHEN approaching retirement is set up your remote Social Security account access and, if interested, you can look at your entire lifetime earnings, year by year. It is a milestone chore that inspires a stroll down memory lane and, more importantly, a bit of self-reflection.

My first "business" was The Party People. I organized a group of friends to serve and clean at parties in my suburban California Bay Area community. Then I ran a swim program at an athletic club. In college, I lagged peers in identifying a career choice and dabbled in a variety of interests. While considering a career in law, I built a public advocacy group for women in the skilled trades and worked for the California Department of Health Civil Rights Office.

When I landed on a career in medicine, that entrepreneurial and leadership nature helped me navigate my status as a "non-traditional" applicant. But despite my meandering pathway into medicine and a career as a physician executive, I really don't ascribe to the "follow your passions" approach to life planning.

In hindsight, I am convinced that regular and humble self-reflection about your strengths and weaknesses is essential. With deep self-awareness, leveraging your talents while methodically shoring up your weaknesses is the best pathway to making meaningful contributions and experiencing a gratifying and satisfying career. The 10,000-hour rule applies to the complex and rapidly evolving field of healthcare executive leadership: there is a lot to know, and disciplined ongoing learning is critical.

Throughout my life, I've always been drawn to leadership roles. I would describe my primary talents as systems thinking, change leadership, and problem solving within organizations. While in medical school I served as president of the American Medical Student Association, which provided me with tremendous learning opportunities and skills development in communications, writing, negotiation, and advocacy. My systems thinking aptitude inspired me to opt for primary care internal medicine and working with people serving as the liaison between them and the broader health care system.

But I needed to balance my big picture system and culture insights with subject matter experts who have deep expertise in any specialty area essential to success. This takes humility. I'm grateful for having been an athlete growing up, an experience that fosters awareness of the value of teamwork. I have generally tried to balance my strengths with the expertise of teammates. Whether in clinical practice or in administrative roles, I have never tried to do it all myself. Rather, I sought to engage a diverse team with a broad array of talents and perspectives. This creates the best outcomes for patients as well as for organizations.

With these key attributes — self-awareness of strengths and weaknesses, respect for diversity of skill and thought, and admiration for mastery — I found myself completing a residency at the Massachusetts General Hospital in 1985 and being recruited into an administrative role with a Massachusetts group practice and health plan. Since that first position 35 years ago, I have served in executive roles at every station along the healthcare "food chain," from patient care delivery to managed care to consulting.

My first job was not highly sought after, a bit of an internship in administrative work back then, doing prior authorization and discharge planning advising with surgeons. Thankfully, I quickly moved on into quality, performance improvement, and measurement, my area of focus for more than 15 years.

After that, I was again in the right place and the right time and was asked to serve as a national judge for the Baldrige Performance Excellence Award, titled the Malcolm Baldrige National Quality

Award in 1999. It was through that highly intensive volunteer opportunity that I gained my deepest exposure into organizational performance excellence.

By 2003, I had gained a formal systems engineering lens through which to approach executive leadership and problem solving that became my world view going forward. It can be boiled down to a few basic questions: What is the purpose of this organization? How do leaders lead? How does the organization design and accomplish its operations? How do they engage their people and customers? And given all that, what results are they getting in every aspect of performance?

I realize my journey was unusual in that I went into administration four months out of residency. Most move from clinical medicine to management in a slower progression but of course all our journeys are unique. No matter how quickly one transitions into a leadership role, there are basic lessons applicable to all.

I decided to write this chapter as if it were a graduation speech as I look back on my life and career, sharing a few pearls I've collected (in addition to using generous amounts of sunscreen at a much earlier age!).

Define your own, personal "true north" early and often.

When I reflect on how and why I was able to develop leadership skills, I realize that it was only when I pushed the *pause* button, or after someone else encouraged me to push it and clarify *who* I was trying to become, that I moved forward and grew as a leader. I am not talking about job title or function, but about the values I believe in and which now, looking back, I am proud to have lived in my work.

For example, I have always believed in being a truth teller, even when that choice could cost me in the short run. As a senior resident, I was on a team that clearly erred and those errors in diagnosis led to harm to a patient. My fellow senior resident failed to appear at the Morbidity and Mortality Rounds. But I did and owned up to the mistake in front of the group. It hurt. I was scared.

People didn't talk to me afterward, at least not right away, and not comfortably. I knew it was the right thing to do. In the long run, the people I respected appreciated my honesty and transparency. I grew as a physician.

Refining true north periodically is about more than your personal values and behavior. It's about the type of work and roles you are best suited for. I was fascinated with measurement and analysis early in my career. I worked in the Quality of Care Measurement Department at Harvard Community Health Plan under Dr. Donald Berwick in one of my first positions. I partnered with Dr. Brent James in developing and delivering curriculum in this area. It seemed clear to me that this area of expertise would be critical to any leader of a healthcare organization.

Today, this and many areas of administration and executive skill are much more sophisticated. When the field shifted increasingly to technology focus, I moved on to focus on culture and leadership approaches, knowing that others with a deeper interest in the IT fields would carry on in building measurement capabilities.

So, remember to periodically hit the pause button, evaluate your chosen path, and carefully assess the skill development options available as you supplement your medical education in these other areas. Sometimes this means gaining additional degrees, but increasingly on the job training and experience are more valuable and less costly to you.

Define your scope and deliverables.

While I realize this is consultant speak (that's what I do full time these days), everyone does need to do this to be effective. Ideally, your organization and your boss give you a job description and assignments to help you define your goals and deliverables. Unfortunately, in my experience, this often is not the case.

Often, physicians are given a problem to solve or a program to design and manage, and this is your opportunity to prove your aptitudes in executive leadership. Do not shy away. Lean in, teach yourself, find mentors, search for examples to benchmark, and go for it! You may learn more from these opportunities than formal degree programs. Know that you are being tested so use those self-reflection skills and seek out feedback from trusted mentors regularly. Document what you and your team accomplish.

The most effective executives are those who can clearly articulate the scope of their responsibilities and define what they will deliver in terms of results with milestones and timelines. In a sense, they are writing their future resumes with what they have accomplished before they accomplish it. Then of course, they deliver.

As physician executives, we are considered "overhead," i.e., every moment we are not seeing patients costs the organization our salaries. Therefore, we must provide measurable value for our time.

Learn process literacy.

When I had the great fortune to serve as a judge for the Malcolm Baldrige National Quality Award (2000-2003), one of my fellow judges from another industry (as they all were) called healthcare "the bastion of process illiteracy in the U.S. economy." What he meant by this was that we are still a cottage industry of individual professionals and we have yet to view all work, including leadership and management, in terms of processes. If you can't define your multidisciplinary, cross-functional work in processes, how can you hardwire, measure, and standardize work? How can you make it highly reliable and efficient?

I coined the term "process literacy" to refer to this major and critical shift in how we think about our work in healthcare. Leaders in the coming decades will think and work this way. It takes the ego out of our organizations because it makes work less dependent on individuals and more likely to be consistently successful. Perhaps that feature is part of the resistance to making this change? Regardless, high-performance organizations and leaders operate this way.

I will say I think we have improved significantly in terms of standard work and hardwiring processes over the last 10–15 years. The progress is noticeable in the organizations I coach with the investment in high reliability and lean methodologies. But this is a never-ending requirement for high performance organizations, including in how they lead. I still see organizations with very chaotic leadership processes, inefficient meetings and communications, ineffective organizational performance reviews.

Build your self-awareness

We all have strengths and weaknesses as well as talents and personal demons. Every one of us. Highly successful leaders foster their personal awareness of these issues over time. This is a characteristic of highly emotionally intelligent people. This takes discipline and can be learned. In many companies, high-ranking executives are provided personal coaches to help them accomplish this. You can create these relationships from people around you, or choose to hire your own personal coach.

See one, do one, teach one . . .

Remember this old rubric of medical education? Thankfully, it no longer applies in most clinical training settings. However, it still operates in administration. Leadership is learned by observing successful leaders and imitating them as opposed to didactic sessions sitting in a classroom or simulation lab. It also is learned through teaching others.

I encourage you to evaluate your teaching options if you are interested in administration. As a supervisor, you will be expected to be a mentor to those who report to you. Take this role seriously and learn from your organizational development and human resources how to be an effective mentor.

The skills required are typically not taught to doctors because we are thought to be "beyond" this skill. It's not true. Just because physicians have deep content knowledge doesn't mean we also know how to manage and mentor people. Those who become good mentors usually do very well in their organizations. They bring tremendous value that generally gets rewarded. People are more grateful for meaningful mentoring than they are for praise; although generosity in admiring genuine strengths of others is always a good attribute among leaders.

Learn to manage conflict.

This is particularly hard for women. We tend to take things much too personally and get too emotionally involved in relationships with others in the work environment. Strong male leaders are often the best role models for learning to manage conflict. The sooner you learn to manage conflict by remaining detached and focusing on the situation as opposed to personal dynamics, the better off you and your organization will be.

Successful leaders and managers are able to defuse and depersonalize conflict, allowing themselves and others to resolve conflicts with minimal emotional drama. If the priority is the patient, conflicts are a distraction and a waste. Leaders who keep the focus on the patient and effective work on their behalf, always rise above the fray in our stressful work environments. And more often than not, if someone is doing something that irritates or angers you, it's not personal. They are not doing it for you; it's who they are and likely they behave that way with everyone else as well. Develop a capacity to let conflict run off your back quickly and you will be rewarded by reduced stress and great respect from your colleagues.

For those of you who aspire to leadership roles in healthcare, the above few pearls will help optimize both personal gratification and contributions to your organization. Good luck!

CLINICAL RESEARCH

*"If the vision you believe in is different
from the status quo, you must be
dogged in your pursuit of that vision,
let your passion drive you forward,
and be resilient in the face of the
obstacles you will undoubtedly face."*

– LAURA ESSERMAN

CHAPTER TWENTY-EIGHT

Persistence, Passion, and Resilience and How to Create Your Own Path

By Laura Esserman, MD, MBA

IF THE VISION YOU BELIEVE IN IS DIFFERENT from the status quo, you must be dogged in your pursuit of that vision, let your passion drive you forward, and be resilient in the face of the obstacles you will undoubtedly face. Such a goal may require an unconventional path and unforeseen forks in the road. Courage, a thick skin, and constant reassessment of the landscape and your place in it will be your constant companions. To make change, there has to be purpose. To get people to follow you, you must articulate a vision worthy of everyone's best efforts.

I've always been a curious person. As a child I loved every subject, but particularly science and theater. Love of music has enriched my life. I have always indulged my creative side – acting in several shows and writing one in medical school, being in a cappella groups during residency, singing my patients to sleep, and writing and performing musical political parody (including a series of shows called *Audacity*). It is important to me to engage in issues larger than me and my own circle — to contribute to and give back to the greater community in which we live.

I've also always been interested in research, but love combining it with clinical care. As a clinician, you make a difference by how you engage with patients. Even if you can't change the outcome of a particular disease, you can influence how someone experiences their care. Clinical trials and research provide the opportunity to improve outcomes; care provides the opportunity to put research into action. Each provides an antidote to frustration with the other.

As a Stanford medical student, I took full advantage of opportunities to pursue research and to explore the amazing interdisciplinary programs available because the medical school was co-located on the university campus. I was interested in basic and translational science but received a research fellowship in the Department of Engineering Economic Systems (now Management Science and Engineering) where Dr. David Eddy had created a program to introduce students to Bayesian statistics and disease modeling (modeling of cervical and breast cancer screening in particular) to make policy more in synch with biology.

As part of that program, I was able to audit Dr. Alain Enthoven's business school courses in health policy and international variation in care to better understand how to translate new innovations into actual practice.

At the time, most clinicians were not interested in health policy, including modeling. They were hostile to efforts to transform medical practice. So I returned to my interest in translational science, working with Dr. Ron Levy, a pioneer in medical oncology and immunotherapy. I considered him to be the most innovative person at Stanford, the most willing to challenge the reigning paradigm, and to learn how to drive lessons from science into advances for patients.

Dr. Levy was a luminary in lymphoma, not a traditionally surgical disease. My goal was to take what he taught me about changing a treatment paradigm to transform surgical oncology and, in particular, the care of women with breast cancer. The standard at the time was to take women who presented with a mass to the operating room and to make the decision, based on a frozen section diagnosis, to perform a radical mastectomy or not. I realized that science had to change treatment and outcomes for women when I heard a talk from Dr. Craig Henderson, "You Do Not Need an Elephant Gun to Kill a Flea." Given the remarkable variation in tumor biology, there was an absolute need to tailor care to biology in the setting of breast cancer.

When I was chief resident in surgery at Stanford, I asked Professor Enthoven to give grand rounds on his just published book *Health Plan*. At the end of his talk, I asked who he felt should be responsible for training the next generation of physicians in his model of competing integrated healthcare delivery plans. The answer required a longer discussion. I met him at his office, and his response to me was, "You will. I want you to come to the Stanford Graduate School of Business as a Hartford Fellow and learn to apply the principles of modern management to medicine."

While flattered, I felt this "right turn" would be unrealistic and inconsistent with the trajectory I had in mind for my career. I'd spent 10 years training to become an academic surgeon, I was preparing to start my own laboratory and clinical program, I was seven months pregnant, and this request seemed to be very far afield.

Professor Enthoven was persistent, calling every week to check on the status of my application. He envisioned training a new cadre of physicians dedicated to improving the quality of medicine and how it was delivered. Not willing to take "no," he explained why this new path was right for me. I spoke to many people about this new opportunity. For the most part, their reactions were negative — especially the medical school dean and chair of surgery at the time who said I would be "throwing away" my career.

However, at the end of 1990, I knew there was about to be a revolution in healthcare delivery. Better understanding of this emerging landscape could bring to life my personal vision for how to drive science and innovation into clinical medicine, to build and promote the notion of learning healthcare systems.

Only a few people agreed: Ron Levy, Peter Bing, and John Collins, chair of surgery, who inspired me to pursue a surgical career. These were people I admired and that was enough, though it still felt like a big risk. I recognized it would give me a very different perspective, and a set of tools few others would have. These skill would complement my broad training in medicine, research, modeling, and policy. What was the worst that could happen? I'd spend a couple of years learning about other business systems and illuminate my view of healthcare delivery.

To reduce the risk of being excluded from the ability to practice my craft (there were few women in surgery at the time), I arranged to work part time as a faculty member in surgery, to ensure that my skills remained current and that I would be seen as someone serious about the practice of medicine. Business school was not an exit strategy from medicine. I realized I needed to send a strong signal. All it required was an extraordinary effort and energy — similar to how I approach every phase of my career and family life.

Thus began my quest to transform the practice of medicine from the business of cost recovery to service and quality, to create learning healthcare systems driven by science, to generate data from outcomes and patient reported outcomes to continuously learn, improve, and create healthcare value. I wanted to focus on disease management — in this case, breast cancer — across the spectrum of care, from translational and clinical science as well as policy.

During this critical period, I learned that medicine is a business just like other businesses: people respond to incentives; other learning systems models exist, driven through data systems providing continuous learning; teams are required to accomplish big changes; and culture is critical to creating acceptance of new ideas for innovation and patient centeredness to thrive in medicine.

Understanding that a culture around these concepts had to be created, sustained, and nurture informed how I built programs around team science. It informed how I built the I-SPY TRIAL network, the Athena Breast Health network, the WISDOM study. It informed how I created a post-baccalaureate training program to expose young people to the importance of teamwork, bringing multiple disciplines together to drive learning through science and data collection, teaching the importance of listening to the patient voice, imbuing them with the responsibility of taking these principles forward as they build their own careers.

Finally, I learned from my wonderful professor and now great friend and colleague, Jeffrey Pfeffer, that power matters. No idea succeeds if you don't understand the political landscape of your organization(s) and are not strategic in your plan to make change.

It is complex and difficult to build an innovative team culture in medicine. For those building a career in medicine, each promotion step is based on individual effort, not the reliance on others. Medicine attracts people who tend to be risk-averse; those who are more risk takers choose venture capital or become entrepreneurs. Finding a path forward to build a different approach to delivery of services can be challenging.

After business school, I was recruited by Dr. Haile Debas in his last weeks as the chair of surgery at the University of California, San Francisco (UCSF) before he took over as dean of the UCSF School of Medicine. Just as I could not imagine at the time going to business school, I never thought I would leave Stanford and all of the roots and connections I had established there. However, when I laid out my vision for the kind of program I wanted to build around breast cancer, and how it could serve as an example in medicine to change our approach to integrating care and research and building learning systems, he simply said with his broad smile, "Well Laura, I think that is wonderful. Why don't you come and do it here?"

At UCSF, I was able to think about the clinical program as a clinical laboratory to bring critical components of a program together as a demonstration. I have, along with a very talented group of people across all disciplines, built an integrated program for women with all stages of breast cancer. We created a place that is patient centered, honoring the voices, concerns and wishes of our patients. We constantly try to improve treatments we deliver. I have created University of California as well as nation-wide networks to advance the science of personalized medicine for treatment, screening, and prevention of breast cancer.

The work is not done — it is ongoing. In order to succeed, I have been able to secure state and federal funding to build these programs, collaborating with California Breast Cancer Research Program (BCRP), National Cancer Institute (NCI), Food and Drug Administration (FDA), Patient Centered Outcomes Research Institute (PCORI), Department of Defense (DOD), Defense Threat Reduction Agency (DTRA), and Biomedical Advanced Research and Development Authority (BARDA). I founded a non-profit foundation (Quantum Leap Healthcare Collaborative) to help advance systems for the integration of care and research. It includes leaders from disciplines outside medicine who want to see learning healthcare systems flourish.

Interestingly, much of what I have created is through informal, rather than formal power. This has required developing relationships, building teams, and engendering trust. It takes enormous energy and persistence as well as an infectious passion for why it is so important.

The key programs include:

I Spy Trials

The I-SPY-2 TRIAL (Integrating Serial studies to Predict Your Therapeutic Response with biomarker Integration and Adaptive Learning) is a precompetitive collaboration among academic, pharmaceutical, biotechnology, governmental (FDA), and advocate stakeholders. I-SPY has revolutionized the approach to oncology trials, bringing phase 2 drug development to the early stage high-risk setting where the goal is cure, integrating early endpoints, screening 22 agents, and demonstrating that improving response saves lives. The I-SPY consortium includes a collaborative, engaged, investigator network at over 26 US medical centers. Importantly, I-SPY has re-engineered the clinical trial process (including contracting, master protocols, IRB efficiency, data collection), accelerated the pace of getting agents into the trial, and reducing learning cycle time.

In early 2022, the trial will evolve to 2.2 — from adapting within the trial, to adapting therapy for each individual. Importantly, we have developed the mechanism to test and qualify new agents while optimizing the treatment for each patient, helping them achieve the very best outcome. We will be able to test new targeted non-traditional chemotherapy approaches first, and if successful, allow people to skip other unnecessary toxic therapies in the face of a complete response (disappearance of tumor).

Through 10 years of study incorporating quality-of-life measures and toxicity, we've devised a set of serial treatments for those who don't achieve a complete response. These patients will proceed to less-toxic and more effective treatments for their specific biology. Thus, in this landmark change in trials, we can deliver optimal care for each patient and test promising new agents.

It also allows us to continue to focus on improving outcomes (through science) for those with less than optimal response. Our goal is to get 90% of high-risk patients to a complete response within the next five years. It is aspirational, but given the pace of change in the field, it is absolutely achievable if we work in concert.

In April 2020, with the emergence of the pandemic, I began working with Dr. Carolyn Calfee, a pulmonary care faculty member at UCSF who had just completed a year sabbatical with me learning about the I SPY TRIAL platform. We hoped to apply the I-SPY 2 model to acute respiratory distress syndrome (ARDS), the final common pathway that leads to death from COVID infections. We replicated the substantial capability of this platform focused on improving cancer care to focus on the rapid development of new treatments for COVID-19.

In four months, we had repurposed our infrastructure, team approach, distributed leadership, and community building, creating a network to screen new agents for critically ill COVID patients. At the start we had the FDA's and COVID RND consortium's commitment to provide promising marketed and scalable agents. Subsequently, we received support from DTRA and BARDA, which allowed implementation of the trial across 35 sites, the integration of real world evidence, and the implementation of the OneSource platform for data collection.

We have tested more than a dozen agents, are integrating real-time biomarker testing to subtype ARDS, and have accrued over 2,500 patients in less than a year and half. We have demonstrated the scalability of platform trials and learning systems. We have yet to substantially reduce mortality from COVID and ARDS, but the distributed network of investigators and coordinators has the energy, passion, innovative spirit and persistence to solve the problem. With time, I have no doubt that they will.

Athena/WISDOM

In 2009, we established the Athena Breast Health Network, an organization across the five medical centers within the University of California. Our goal was to work together on programs that required a large-scale team effort in order to integrate care and research and to drive the lessons from treatment into the arena of screening and prevention. The leaders at each of the institutions across UCSF, USCD, UCD, UCI, and UCLA have continued to work together for over a decade, driven by the common purpose to provide a better approach to breast cancer care, screening, and prevention. This network has spawned the WISDOM study: Women Informed to Screen Depending On Measures of risk.

There have been rapid advances in our understanding of inherited risk extending beyond the relatively rare inherited single mutations that confer high risk. Over the last decade, we have learned the importance of low risk variations in genes people inherit (single nucleotide polymorphisms or SNPs) which, when combined, comprise polygenic (multiple genes) susceptibility risk or a polygenic risk score (PRS). Increasing information on polygenic risk will continue to improve our ability to predict the risk of breast cancer as well as many other diseases.

In the WISDOM study we are testing the traditional one-size-fits-all approach to screening, against an approach tailoring screening and risk-reduction recommendations based on each individual's personal risk. In the personalized arm, we use both polygenic risk and mutations as part of our approach to assessing risk.

It is essential that we transition to a platform that can accommodate the rapid emergence of new knowledge about SNPs so we can improve our ability to identify specific variants associated with risk across diverse ancestral populations and apply new knowledge about predictors of aggressive cancers. By improving understanding of what drives these aggressive cancers, we hope to learn how to prevent and treat them better – especially in women under age 40 who are currently not being screened. This can only be done if we can predict populations at risk. We also need to reduce over-diagnosis of indolent cancers.

OneSource

OneSource is an initiative to integrate care and research. The goal is to streamline the collection and distribution of patient health data. While electronic health records have been an important step forward, they are not sufficient to help transform medicine to a business around quality and quality improvement. From the time I left business school, I was convinced that without tools that enabled the capture of data as a byproduct of care, quality improvement (QI) would not be routine in medicine and that knowledge turns would be slow.

At the heart of the problem are the lack of data reconciliation, complexity of systems integration, and abundant interoperability gaps. While electronic, clinical trials are carried out by coordinators copying data from clinical care into the research systems. Trials are complex and onerous. Across the country only 3% of adults participate in this engine for learning and change. Doctors, researchers, and patients are trapped in an inefficient system that not only generates high cost, but also creates barriers to trial and registry participation.

I have worked on different approaches to solving this problem over the last 30 years, have partnered with many companies, both big and small. Michael Bloomberg once told me that the problem with healthcare was the lack of concentration of capitol. He might be right. However, there is an open source solution that can radically simplify our approach, and make the transformation of the clinical care process possible.

For the past six or seven years, our strategy has been to partner with the FDA to build a process that would provide them with the data they need to evaluate trials and for us to integrate the data collection seamlessly into the process of care. OneSource is a radical simplification that utilizes the concept of a "checklist" of essential clinical data that all stakeholders require (clinicians, researchers, epidemiologists, clinic managers and so on), with global data standards beneath terms that are familiar to clinicians. This is what allows the integration of care and research. By layering in a clinic process redesign, the clinical data can be entered at the point of care, enabling the identification of critical information, tracking of care progress, and organizing. This approach allows for the entry of critical clinic data once — by the clinician and/or the patient — and serves as the authoritative source. In this way, data is entered once at the point of care and can be used many times, thus providing access for trials, QI, and research.

Ultimately, the vision for OneSource is to create a quality management infrastructure in medicine to enable users to improve healthcare quality, accelerate clinical research, and advance healthcare value. We have partnered with the FDA, the Center of Excellence in Regulatory Science and Innovation, the UCSF Information Technology leadership, and BARDA on the implementation of this effort. We envision that this can be an open source effort that brings about a sea change in how we approach clinical care in the era of personalized medicine. It is now operational in eight of the COVID sites, and hopefully by the middle of 2022, we will have it operational across all of the sites participating in I SPY 2.2 and I SPY COVID.

Will this be sufficient to create change? Not likely, but it may just provide a visible demonstration of what is possible, and that indeed may become the tipping point.

The BCC Internship Program

The premedical UCSF Breast Care Center Internship Program is a highly competitive program. We offer recent undergraduates and post-baccalaureate graduates the opportunity to gain 1-2 years of experience contributing to progress in basic science, clinical research, and patient care. Our vision is to sustain our program as a demonstration of a "Premedical Corps," similar in spirit to the Peace Corps or Teach for America.

In such programs, young people work as research assistants while gaining experience working in areas of high need for a few years before continuing their educational and professional journeys. One day a week, interns help patients prepare for their appointments by developing a question list, then taking notes for then as a "patient scribe." This provides the critical perspective of listening as a patient advocate, to understand first-hand what it is like to be on the other side of medical care. The program provides planned turnover in the research staff and includes a robust training program, with overlap from one class to the next.

This program, created in 2005, has grown every year to include more robust experiences, larger and more impactful scientific research, as well as more hands-on training with patients and mentors. The program enables us to have planned turnover and a very stable work force. I based this on my going to business school after completing medical training. My maturity from the perspective of having worked in another domain enhanced the graduate school experience.

As a result of my MBA training, I have been able to provide a perspective on the importance of integrating care and research and the need to possess persistence, passion, and resilience. I've gone on to work with many interns as they became faculty or entrepreneurs in the field of medicine. For me, there is nothing more rewarding than helping launch someone's career. Perhaps the most lasting legacy anyone can have is to see his or her ideas carried on by the next generation.

On Passion and Persistence

You must be willing to take calculated risks. It isn't easy to change paradigms. If you want to make change, you have to be willing to continually work at it. If you're passionate about bringing positive change, you're much more likely to weather the inevitable storms you'll encounter. Passion and persistence are essential, but must be supplemented with the requisite skills in leadership. For me, finding a coach helped make me a better leader. If you want to excel in anything, I believe you must train and be coached. Leadership is no exception.

I have set about to change some of the standard care approaches preventing progress. Not all of these changes have been welcome. Over time, I've learned how to approach change by finding the win-win for everyone. In the mid-1990s one of my first tasks was to integrate all the disciplines and have one place where patients could go for their care so they didn't have to cobble together all of their care themselves. I was able to do this because Dean Debas, along with the hospital CEO, gave me the authority as the program director to make the change. However, to alter the order of treatments I had to convince surgeons and medical oncologists to change.

I was fortunate to have great colleagues. One in particular who came to UCSF when I did was Dr. Hylton, who was building the sequences for what became breast MRI. Together we showed how differently people responded to treatment, making a compelling case for changing the standard approach to treating breast cancer which has been starting with surgery first and then using "adjuvant" therapy after. Taking the tumor out first precludes the ability to learn about an individual's response to therapy and pushes the field to adopt standard guidelines for all patients, instead of tailoring to response. It has required going up against powerful status quo advocates. Making change is a long game, requiring persistence and passion.

The same is true for the treatment of stage 0 or "in situ" cancer. This is largely a diagnosis that came about when we started population mammographic screening. Standard of care is to operate on all women presenting with this condition. But this is an approach that is hugely frustrating to women and the data suggest that for many, it is overtreatment. Again, starting with a careful surveillance program, using imaging to assess response, we've shown that there is a different and better path forward. Importantly, this can provide the path for personalized prevention and treatment.

Breast cancer screening recommendations are confusing and controversial. Despite our best efforts, 40,000 women in the United States die every year from breast cancer. We can and we must do better. If breast cancer is not one disease and every woman does not have the same risk, it doesn't make sense to take a one-size-fits-all approach to screening. It uses enormous resources and affects every woman. We should be focusing on how to improve our approach. Unfortunately, largely because of politics, this has become extremely challenging. All attempts for change have engendered great criticism and antipathy from many in the imaging, medical oncology, and philanthropy communities.

However, over time, I've learned how to better express concern and the desire to provide better options going forward. Using the example of the cell phone, I explain why it is so very important to integrate screening with risk assessment and prevention. Thirty years ago the only way to call someone when you weren't home was to use a pay phone. Today almost everyone has a smart phone. New information, new technology brought that change. In the same way, three decades of data demonstrating that breast cancer is not one disease and that women have different risks factors, requires change in the way we approach breast cancer screening. Hence the WISDOM study.

Many in the radiology community have not supported the WISDOM study. For this reason, we decided to run it as a patient-centered initiative. Internists have increasingly supported us. We have had to be resilient and continue to find the right platform and approach. Despite the pandemic, over 43,000 women have consented to participate. Hopefully that number will double in the next year. This study has required passion, persistence, and resilience as well as a belief that a new approach to screening and prevention will provide a much better path forward (if you are reading this and you are between 40 and 74, and have not had breast cancer, please go to WISDOMstudy.org and join us!)

The final example of leadership is the need for tools that integrate care and research. Trying to create change is not possible without the buy-in and cooperation of hospital and Information technology leadership. The work with the FDA created the basis for the interest in trying to make OneSource feasible at UCSF. It was not enough to say that we wanted to learn from every patient we see. It was essential to have a powerful ally who also saw the enormous value and transformative power of enabling data to be collected once — at the source — in a format that would not only serve clinicians and patients, but seamlessly populate clinical trial systems.

This has the power to streamline both clinical and clinical research processes. And it will enable decision support to be more readily available, including clinical trial matching systems such as the one we built in breast cancer (Breastcancertrials.org). We have not yet accomplished the transformation of healthcare practices, but I hope that interest in this approach will exponentially grow over the next 5-10 years.

I believe the changes we are advocating will make an enormous difference for people everywhere. That is what fuels me. Passion for what you are doing is essential if you are to weather the many battles required to make meaningful change.

On Work/Life Balance

I met my husband, Michael Endicott, in college when I was 19. He is also passionate about the world around him, an environmental activist, lawyer, and political consultant who has now developed a second career as an artist — a photographer. We have been particularly lucky to share many interests, including a love of the outdoors, politics, reading, and family.

Michael has always been incredibly respectful of and supportive of the work that I do. One could say this is lucky — and indeed it is — but I would never have married someone who didn't celebrate the things I was passionate about and respect the person I was and am. Our house is always full, with many projects and people visiting or staying with us (visiting students, colleagues, artists). I love to cook and find that all ideas blossom over good food!

My two children are the love of my life. My eldest, Marisa Endicott, is a very talented writer and investigative reporter. She will be an investigative columnist for the Santa Rosa *Press Democrat* as of January. My son is completing his third year at Berkeley Law focusing on juvenile justice reform and will be a public defender working for the Bronx Defenders starting this summer.

I am incredibly proud of them. They are independent and feisty thinkers with big hearts and amazing appetites for growth and learning and a desire to make the world a better place. I have learned so much from them, and am intensely interested in the story they are writing with their lives.

I worked a lot and had crazy hours — and still do. We ate late, but always together as a family. When I traveled, I took a red eye and tried to return the next night. Once a year I took each child out of school to take a business trip with me. We read books aloud until they went to college. To this day we pick one to read on family vacations. My family knows that I love them and that working on other important endeavors doesn't diminish that love.

As for work-life balance, I can only quote what my son told me when he was 16: "Well Mom, I would not say that anything about you is balanced, but somehow you make it all work."

My advice to young women building their careers: Make sure you get enough help, even if you have to go into some debt for a while to do so. You need someone to help run your household so that you'll have time to be with your children whenever you get home. Remember, there is no one way to do things. Do what works for you and your schedule; don't be wed to a schedule that someone writing advice books insists is the best path forward.

On Resilience

Since the beginning of my career, I have had a vision for what I want to do — not the specifics, but the concepts. I wanted to build a patient-centered, science, and data-driven program where innovation could flourish, where the pace of change in medicine could keep pace with scientific advances, where we would learn from every person we cared for, and that value to patients and shared decision-making would be paramount, where we would have data to challenge reigning principles, and to discover options more acceptable to patients than those we offered when I finished my training.

There have been innumerable times when the steps toward this vision were not successful, when the ideas did not pan out. Every time a door is closed it is important to reflect on why. My approach has always been to regroup and find the next open door (or find one that is slightly ajar and open it!). Pivoting often gets you to a better place faster.

I never doubted the vision I had was the correct one. The many grant and manuscript rejections or snubs from those in powerful positions can certainly be hurtful or annoying. But at the end of the day, no one sees that. They only see what has gone forward, what has been published, what paradigms have changed, and the success of the people you train. Rejections simply spur you to re-examine the

332

principles underlying the ideas and topics, to refine your analyses, and to continue to improve and push forward with renewed effort, clearer data and more compelling explanations and analogies. Over time, the body of your work and that of your colleagues creates a force for change.

The lesson is that each rejection has something to teach you. It is not a cause for giving up your ideas or dreams, but merely a temporary setback. That is true of leadership positions as well. When specific leadership positions did not come my way (in some cases because people thought I was perhaps too focused on my mission), I was able to pivot and move my efforts to focus on programs and projects that specifically advanced my vision for personalized medicine, and learning healthcare systems. It was probably lucky for me, as I might not have been able to dedicate the necessary effort to bringing the large scale endeavors to fruition. When things don't go your way, look for the silver lining.

Nevertheless, it is important to possess sufficient power to make change. When I couldn't quite find the right community to lead to create this vision, I created networks that could advance the vision — I SPY, ISPY COVID, Athena, WISDOM — based on the goal of creating a continuous learning engine able to drive change more rapidly. It is important to find ways to take the principles of building infrastructure that are flexible, re-useable and efficient — not to build one trial or enter one patient's data, but to build a platform that supports learning so our efforts can be spent driving change and improvement. I've learned that both formal and informal power are critical. Informal power requires more cogent and compelling arguments to drive change forward. And that is good discipline.

Ultimately, the road to change requires inspiring young people to dedicate their lives to the same type of vision. That is what will change the field. And that is why I cherish the internship training program, and now the T-32 training grant, and my role as a mentor for countless students, residents, postdoctoral fellows and faculty.

There is much left to do. The future is unwritten. I am excited to keep turning the pages to see how the story turns out.

CHAPTER TWENTY-NINE

Empowering Ourselves and Others

By Katherine Neuzil, MD, MPH

THIS IS THE YEAR THAT I TURN 60. It is difficult to comprehend. My age is more than a decade beyond the age of my parents when they died – mid 40s for both of them. Ironically, it's the age when, like many women, I suspect, that I can fully dedicate myself to personal goals and the legacy I wish to leave.

It is also the time to travel more, to play more tennis and to enjoy my good health, knowing the latter is my greatest privilege. After decades of school, training, and raising three kind, independent children with goals of their own, my last child graduated from college this year. I am an "empty nester" and looking forward to the freedom and opportunities that provides.

I was raised in a middle class, blue-collar family in the Maryland suburbs of Washington, DC, in what many would consider a traditional upbringing. My father, the oldest son of Croatian immigrants and a high school graduate, was savvy and driven — a self-employed small businessman with several contracting/construction companies. He learned the trade as a US Navy Seabee in World War II.

My mother, the daughter of an Irish alderman and a homemaker in Pittsburgh, did it all. She was a high-energy, independent woman who, in addition to caring for her four children and the household and volunteering at school, helped my dad with his business and worked outside the home during a few lean years when most of our disposable cash was in my dad's business.

My brother and two sisters and I — I was number 3 of 4 — went to Catholic school and grew up in a close community. Academic excellence, respect for others, and dedication to family were expected. I loved to read from a young age; and biographies were my genre of choice. I was in awe of Helen Keller, Abigail Adams, Clara Barton, Harriet Tubman, and Louisa May Alcott. Every yearbook in grade school attests to my goal of becoming the first woman president — a goal that is more achievable today than it was when I was 10 years old.

The nontraditional part of my upbringing came in my adolescent years. My father died of rapidly progressive cancer when I was 12, and my mother died of a brain hemorrhage when I was 14. This landed me in "Orphans Court" where my younger sister and I testified that we wanted to stay in our current home and live with my brother, then only 22 years old, and my sister, 20 years old.

My brother became my legal guardian, and life went on with a gaping hole that was rarely discussed, and lots of hard work and odd jobs by all of us to pay the bills. I chose to stay in my all-girls Catholic school and work to pay the tuition because I enjoyed the friendship, environment, and freedom that came with an all-girls education. I appreciated the uniform that hid my inability to afford new clothes, the lack of posturing for the boys, and the ability to be involved in sports and leadership roles without gender boundaries.

Next, it was on to the University of Maryland, College Park, where as a Maryland State Scholar I was able to attend school tuition-free. The odd jobs continued — refereeing basketball, cleaning houses, working at the Student Health Center, lifeguarding — to pay my living expenses. There wasn't a lot of time for political involvement or even career counseling.

My love and aptitude for science and my experience with two personal medical tragedies had me headed toward a nursing career. A former high school teacher asked if I had ever considered medical school – honestly, I had not. That type of career was never part of my world. But I followed up on the idea, and long before the internet, I researched medical schools.

I applied to five schools because I could not afford the application fees of more. I went to only two interviews because I couldn't afford out of state travel, and was thrilled and overwhelmed to be accepted to Johns Hopkins University School of Medicine. I initially turned it down for financial reasons, and am grateful to the financial team at Hopkins who worked with me to provide a combination of scholarships and student loans that eventually allowed me to accept the position — a decision that would change my life in many ways.

My years at Johns Hopkins were the first time I had the freedom to focus on my career goals and I saw the world as offering endless opportunities. Infectious diseases and vaccinology became an immediate favorite; it was amazing to me that we had the scientific ability to prevent disease in entire populations.

This was the mid-1980s, and the world was also grappling with a new virus and a new disease: AIDS. I cared for many tragic cases of AIDS as a student and beyond, and witnessed stark health inequity for the first time. I attended many of my patients' funerals. It was impossible to not be changed by that epidemic.

I met my future husband at Johns Hopkins — we married two days after graduation — and headed to Vanderbilt University to begin what would be eight years of training for him in vascular surgery, and seven years of training for me in infectious diseases and public health.

Honestly, we moved to Nashville with more than a little trepidation. My husband Dan was from Seattle, and I had lived my entire life in Maryland. The culture and reputation were different. The newspaper was, well, a local newspaper, with local headlines rather than national politics to which I had been accustomed growing up with the *Washington Post*.

What began with hesitation ended with a love of a city and community that exists today. Southern hospitality and friendship is real, and Dan and I were welcomed into the community with more barbecues, pool parties, and casseroles in the first few months than we had experienced in our young lives.

At Vanderbilt, I established professional relationships that have become lifelong friendships. My mentors at Vanderbilt read like a catalog of Who's Who in Infectious Diseases and Vaccinology, and three decades later we have come together to fight the COVID-19 pandemic. I have always appreciated my great fortune to have trained with and been supported by this stellar group of individuals.

While still in training, my husband and I had two sons and our world was changed for the better. This is one of the most tenuous times for women faculty — those years with young children. It is tempting to move to part-time work or to careers with defined hours. I wouldn't be truthful if I said I never considered it. However, I loved what I did, and I hoped that my career would be long. I wanted something that would challenge me for 30 years or more.

The additional benefits to my family were children who grew up with "normal" being two full-time working parents, sharing the housework, and the school and sports drop-offs. We both fell asleep while reading the kids their bedtime stories. There was certainly a division of labor between my husband and me: I was better at play dates and filling out the school forms and he usually handled the yard work and the dog walks. We both made meals and did the dishes; he coached the baseball teams and I coached the basketball teams. For the most part, however, duties were shared equally. I smile when I see my grown sons sharing housework as the norm and not the exception.

Without family in Nashville to help, the work-life balance and finances were challenging and a good night's sleep was rare. The next juncture in our lives came when training ended. We loved Nashville, but we missed family — Dan's in Seattle and mine in Maryland. We wanted our children to have extended family, so we chose to move to Seattle so the children could be near their only living grandparents.

Dan had a job when we moved, and I did not – leading several of my mentors to caution about "following my husband." But I was confident, and I wasn't moving just anywhere; I was moving to one of the epicenters of the infectious diseases universe: the University of Washington, and the start of the Bill and Melinda Gates Foundation's work in global health. I had no choice but to be independent of my mentors back in Vanderbilt and to establish my own research in Seattle. In a division heavy with critically important HIV and sexually transmitted diseases work, I studied vaccine-preventable diseases of children and adults.

The first year in Seattle was not easy, and looking back. I am fortunate to have faced this year with the energy of youth! I was pregnant with my third child, living in a new city, working in a new job. Of course my number one stress continued to be childcare – something that will resonate with women two decades later.

We had a series of unfortunate events: two stolen cars, a sewage disaster, an electrical surge that fried all of our appliances. I recall my husband and I walking into Sears with two young boys and a newborn, pointing to the first refrigerator, oven, and dishwasher we saw, and saying, "We'll take one of each." We gradually become part of the school and neighborhood communities there, and it is impossible to thank every person who stepped forward in my life to help in big and small ways — another group of friends whom I will cherish forever.

Meanwhile, on the career front, my daughter made her first trip to work with me when she was three days old so I could meet with new colleagues to get the Shingles Prevention Study off the ground. Meanwhile, my mentors back in Vanderbilt continued to push my career along, recommending me for policy committees, journal reviews, editorials, and talks, and listening at the other end of the phone when the day was particularly challenging.

After seven years with the University of Washington, another opportunity came along: to lead the Rotavirus Vaccine Program at PATH, a global health nonprofit based in Seattle that worked closely with the Gates Foundation. Here in the United States, we had just recommended vaccines to prevent rotavirus and human papillomavirus. At this time, children in other countries did not have access to these vaccines, even though their morbidity and mortality from the consequences of these infections was greater.

This was a big step. I loved academics, and had just been promoted to associate professor. Would I be able to return to academics? Would I forever scar my children by traveling too much? In the end, I was inspired by the mission of PATH and motivated by the opportunity to take my learnings from domestic vaccine research and apply them internationally. I took the job at PATH. With the support of the University of Washington leadership, I retained my academic appointment there so I could continue to teach and to mentor students and research trainees.

Professionally, the next decade was one of the most memorable of my life. I traveled the world, met new people, and did impactful work on rotavirus, human papillomavirus, Japanese encephalitis, influenza, and other vaccines. My family and friends supported me throughout, and for four of those years we had live-in au pairs who cared for our children and broadened their horizons.

I traveled to dozens of low-resource countries and collaborated with leaders in countries around the world and with colleagues at WHO, CDC, NIH, GAVI, UNICEF, domestic and international vaccine manufacturers, and the Gates Foundation. At PATH, I learned leadership and business practices that I had not learned in academics. While not the major emphasis at PATH, I continued to publish peer-reviewed manuscripts, hold leadership positions in professional societies and policy committees, and lecture nationally and internationally.

My children were able to accompany me on occasion, although not as much as I would have liked given their school and extracurricular schedules. I have a treasure trove of stories: encountering a family of warthogs while jogging, being a stowaway on a South African tour bus in Senegal, and eating some interesting (and delicious!) food. My most gratifying moments were in the later years, seeing children receiving vaccines on which our team had worked. I always (and still) bring beach balls for the kids — they pack easily, can be "assembled" in the field, and yield lots of laughs. Of course the staff at Target are always puzzled when I empty their shelves of beach balls just before a trip.

In 2015, I had the opportunity to return to Maryland to lead the Center for Vaccine Development and Global Health at the University of Maryland School of Medicine. A renowned institution, they were recruiting a leader to succeed the founding director, a legend who led the center for 40 years. The goals of the CVD aligned with my own: achieving health equity through research and delivery of vaccines domestically and internationally.

A primary driver for my interest in returning to academics was to nurture the next generation of vaccine leaders. My mentors had been so generous during all stages of my career; it was my turn to do the same. While not intentional, most of my direct trainees since joining CVD have been women. I am as inspired by them as I was by my mentors. These women are resilient, innovative, dedicated, and independent, and I am convinced they will change the world.

What did I value in my mentors? While I always appreciated the advice and support that they gave, what I valued most were the opportunities they provided for me, the ways they empowered me, and the confidence they gave me to take chances and make the bold next step. We need to create opportunities for others. I am confident the next generation will rise to the challenge. And perhaps we will finally get that first woman president.

PROFESSIONAL ORGANIZATIONS: AMWA AND JOINT COMMISSION

"Building a team starts with a foundation of trust, and from there, it's important to tap into each member's passions and strengths to optimize their contribution, rather than force an agenda that can feel like drudgery."

– ELIZA CHIN

CHAPTER THIRTY

When the Detour Becomes the New Road

By Eliza Chin, MD, MPH

WHEN I STARTED MY CAREER IN MEDICINE, I thought that my path would be linear. After all, everything up to that point had been with a direct goal in mind. Looking back, I couldn't have been more wrong. And as I reflect on the past two-and-a-half decades, sometimes I am amazed at the zig-zagged route I have taken. Yet what seemed then like a series of detours, somehow through chance and circumstance have led me to where I am now.

Motherhood

As a third-year internal medicine resident, I had my future mapped out. I had been accepted to Columbia University's General Medicine Fellowship (which included a master's degree in public health) and would be joining my husband, a reconstructive surgery resident at New York University. But when I became pregnant with our first child, I realized that having a baby at the beginning of a two-year fellowship, affording quality childcare, and living in New York City on two trainee salaries was going to be hard enough, not to mention the responsibilities of patient care, resident teaching, public health courses, and research.

In order to pay both rent and childcare, it became clear that one of us would need to get a job with a real salary. One of the hardest decisions I would ever make was to send a resignation letter to my future fellowship program director. Even though I knew that it was the right decision for me personally, I felt that I had let the program down.

But then what next? Finding a clinical job in a city where I had no connections turned out to be harder than I had expected. Besides the Yellow Pages, I really didn't even know where to begin. In the spring, I found myself at the Society of General Medicine Conference, and a mentor told me that the same fellowship program director, when he heard that I was looking for a job, had encouraged me to talk to him.

To this day, I will be ever grateful to Dr. Steven Shea. Not only did he offer me a position that allowed a start date four months after my delivery date, but he allowed me to work 75% time and join the division as a clinician educator. I had not seen myself as qualified to apply for an academic position, but here was an unbelievable offer. I was even able to enroll in the MPH program part-time and thus complete the master's degree program during my years at Columbia. While one door had shut, another had opened.

Voices of Women in Medicine

Shortly after the birth of my second child, I found the juggling act of managing a career with family to be even more challenging. My husband was still in his seven-year joint surgical residency and his hours were long and unpredictable. How had my physician mentors made it look so easy? Though I eagerly read books about being a working mother, the demands of being a physician mom seemed to be different. I yearned to hear from other women physicians and secretly dreamed of one day compiling a book of stories. This was the era before social media and blogs.

That dream would sit dormant for over a year and likely would have remained a figment of my imagination had I not stumbled across the piece "Doctor's Daughter" in the *Annals of Internal Medicine* in 1999. Reading another physician's story made me realize that others might also want to share their experiences. And so began my journey as a physician writer with the help and encouragement of my colleague and mentor, Dr. Rita Charon, then director of the Program in Narrative Medicine at Columbia University, and Janet Bickel, then an associate vice president and director of women's programs at the Association of American Medical Colleges.

In the days before social media, outreach was through snail mail, email, fliers, and word of mouth. The book project would become my main link to fellow physicians during the years I was a stay-at-home mom as we relocated the family for my husband's fellowship training and practice. I became inspired with the stories of women in medicine and delved into historical writings to learn more about the pioneer women physicians who had forged the paths before us. My anthology, *This Side of Doctoring: Reflections from Women in Medicine,* was published in 2002.

Association Leadership

My desire to connect with women physicians led me to the American Medical Women's Association (AMWA). My first AMWA meeting in Atlanta, Georgia, in 2003 was the first time I traveled without my three young children. Within AMWA, I discovered a community of likeminded peers and mentors. That meeting would be the start of a decade of volunteer leadership, first as a branch president and later as a committee chair and board member. I was inspired to be part of an organization with nearly a century of legacy. I aspired one day to join the line of luminary women presidents, from the founder Dr. Bertha Van Hoosen to renaissance physician Dr. Esther Pohl Lovejoy, to New York's first woman ambulance surgeon of New York City Dr. Emily Dunning Barringer, to my mentor Dr. Leah Dickstein.

But I also knew that the organization was challenged by limited staffing, recent tax law changes, and the struggles that every non-profit faced after the 2008 stock market crash. Years earlier, some in AMWA had even questioned whether the organization had served its purpose and could retire to a glorious sunset. I began to worry that if I waited too long, there might not be an organization to lead, so despite being the youngest candidate in recent years, I threw my name in for president-elect.

At that time, I was working part-time as a primary care physician and a utilization review consultant. Compared to others, I had no high-ranking academic title or decades of work experience, but I had a deep passion for the mission of the organization, an unflinching work ethic, and a willingness to embrace new ideas and partnerships.

So began my presidency of AMWA in 2010-2011, at a time of enormous healthcare reform and exciting changes at on the national level within the White House and the Department of Health and Human Services. Over the next few years, AMWA continued to grow as a new generation of physician leaders invested their time, resources, and passion in the vision and mission of the organization. I continued to remain involved in various leadership capacities and will always credit AMWA for providing the training ground where I first understood governance and learned to use parliamentary procedure, manage budgets, and interpret financial spreadsheets.

Reentry to Clinical Medicine

After staying home to raise my children during our family moves, I decided that it was time to return to clinical practice. I sent my resume out locally and interviewed with a few groups, but my desire for part-time work ended up being a barrier for any serious job prospects. It was a year later when one practice contacted me again. Would I be interested in providing primary care in a senior care community?

While I had not trained specifically in geriatrics, the practice set up could not have been better, so I enthusiastically accepted. Later, additional per diem work opened up in an occupational medicine clinic. Over the next decade, these two areas of work would constitute my part-time practice, allowing me the flexibility to adjust my work schedule around school hours. I came to love geriatric medicine, and the relationships I established with both my patients and their families would constitute some of the most formative years of my career.

Being in an off-site satellite allowed me the luxury of spending time with patients to provide the quality of care that I felt was necessary during these important years of a patient's life. Later when I stepped into a medical director role, I gained insights to the challenges within our healthcare system and sadly also the realization that physicians, like nurses, were often considered dispensable, as easily replaceable as the next – despite the intangible losses with each upheaval.

Association Leadership Reprised

Two years after my presidency of AMWA, another opportunity opened up within the association. A call had been put out for a part-time physician executive director. I knew at once that this was the job that I had unknowingly been working toward during all my years as a volunteer leader. While I didn't necessarily have formal business training, my recent presidency and past participation on key committees had provided intense on-the-job training. And there was not a facet about the organization that I did not know. Years of volunteer leadership had fortuitously paid off.

Taking on the role of executive director was like being the founding entrepreneur of a start-up company in more ways than one. Beyond an association management company and a cadre of dedicated volunteer leaders, we had little support staff. But within the leadership there was a deep sense of connection and mutual purpose. I felt like an intern all over again, both in terms of salary and schedules. Yet despite those limitations, I had never felt more professionally fulfilled. The alignment of my work and my passion had never been so well matched.

Thanks to the commitment of the leadership, each year was more successful than the next. We began to realize that not only was AMWA still relevant, but our voice was very much needed to advocate on issues that directly impacted women physicians. Over the past eight years, we have expanded membership and built up a revenue base to add staff and new programs. We are tackling relevant issues like physician fertility, gender equity, and physician mental health. Three years ago, we outlined a new strategic plan to lay out a roadmap for the future. The years of hard work had been worth it, and we set our sights on the vision for the next century.

Lessons Learned

I've learned that organizational leadership is vastly different from individual leadership. This can be more challenging for us as physicians because we are accustomed to leading clinical teams and being solicited for our individual expertise and perspective. Serving an organization, however, requires a different set of metrics and a putting aside of one's personal opinions to represent the position of the association. For physicians, this can take some adjustment, but for most, it is a skill that can be learned.

I've learned that building a team starts with a foundation of trust, and from there, it's important to tap into each member's passions and strengths to optimize their contribution, rather than force an agenda that can feel like drudgery. Discovering Patrick Lencioni's work was a gamechanger for me, both to understand why things weren't working and find ways to harness the natural gifts of each leader. I gained keener insights as to what areas of work were likely to lead to burnout for both myself and my colleagues. This perspective is particularly important in an association like AMWA, because when volunteer work begins to feel like a grind, that is about the fastest route to disengagement. The process also highlights the fact that everyone has a strength that is needed for the team to succeed. The key is to find and engage those strengths.

I've seen that teamwork is easier if everyone is following the same North Star. This concept is easier to understand in sports when the goal of winning the game is apparent to all. Within organizations, however, team members may come with priorities of their own. In those situations, it's important to ensure that the mission and goals of the association come first.

When everyone is working toward the same goal, differences in opinion are welcomed as diverse perspectives and robust conversations to achieve the best solution can take place. There are no winning or losing viewpoints because all perspectives have been critical in reaching a final consensus. When goals are different, however, differences in opinion are seen as dissension and can lead to some feeling like winners or losers, or worse yet, to a breakdown of the team's trust.

I've realized that partnering with others helps you get to the same goal faster. I'm a big believer in sharing both the work and the credit, because lifting each other up means that we all go farther. Leadership does not have to mean ownership; in the nonprofit world, the former is far more important.

I've seen that equity has many shades. As an Asian American and daughter of immigrants, I am all too aware of the biases that exist still today. Yet even as one often dismissed as being part of the "model minority," I know that my ethnic heritage has been part of my consciousness for as long as I can remember. Would my input carry more weight if I looked different? Probably. Have I ever recruited colleagues to convey a message because it might be heard differently? Definitely.

Finally, I've learned that executive coaching works. I never thought that I would have the time nor resources to incorporate coaching into my life, but now I can't imagine doing my job without it. What finally motivated me to seek coaching was the need for mentorship in navigating complex organizational dynamics, and what I gained as a result were lifechanging insights about leadership, team building, and communication.

I now see coaching as a vital part of leadership training. Without it, directing an organization is like learning chemistry without the lab. Simply understanding principles may not always be sufficient. Having them reflected back through coaching helps us apply those principles to the work that we do and the relationships that we build.

Giving Grace

There is no doubt that the past few years have been tumultuous, both within medicine and society at large. This is most certainly a time of change and a time of learning, no matter one's age or experience. It has been a humbling experience. Perhaps because I am on the "learning" side of the continuum, I often feel that we as a society – and as a profession – don't give each other enough grace, or enough time to grow and change. It's like teaching someone to ride a bike but expecting success on the first try.

And then there is the compounded challenge of social media. Failing is hard enough, but when one person's failure becomes another person's public messaging platform, it magnifies that experience of failure a hundredfold. Yet it doesn't have to be a zero-sum game, does it?

Maybe if we all took the time to listen more actively, walk a mile in another person's shoes, realize that we each have learning of our own to do, we can be more generous in giving the grace that will help others grow and move forward in their own journeys. That is the type of leader that I aspire to be.

Gratitude

It's been eight years since I stepped into the executive director role in AMWA. I love where I am now — to have work that I relish every day (albeit long days) is a gift. To be in a role that allows me to innovate, forge meaningful relationships, and make an impact in healthcare was not even a "job" I thought possible when I first set out as a physician. I still have a small hand in the clinical world, as medical director of an assisted living community. Though I no longer have direct patient care responsibilities, I feel fortunate to be working with colleagues who value my input and contributions.

I have often admired other physician leaders for their bold career moves. Although my journey has also evolved over the years, those transitions have been mostly gradual and often serendipitous. Yet somehow, despite an unconventional path in medicine (which at one point admittedly felt stalled and even backwards), I have finally come into a career that has been deeply rewarding.

For one who gave up personal goals in the early years to focus on family, it has been an unexpected gift to have a career where I can nurture my own aspirations, even as my children come into their own adulthood. My advice to others is this: never be afraid of exploring the detours along the way, even if they don't promise the traditional metrics of success. If it is your passion, that detour may very well end up being your new road.

CHAPTER THIRTY-ONE

You Are Worthy of
Your Dreams

by Ana Pujols-McKee, MD

I AM THE DAUGHTER OF PEPE AND DONA PACA, an electrician and a teacher who migrated from Puerto Rico to New York City. Like many others, they came in pursuit of better opportunities for their growing family.

My two sisters and I were raised in the South Bronx and spent many summers in Puerto Rico with our cousins and extended family. Our home was a very traditional Puerto Rican home. Spanish was the only language allowed. I learned English in school.

Education was highly prized by my parents. There was never a doubt that the three daughters would receive a university education. As small children we were frequently asked, "What are you going to be when you grow up?" My sisters would answer "a teacher" but I shouted out, "a doctor."

Over the years I witnessed The South Bronx deteriorate into a drug-infested community where survival was challenging. Abandoned residential buildings were popping up everywhere and fell victim to arsonists. It was common to see five-story buildings go up in flames. When the fires were squelched, we were left with the dark skeletons of vibrant, once-occupied buildings.

The schools were a mirror image of the devastation that existed outside their doors. By the time I entered junior high school, the conditions in the schools had deteriorated beyond belief. This was not a school with sports teams, science labs, or art studios.

I remember hearing screams in my school after someone found a fetus in the bathroom, and the horror of a desk being thrown out of a fourth floor window. But the saddest thing of all was a student trying to murder a teacher with a knife in a hallway packed with students. These memories still haunt me.

Since I was considered a good student I was placed in advance classes with the best teachers. The irony was that the school was in such a state of disrepair and hopelessness that even the teachers who were considered the "best" were woefully inadequate. For my science project in seventh grade, my science teacher had me cook "arroz con pollo," a traditional Puerto Rican dish for him. I knew then that the science teacher was incapable of teaching science and that he therefore turned his attention to other meaningless things. Not having a sound early science foundation left me feeling insecure and that would trouble me for years.

My parents were my salvation. They were two uncompromising individuals who were fully committed to raising three successful daughters regardless of what was lurking in the neighborhood. My parents worked hard to try and overcome what we did not get in the classrooms. They provided us with encyclopedias, numerous musical instruments, music classes, and travel.

My teachers in the South Bronx never believed me when I would report back on my summer vacation trips to Canada, Cuba, Dominican Republic, and Puerto Rico. Their disbelief was based on their impression that children in the South Bronx never crossed the Bronx River — never mind got on a plane.

My parents were masters at inspiring us. They repeatedly told us we could be whatever we wanted to be and they taught us that we were worthy of our dreams. My father focused his attention on giving us a sense of presence and pride. He taught us that we deserved to be acknowledged and not ignored. He had training sessions where we would role play how to stand and walk proudly, how to look a person in the eyes, and how to manage our timidity. These days, I smile right before I enter a board room, remembering the care he took to prepare me for that moment.

I dreamed of becoming a physician for as long as I can remember, and I still marvel at the boldness of my dreams. I envisioned myself the physician leader of a large clinic in the South Bronx that I would build to serve the community.

When it was time to start high school, I was assigned to a high school in the northern Bronx as part of the school district's effort to integrate public schools along with other Black and Brown students from the South Bronx and Harlem. By the time my senior year came around, I was in a fast pursuit of my dreams. I made it a habit to try and meet with my high school college placement counselor once a week. I was relentless in my effort to get guidance on the college application and selection process.

My parents were unfamiliar with the college admission process on the "mainland," so I was left with no alternative other than to rely on the counselor. Each week when I would ask for time to talk to her she responded in the same manner, "I don't have anything for you." I never understood what "anything" was. I was simply seeking information and direction.

One day, I entered the room after knocking on the closed door. As I opened the door, I saw a group of seven white students sitting in a circle accompanied by the counselor and a white man in a business suit. I was met with her alarming command, "Don't come in, this is a private meeting." Stopped in my steps, I turned around but then heard the man in the suit tell the counselor, "Please let her in. Remember I told you that I came here to recruit minority students."

His name was Edward Walsh, a recruiter for the State University of New York at Binghamton. He is the reason I attended the university. Even today, my stomach turns when I think that a guidance counselor would harbor so much hatred that she would deny a child an education and an opportunity to improve their life circumstance. Unfortunately, individuals like this are still influencing the lives of our children today.

University life for a minority student was not easy in the 1970s. I was immersed in an unwelcoming all-white community where I was essentially invisible. I had to learn how to navigate this highly segregated environment. Along with the thousands of white students were a couple of dozen Hispanic and Black students. The minority students studied together, supported one another, and functioned as an extended family.

I learned years later that the white faculty did not support having this small group of minority students enter the university. They argued that we were being set up to fail. We were not worth the effort. Decades later, these same minority students held a reunion. My only sorrow was that the white faculty was not there to see what we had become. I was surrounded by accomplished social workers, physicians, school superintendents, school principals, professors, and educators. One of my classmates was solely responsible for raising 20 foster children and today holds the title of "grandfather" to their children. This reunion was humbling — to be among "those who were not worth the effort" and to be in awe of what we had become.

Upon entering medical school at Hahnemann University–Philadelphia, I had to work hard to catch up and build the foundation in the sciences that was missing. I suffered insecurities, struggles with feeling I was not good enough, and worse, the "imposter syndrome." This is the fear that one day I would be "found out" that my degrees were never fully earned. This fear persisted for years. I carried this heavy burden of worries along with this crazy syndrome and all of the insecurities that I had been "programmed" to carry for years. I had to create my own anecdotes and remedies to move forward. Indeed, they too were my salvation.

Exams in medical school brought tremendous stress and fear. But I remembered the inspiring voice of my father. His encouragement was what anyone would wish to hear before going into battle. I never failed to call him before an exam. The conversation was the same almost each and every time. "Dad, I have an exam and I am scared I will fail." Then he would deliver a sermon for battle. I had heard it all my life, but each time it forged my armor and shield and prepared me for the win. The lesson here is this: Whatever is your weakness, look to your loved ones and find your strength in them.

I graduated from medical school in 1979 with honors. That did not matter. I started my residency in internal medicine at Presbyterian Medical Center in Philadelphia with the same emotional baggage that I had been programed to bear. The "found out" syndrome followed me into the ICU when I covered it during night call. It was there when I took care of patients in the emergency department, and it threatened to cripple me during the morning rounds with the chief of medicine.

During rounds one would have to present the differential diagnoses of patients admitted, along with the rationale for the treatment options chosen. I learned to manage this fear and rely on the early lessons taught by my father: Look the chief in the eye, stand proud, and deliver the facts.

I was now married. My husband, a lawyer, was always extremely supportive and helped me to further develop my courage. I learned that it was okay to be afraid, but how one manages the fear is what makes the difference. That difference is courage. I was fortunate to have a husband who championed me along the way. I have never taken the support of family for granted. Without it, I doubt I would have been able to fulfill my dreams.

Towards the end of my residency, I had become increasing alarmed by the two hospitals in which I was training. Although both hospitals had the same name, one hospital was for white patients, all admitted to the newer building and cared for by white private physicians. The second hospital was for people of color who were admitted to the old building, to be managed by a resident in training.

This was a common practice at that time, which means many physicians today had institutional racism hard wired into their training. It would be wrong to assume that separate care was equal care. This separation of the races was a significant driver of disparities in healthcare that persists today.

Outpatient care resembled the care in the hospital. White patients were predominantly seen in the private offices of the white physicians and people of color were seen in the residents' clinic. This segregation made me uncomfortable and was a source of distraction during my training. I wanted to do something about it but wasn't sure what I could do.

Toward the end of my residency it became clear to me that to make the magnitude of difference I wanted, I needed to become a skillful physician leader. I became an affiliate member of the Robert

Wood Johnson Fellowship Program at the University of Pennsylvania and studied healthcare administration.

At the same time, I convinced my chair of medicine that I would be the right person to lead the resident medical clinics. He conceded that improvements were needed and hired me as the medical director of the clinics. In my heart and mind, this was the opportunity I was hoping for. I could change the formula from separate and unequal care to separate and better care. I had taken my first step toward becoming a physician leader. I could potentially impact the lives of many not just the few patients under my direct care.

I began organizing the clinic, engaging the clinic staff, raising expectations, shortening waiting times, and improving the over-all experience of our patients. In the first year, we automated the scheduling process with one of the earliest versions of informa-tion technology. It was fulfilling work and I adored our patients. Eventually it was time for me to start my own practice.

My husband and I were now busy with our careers and raising our two daughters. We needed help. We turned to our moms, who were both in their early seventies, living alone in separate cities, and we asked them if they wanted to relocate and help us with the children. It took no convincing.

We purchased a four-unit house and offered each of them their own apartment. They both chose the largest apartment and decided to live together in it. They lived as roommates and enjoyed a great friendship for 25 years. Our extended family now included "The Moms" as they were known. We vacationed together, gathered with friends together. It was truly enviable.

In the mid-1980s, I began my own practice, which quickly blos-somed. Over the next several years, my partner and I had grown our practice to consist of three offices and a staff of 16. I chose to practice part time because I wanted the flexibility to be able to accept other leadership opportunities that I believed would come along.

That next opportunity did come along as I was asked to serve as the medical director of the Philadelphia Department of Public Health Ambulatory Care Program, which consisted of eight free-standing clinics and a medical staff of 70 physicians. These clinics were the only source of care for thousands of underserved Philadelphians.

During my tenure as a medical director, I grew professionally and learned some of the hard lessons on what it takes to lead. I learned that earning the respect and trust of those you lead is essential. I focused my attention on improving the quality of care by putting in place physician education programs and protocols, and implementing a quality assessment program.

My accomplishments did not go un-noticed and soon the health commissioner and other officials were asking me to assess the quality of healthcare in the county prisons and conduct an evaluation of the healthcare needs of a homeless community living in an underground train station. I was selected to serve on committees at the FDA and NIH.

The NIH committee worked on selecting sites of HIV care across the country for funding under the Ryan White Act. My FDA work consisted of being part of an advisory team that would participate in an expedited approval process for HIV therapies. I enjoyed my work, the dedicated clinicians, and the national impact of my committee work with the FDA and NIH. All of these opportunities came my way while I was medical director of the ambulatory program for the health department. Nine years had passed, and I knew it was time to move on to the next opportunity.

Many colleagues could not understand my decision to become medical director for Blue Cross Blue Shield. I viewed it as an opportunity to learn the "ins and outs" of risk contracting, which at the time was a form of healthcare financing that was rapidly growing in many markets. I was thirsty to learn all aspects of healthcare. I spent nearly two years there and became skillful in the strategies that were necessary to succeed in risk contracting

With that came another opportunity. The University of Pennsylvania Health System offered me the position as medical director for their managed care program. My responsibilities included helping physicians improve performance with their risk contracts. The program eventually failed for many reasons, but mainly due to the lack of information technology infrastructure necessary to support and provide timely information to guide clinical decisions.

As that door closed another opened: the opportunity to serve as chief medical officer for one of the Penn Medicine hospitals. It was the hospital where I had trained and built my practice.

Leading the patient safety and quality improvement efforts was challenging. I had to quickly learn how to convince department chairs and "the rainmakers" to standardize and improve processes and to work in teams – which was even more difficult. I had to use all my leadership skills plus more to move the organization forward.

During my time there, I received two interesting calls from the governor of Pennsylvania; the first was to ask me to serve as the state's secretary of health and the second was to chair the Pennsylvania Safety Authority. I declined the first and accepted the second.

I had become a servant leader; my confidence was strong and I was no longer afraid of being "found out." I could now walk into a room with confidence regardless of who was there or what I had to face. I now knew that I had earned my place at the table. It took me many years to successfully de-program myself and rid myself of those insecurities and that crazy syndrome.

When I was asked to join the Joint Commission as their first chief medical officer and executive vice president, I immediately saw the opportunity to influence and improve healthcare at a national level. Despite the advances in medicine and its technology, there has not been an equivalent advancement in the application of safety science and improvement science. Erroneous surgeries still occur at the same rate as they did years ago, and healthcare-acquired infections continue to kill or extend the hospitalization of thousands. I live every day with a sense of urgency to hasten the pace of improvement in healthcare.

My work has allowed me to meet and work with extraordinary leaders in healthcare. I have had the opportunity to continue to grow, learn, and teach others as well. As I see it, I may be far from the South Bronx, but I am right in the center of the dreams that little girl had in wanting to serve the community.

FUTURE LEADERS

*"A medical career should
not mean the lack of family
and friends, but rather
a path to relationships,
service, and purpose."*

– DANIELA SOSA

CHAPTER THIRTY-TWO

Life Has Taught Me to Strive for Purpose and Service

By Daniela Sosa, MD

WHAT DO YOU WANT TO BE WHEN YOU GROW up? When asked by curious adults, I gave a typical childish response: "famous pop star." Yet, I knew even as a youngster that I had to change my answer. First, I was a self-aware kid. My singing voice was not going to cut it. Second, because I wanted approval from adults asking the question, my answer had to be serious. Last, since I knew how difficult it was to be poor, my choice had to be a career that would allow me to live my life without worrying about having enough money. Thus my answer changed to "lawyer." It was serious, but it never felt right.

Fortunately, fate soon put me on the right path. My brother was enrolled in an affordable baseball summer camp. Girl were not allowed. Since my mother could not afford childcare she brought me to her office where she worked as front desk secretary for a rheumatologist. It was the boring days in the back of the office where I learned to file charts, discovered an insatiable appetite for reading, and where "lawyer" became "doctor."

The doctor-patient relationships I observed were inspiring. I discovered that I, too, wanted to help others feel less pain. As the years passed and my answer never changed, the adults' responses soon evolved from enthusiastic approval to questioning whether my choice in medicine would get in the way of raising a family.

Nonetheless, I persisted. At first, it was due to female role models who had a strong work ethic, combined with my desire to get out of poverty; then, it became a drive for purpose and service. The road was long and rocky, but I would not trade it for anything else.

First, because both my grandmother and mother were strong women who diligently worked to provide for their families, it never occurred to me that women could not do certain jobs. While still living in Cuba, my grandmother divorced my grandfather – something her family and friends did not support. As a working single mother she raised three daughters. After immigrating to America, my mother divorced my father and found herself in a new country with two small children — me and my older brother Emmanuel. Born in Cuba, I was only five when I came to America.

From the moment my mother entered the United States, she was always working — first as a waitress at a 24-hour pizzeria, then as a secretary. It was not until my brother and I were adults that she confessed how at times she skipped dinner so that there was enough food for us. I knew we were poor, but never suspected we were that poor.

My life circumstances taught me the importance of financial independence. After a few years in the United States, my mother met my stepfather. Though kind, he was a man with a troubled past that unfortunately led him to develop alcohol use disorder.

My determination to escape poverty was not simply about owning nice things or not having to live paycheck-to-paycheck, but the desire to be independent. My mother never imposed any career choices, but did teach us that education was the key to the American dream. I remember being shocked by high school classmates who decided not to go to college. To me, this was not an option and a waste of an opportunity.

I knew that getting into medical school would take hard work, and I was ready. I had seen my mother sacrifice her adult life for us and was determined to pay it back. I studied relentlessly in high school to get a full-ride college scholarship. I didn't go to parties or date until my senior year and only after acceptance letters were in my hand. I didn't experiment with other career choices or hobbies and even stopped reading for fun. My entire life was dedicated to studying, but I never thought I was missing out on anything since my small group of friends had similar life experiences. We were all raised by single moms and knew we had to do well in school to get into college.

I was accepted into great schools offering partial scholarships, but my full-ride scholarship only pertained to public Florida schools. Moreover, I would still have to take out loans and work extensively to be able to afford to move out. The smart choice was to live at home and go to Florida International University (FIU), the public university nearby.

At first I was gutted. I wanted the prestige and reward for my hard work. However, six months into my freshman year, I realized that everything happens for a reason. My stepfather was diagnosed with stage 4 terminal lung cancer. I spent spring semester going to class in the mornings before rushing to the hospital in the afternoons where I would stay with my stepfather while my mother went home to shower and rest after spending all night and morning with him. He died soon after the semester ended.

After my stepfather passed away, it was as if a light switched off. I led the typical college life with newfound freedom from a hostile environment created through living with a person with alcohol use disorder. I still wanted to be a doctor, but thought in the end, it would work out. My lack of tenacity and determination cost me two gap years and my self-confidence. I didn't apply for research positions during college because I didn't think I could do it despite doing well and being excited about my science classes. It took me a year to sign up for the MCAT. After taking it the first time I impulsively chose not to score my exam. The second time I took it I scored it but only because I didn't know how I would explain this to an admissions committee. My self-doubts left me frozen in place.

I knew that if I didn't get my act together, I would let my mom's sacrifice go to waste. I resolved to fix my predicament by reverting to the studious girl from high school. Looking for structure, I decided to join my best friend at the gym. I obsessed over becoming the healthiest version of myself. This meant an exceptional high-intensity workout routine, the "cleanest" diet, and reading up on any self-help book I could get my hands on.

I admit, I went too far at times, but I am thankful for this era of my life because it introduced me to health and wellness. It helped me adapt from a fixed to a growth mindset, provided an outlet to care for my mental health, and gave me the necessary structure to get accepted to and survive medical school.

Once in medical school (FIU), I couldn't believe I'd made it. In my mind, my acceptance was a fluke, so I had to do everything in my power to graduate. I remember my first day of class telling myself to continue working hard. After every exam and at the end of each course, the school sent out reports letting us know where we stood compared to other students. I was always surprised to learn that my score was above average. I felt it was only because I was studying so much, which fueled my "all work, no play" mentality.

I was convinced my superpower was my ability to concentrate for hours. I could study all day without a problem. I just had to keep up my routine. Four a.m. workouts, then class/clinic, followed by studying for whatever exam was looming until my 8:30 p.m. bedtime. I kept up this routine and made it a point to get at least seven hours of sleep for the majority of my time in medical school. However, there are only so many hours in the day, and this schedule left no time for family or friends.

During my fourth year, I experienced burnout that no amount of meditation cured. I had come full circle to where I had been after graduating high school and college: feeling sad and disconnected despite being at the top of my class and having high scores on my step exams. I realized I had sacrificed balance. While I was obsessing about studying, my colleagues had managed to make lifelong friends, meet their significant others, and make amazing contributions to the community. Unlike me, they were thriving.

I was lonely, and I only had myself to blame. The fear of failure, imposter syndrome, and lack of confidence has been a constant theme in my life. I had been living a life stuck on survival mode, without joy or purpose.

When the COVID-19 lockdown began, I suddenly found time for myself. As I emerged from the medical school bubble, I found that the entire world had slowed down. There was no gym or clinic to attend. I started taking afternoon walks, listening to podcasts, keeping up with current events, even reading for fun again. I think during this time I finally allowed myself a true break — not only from a hectic schedule, but also from my crippling expectations. This allowed for self-reflection and I realized I was lacking purpose and self-compassion.

During medical school I had had the privilege of meeting many wonderful compassionate female role models who are fighting for a better world. Now in lockdown, it was as if all their lessons I had been ignoring entered my psyche at once. I began to yearn to help in ways I never thought I had the power to do. I decided that, like them, I wanted to make positive contributions to society and be a part of something bigger than myself.

Through these reflections, I began to think about my values, what I truly wanted in a residency program, and sought ways to step out of my comfort zone. One way would be to become a student facilitator of a two-week elective offered at my medical school.

Aptly named Seminars for Physician Leaders, this was a transformative experience. Not only was I exposed to roles I didn't realize were available, but I learned many valuable lessons. I co-facilitated these seminars with my colleague David, in the Spring of 2021 amid political, social, and civil unrest due to a pandemic, racial injustice, gun violence, and rampant misinformation.

We were adamant that a conversation about racism and advocacy needed to happen, and since perfectionism isn't a habit one can easily drop, I expected to have a perfect conversation. It turned out to be a lot messier. At first I felt that I was a failure because I hadn't been able to control the process. However, the leader of the seminar taught us ways to approach people whose views might be different from yours. She explained that having serious conversations is more important than the fear of looking foolish. The course provided opportunities to practice key leadership skills such as effective communication, problem solving, teamwork, compassion, and empathy.

While the COVID-19 pandemic brought devastation, it actually gave me the remedy to my burnout. The space it provided allowed for less rigidity and better relationships, and has been a key in my becoming a better human. I hope to continue to achieve this during residency. I understand at times this will be difficult, but with practice, I hope to achieve this goal.

In addition, the pandemic changed my specialty plans. Before entering medical school, I had chosen pediatrics but fell in love with the complexity of adult medicine during my clerkship. I realized that as a pediatrician, I would be missing out on the adult patient-doctor relationship that had initially inspired me to become a doctor. As an adult doctor, I'd be missing the beauty of pediatrics. Ultimately, I resolved this dilemma by applying to combined medicine-pediatrics residency programs. I chose programs where I knew I would receive the best training in both fields with the addition of being around people who cherish social connection and kindness. I matched with the University of Michigan in Ann Arbor.

My hope is that as a resident I can show future and current student doctors that they don't have to feel as though the path to success is one of loneliness and self-sacrifice. A medical career should not mean the lack of family and friends, but rather a path to relationships, service, and purpose.

Now, as I look to the future, I envision a world where doctors and other medical professionals can be active leaders for their community. Today more than ever, it is important to act on our values and duty, whether through political or media advocacy or everyday actions when speaking and doing.

The COVID-19 pandemic highlighted the need to address racial disparities, mental illness, malnutrition, and climate change. I am especially passionate about establishing anti-racist, sustainable, and healthful systems for underserved communities. While I agree with Hippocrates that food is medicine, it is only one piece of the puzzle. Communities need to have access to healthful foods, but they also need safe neighborhoods to live in, good quality air to breathe and water to drink, as well as outlets for stress through nature, mental health professionals, and social connection.

I hope to be a part of this new world where confidence in the medical community is restored via the act of listening, welcoming all humans, and becoming true partners with the community to help solve these issues. I aim to help the community I serve reach its goals and through this provide others with what all the strong female mentors in my life have given me — an example of what women and immigrants can do.

CHAPTER THIRTY-THREE

Learning to Embrace Imposter Syndrome

By Janelis Gonzalez, MD

ODDLY ENOUGH, I NEVER SAW MYSELF AS A LEADER.

I was born in Hialeah, Florida, a small, predominantly Cuban city in South Florida. My parents were both Cuban immigrants and I was raised in a pretty typical middle-class household.

While growing up, my fondest memories were the times spent at the five-acre farm my grandfather owned near our home. My brother and I would visit nearly every weekend to help feed the livestock. My grandfather's understanding of the animals always fascinated me. Almost instinctively, he just knew what ailed them and how to fix it. This is where my love for medicine first began. He showed me the importance of the physical exam and the subtleties that illness can sometimes possess, as well as the rewarding sense you get from helping something recover and get stronger.

When I was 16 years old, my mother was diagnosed with breast cancer. Needless to say, it was devastating for our family, and it turned my life upside down. My mother was the embodiment of strength to me. She was the pillar of our family and managed to keep our chaos in check. Getting my brother to his baseball games on time, practicing with me for my spelling bee, listening to our childhood heartbreaks — she could do it all.

We approached her diagnosis head-on and united as a family, taking her to chemotherapy and radiation sessions and doctors' visits. I made it a point to try to go to every visit I could. At the time, I didn't understand much about the science of her treatments, so I'm not sure how useful I could have been, but it felt as if it was the only control I had of the situation.

Despite that sense of helplessness, I did notice the incredible impact every medical professional had on my mom and our family. The time anyone would take to bring extra blankets or snacks, adjust her pillow while she sat for chemotherapy, get to know her name and our family, and even sit down to explain what was happening in a way we could all understand always felt like a weight had been taken off our shoulders.

Understandably, the experiences were not always positive. There was a fair share of poor bedside manner, but this emphasized to me the importance of the medical professional's role in the way a patient (and a family) experiences illness. This was when I decided that medicine was truly my calling. I wanted not just to help people heal from illness, but also to help them on their journey *through* their illness — no matter where that journey ends.

Sadly, my mother would eventually succumb to stage IV breast cancer after a year and a half of treatment — she was 45. Not a day goes by that I don't remember my mother. It was her incredible example that continued to push me to pursue my dream of becoming a physician.

A few months after her passing, I graduated high school and decided I wanted to stay near my family for schooling to help us all heal; I couldn't bear the thought of leaving after everything we had been through. I was lucky enough to receive a full-tuition scholarship to Florida International University, a local public university in South Florida, where I would go on to complete my undergraduate studies in biology with a minor in chemistry (as do most pre-med students).

As I neared the end of my bachelor's degree, I quickly realized I didn't want to go straight into medical school. I hadn't lost my motivation, I still had my eye on the prize, but I knew how intensive medical school was and how much less time I would have outside of the classroom or hospital once I began, so I took a "gap year" to regroup.

That year, I took a job at the Pre-Health Advising Office at FIU as a secretary. I spent my time advising undergraduate students —

preparing their applications for medical and dental school, revising CVs and personal statements, and helping with mock interviews. It was a year of a lot of growth for me as well, during which I put my own application together.

Ultimately, I was drawn to stay in the community within which I was raised and was awarded a full-tuition scholarship for FIU Herbert Wertheim College of Medicine. I was quickly swept into the pace of medical school as one would expect ("drinking from a fire hydrant" and all that). But one of the most intriguing aspects of FIU HWCOM was the fact that as a very young school (founded by the Florida Board of Governors on March 23, 2006; the first graduating class was in 2013) there were lots of opportunities to create change and have a hand in our education.

I became involved as vice president of the Class of 2018. In that role, I had the opportunity to meet frequently with school administration to discuss feedback from our class for everything from exam schedule changes to curriculum innovations. FIU's connection and stronghold in the community served me well throughout my medical education. I worked with many different hospitals and physicians from all walks of life who served to create my view of the healthcare system.

It was probably around the third year of medical school, as I entered my clinical practicum, that I had my first run-in with something that would be a recurring theme in my professional life: **imposter syndrome.** It was a topic that I had heard in passing during many wellness talks in medical school. Defined loosely, it was the sense of being undeserving of your accolades to the point of feeling like a fraud. Defined more specifically, it was (and often continues to be) my biggest obstacle throughout my medical career.

I don't know exactly why I started getting these feelings when I started my practicum, but reflecting on that year, I'm sure the prospect of rotating in a cohort with other brilliant medical students in my class was a prime factor. I distinctly remember the anxiety I felt with every new rotation, the feeling of starting from the bottom of the totem pole yet again with a new attending with new expectations and inevitably being compared to my peers. I remember feeling like

I had "slipped through the cracks" of the admitting process and shouldn't be in the same tier as some of my classmates.

I wish I could say I had an inspiring reflection one day that made me forget all about my imposter syndrome, but I'm afraid the truth was more . . . practical. I would tell myself to find evidence, clear-cut objective data, of my failures, of my inability to keep up with my classmates. And often, when coming up shorthanded, I'd understand that I couldn't possibly be alone in my anxiety with each new rotation. And so, I started reaching out to other classmates I felt comfortable with and asking them about their experiences.

I think too often we're expected to keep silent about our misgivings or doubts because we have patients depending on us, but I can't think of any group with a more shared experience than medical professionals. It's key that we communicate these feelings, for the sake of ourselves and for the sake of our patients.

I ultimately graduated medical school with a newfound confidence. I can still remember my graduation day and the pride swelling within me that made me feel like I had finally accomplished my dream — I had officially achieved my MD and I had matched in internal medicine at a wonderful program, the University of Florida, another stronghold in the north Florida community. I knew this program would help me become the doctor I had always wanted to be. Shortly after graduation, I was engaged to be married to my life partner and rock and we were off to a great adventure in Gainesville, Florida.

As I approached the infamous July 1, I could feel the same sense of anxiety return – I was back at the bottom of the totem pole once again. I can remember it as if it was yesterday, showing up to the hospital at 5:30 a.m. to pre-round on patients at the VA hospital. I didn't know how the EMR worked, I didn't know how the rooms were organized. Heck, I barely knew how to evaluate a patient!

Luckily, interns who felt the same way surrounded me. I quickly found myself in great company. We were able to talk about how we felt. I still remember asking my senior resident on my first day (bless his heart) if I could order acetaminophen for a patient with a headache. I still laugh when I put in that order.

Time went on and my efficiency improved. I started to feel more comfortable in my role within the team. As I met with my advisor, Dr. Lo, throughout the year, we created a deep bond. She was my clinic preceptor as well as my confidante about my ongoing imposter syndrome anxieties. Having her as my mentor proved such a vital resource in battling these anxieties throughout residency. She made me understand that many successful individuals experience these same feelings — that it didn't have to be viewed negatively. She challenged me to channel the energy from my imposter syndrome into keeping myself constantly invested and detail-oriented with my care of patients.

At the end of my intern year, we reviewed my evaluations and feedback. I remember her asking me what I thought about becoming a senior the following year and I froze – there was that feeling again, the sense of inadequacy. I told her, half-jokingly, that I couldn't believe the program trusted me to oversee interns (self-deprecating humor is my forte). She quickly replied that she never had any doubt I could be a star senior and that I should feel the same. I would later go on to win PGY-2 of the Year, an award selected by my co-residents to recognize the second-year resident who exemplified outstanding teaching, leadership, and collegiality. That award is still one of my most humbling experiences in residency.

Near the end of my second year, our program administrators selected me to take on the position of chief resident, a 4th-year position. Having a passion for medical education, I couldn't pass up the opportunity to learn the inner workings of a great residency program like UF. And that is where I find myself today, at the beginning of my chief resident year.

Being a chief resident has certainly brought me a new perspective, one of advocacy. Having just been in the resident role, I find my voice is stronger now that I have knowledge of how the program functions in a more practical sense. This has allowed me to continue to make changes for the better.

As luck would have it, I would enter my chief resident year on the backdrop of the largest surge of COVID-19 cases since the start of the pandemic. One month into my new position, with the overwhelming surge of patients, I had to figure out how to mobilize our residents to supplemental inpatient positions. While many of our residents' willingness to volunteer their time in elective rotations for more intensive inpatient or ICU rotations has been truly awe-inspiring, the chief residents have been tasked with the challenge of ensuring that their mental wellbeing is maintained above all.

Too often, we are expected to fill unrealistic surge responsibilities by hospital administration. This can put the mental health of our residents in turmoil. The challenge lies in finding that happy medium between responsibilities that have to be met and what we can do as a program without ignoring resident morale and well-being. It's been a daunting task, but one that has shown me the inner workings of the medical education system in a new light and pushes me to continue to learn more and, by proxy, advocate more.

So where do I hope to go from here? I plan to practice as an outpatient general internist in South Florida to allow me to be closer to family again. In terms of leadership, I aspire to continue being a part of creating the next generation of physicians through medical education. And though still unsure in what capacity, I would love to work in an academic residency program where residents and medical students alike can challenge me. It is this challenge that I've found drives me in my career, and I wouldn't have it any other way.

I'd also like to pay forward all the wonderful mentors I've had throughout my career by focusing on mentorship to students and residents. It's my hope that I can help others overcome the mental blocks of their imposter syndrome and learn to embrace the driving force behind it. Finally, I aspire to show compassion in everything I do and never forget the impact I can have on patients and their families as they journey through their lives and illnesses.

CHAPTER THIRTY-FOUR

Coaching – What's in It for You?

By Margaret Cary, MD, MBA, MPH, PCC

AFTER READING ABOUT THE MANY ACCOM-
PLISHED women profiled here, some of you may
feel that you could use help with your own
careers in order to move into leadership roles
within health care. Working with a professional
coach is one way to facilitate the process.

The term "coach" was first used at Oxford
in 1830 to describe the tutors who "carried" their students through
exams. The first reference to sports coaching was in 1831. Executive
coaching has been around for several decades. As executives ascend
the corporate ladder, colleagues providing constructive criticism tend
to drop off. At the same time, those ascending the corporate ladder
often become less inclined to listen to others' observations about
their management and leadership skills.

Who do these executives have to give them honest appraisals, to
help them consider options, to ask the questions no one else asks?
That's what coaches do.

"A masterful coach is a vision builder and value shaper who
enters into the learning system of a person, business or social institution with the intent of improving it so as to impact people's ability
to perform" (Robert Hargrove in *Masterful Coaching*).

"Coaching is not telling people what to do; it's giving them a
chance to examine what they are doing in light of their intentions"
(James Flaherty in *Coaching: Evoking Excellence in Others*). The
International Coaching Federation (ICG) defines coaching as partnering with clients in a thought-provoking and creative process that
inspires them to maximize their personal and professional potential.

Imagine someone who is your curbside "consultant" for management and leadership challenges and learning. Someone who gives you their full attention when you speak, who asks you questions designed to help you figure out your own solutions. Someone who gives you unvarnished feedback, questions your motives and pushes back when beneficial to you. Someone who is always in your corner, who shares articles, books, exercises and asks, "In what other ways could you approach that?"

That's what coaches do.

Through much of my professional life, people have come to me for advice. I listened, occasionally asked for clarification, and then offered my solutions — emphasis on "my." Problem solved, on to the next.

As a physician, I was trained in differential diagnosis. Patients came in. I listened to symptoms, considered signs, performed a physical examination and listed all diagnostic possibilities that came to mind. I used deficit thinking to eliminate them one by one until I arrived at a few options. I ordered tests to eliminate some of these and investigated the handful that remained until I arrived at the diagnosis.

Leadership and management don't work like that.

A friend recommended I work with her executive coach.

"Coach? What are you talking about? I'm not in competitive sports."

"An executive coach, a trusted confidant, someone who offers a different perspective and who can help you sort possibilities"

"I don't think I need that. I have all the degrees I need and make my own decisions. I'm straightforward. I don't want to lose that."

She smiled.

My coaching journey began, from coaching client to coach (see Chapter 3 for my personal story). In the last edition, my engagements were exclusively one-on-one. Now, in addition to individual coaching, I'm focusing on team and group coaching to unlock a group's potential and amplify collective intelligence — synergy. Key to this is clear communication among all members — open dialogue, sharing concerns and fears, and working with constructive challenges.

Non-physician career managers and leaders enter management in their 20s or early 30s. Their mistakes can be excused with "She's young. She'll learn. She has a good mentor."

Physicians generally enter management roles in their 40s or 50s. Our management skills are compared with non-physician managers of the same age, but physicians haven't had two decades to make management mistakes. We've been too busy learning medicine and seeing patients. We make the same mistakes non-physicians make early in their careers. We're developmentally delayed. What we've been taught in medical school and residency is 180 degrees from many of the skills needed to be an effective manager.

For example, as practicing physicians, we tend to be risk averse. Making a mistake as a clinician could cause someone to get sicker or even die. Our role as healers depends upon our being The Expert. On the other hand, taking risks is inherent in management and leadership.

Likewise, listening to alternate views is a critical leadership skill. Unfortunately, many physicians become so vested in their careers, in diagnosing illness and being healers that they find it difficult to listen to alternate views. As I was, many of my physician clients are proud of the fact that they are straightforward, pull no punches, and ask directly for what they want. Managers and leaders need to be collaborative communicators.

Some of those strengths we have as solo clinicians can keep us from developing other skills we need as managers and leaders. As an executive and leadership coach for physicians, I hold a mirror in front of them and ask questions to guide them in developing their own solutions.

My clients often ask for specific skills, how to manage their time, how to work with their bosses, how to manage conflict. As physicians, the most common challenge we have is learning to control our limbic systems, in order to avoid our automatic, unthinking responses.

Chris Argyris, professor emeritus at Harvard Business School, wrote "the smartest **people** find it the **hardest to** learn."

Medicine is filled with brilliant people.

You can lead from anywhere. You don't have to be at the top of the organization chart. You can also lead from below by working with your boss as a team. Authority is about titles and organization chart positions. Leadership is about integrity, being competent in your field, and being comfortable in your skin. You choose the perspective through which you view the world.

One of the issues that may discourage physicians from considering coaching is time and access. Coaching can be done in person, through Zoom and over the telephone. With our erratic schedules as physicians, we often find it easier to use Zoom and the telephone, supplemented by in-person sessions if appropriate.

Unlike medicine, coaching as a profession isn't as regulated – yet. The International Coach Federation requires coach-specific training to become credentialed and continuing education for credential renewals. We're still in the early days of standardization and establishing requirements for coaches, sort of pre-Flexner Report status. So, what should you look for when you select a coach?

1. **Coach-specific training from a respected, reputable organization or from an organization that has been accredited by a reputable organization, such as the International Coach Federation (ICF).**

   When I decided to learn to be a coach, I wanted a program associated with an accredited university. At the time, Georgetown was the only program that showed up in my searching. I also wanted an in-person program with interaction, rather than an online program.

   Coaching is not therapy, mentoring, or consulting. If you think of therapy as archaeology, mentoring as advice and connections, consulting as others' solutions, then coaching is architecture. To follow that analogy, like an architect, a good coach works with you to help you construct your personal future, guiding you in reflecting on how you approach challenges.

   Just as when choosing a physician, you need to find the right fit. It's your engagement and it's your future. It is tempting to ask for advice and solutions. You won't own your decisions if you don't figure them out for yourself.

2. **Your credentialed coach should have had mentored, supervised coaching by a credentialed coach, as well as at least 100 hours of coaching experience.**

Atul Gawande wrote in his 2011 *New Yorker* article about the importance of engaging a coach in his own career. His coach was a retired surgeon with more experience than Gawande, someone able to observe his surgical skills and offer suggestions for improvement.

In learning to be physicians, we start by learning how to interview patients. In the beginning it's overwhelming to probe for answers to sensitive questions, to insert ourselves into our patients' lives, even as we realize it's a privilege. Our learning curves are steep. Like learning to ride a bicycle, eventually talking with patients becomes second nature. I'm an emergency and family medicine physician. If I took a long weekend course in neurosurgery would you let me cut your head open?

3. **Your coach should use techniques with evidence for their effectiveness.**

Yes, evidence-based methods apply here. A good coach will keep current with management and coaching literature and will modify what s/he does, just as with medical practice.

Finally, how will you know if the coaching has "worked" for you? The best way is to get feedback from others before your coaching session and after. The process takes months, much as learning any new skill. Your answer is always the same after asking for feedback: "Thank you." No blaming, no defensiveness, no excuses and no explaining. Just "Thank you."

Management 101 is hard. Leadership 101 is harder. Coaching continues to move me toward more authenticity and vulnerability, as client and as coach. The coaching approach works for managers, leaders, and parents. We physicians are eager, lifelong eager learners. Those of us who wish to become managers and leaders can learn the necessary knowledge base and skill set, just as we learned anatomy and genetics, how to interview patients and take blood pressures.

Sometimes we just need a little help, someone we trust who asks the right questions to help us find our way. That's what coaches do.

You can read some of Dr. Cary's coaching essays at https://libraryofprofessionalcoaching.com. You can view a five-minute video of her presentation on executive coaching at the 2012 annual meeting of the American College of Physician Executives (now American Association for Physician Leadership) at http://youtu.be/653anCaWwNk. Contact her at drcary@thecarygroupglobal.com.

In 2021 she was named one of 20 top coaches in Washington, DC (influencedigest.com) https://bit.ly/3oVXopQ

CHAPTER THIRTY-FIVE

Final Words

By Deborah M. Shlian, MD, MBA

ALTHOUGH WE HAVE USED THE TERM *manager* and *leader* interchangeably here, technically there are differences. According to John P. Kotter in his classic *Harvard Business Review* article, "What Leaders Really Do," "leadership and management are two distinctive and complementary systems of action. Each has its own function and characteristic activities. Managers optimize the organization and its people to meet strategic goals while leaders drag the organization and its people kicking and screaming into a strategic future." The real challenge, he says, is to combine strong leadership and strong management and use each to balance the other.

This book profiles women physicians who are both managers and leaders. They understand how to use processes and procedures to manage the complexity of large organizations and how to exercise leadership to motivate and lead others through change and uncertainty.

The questions so often asked by women physicians aspiring to management is, "How can I enter the field" and "How can I move up the ladder?" The fact that doors to leadership in organized medicine have swung open is only half the battle. Women have to be willing to walk through those doors.

The women profiled here are intentionally a diverse group. A couple are nearer to the beginning of their management careers, others are midway, several have reached senior level positions, and a few are close to or have already retired. Some are married, some are not, some have children, and some have none. Some are surgeons by training, others are primary care doctors. While each of the women physicians presented in the preceding pages is unique, working as physician managers in virtually every type of healthcare organization in the US, their stories share some common themes. I've put together several helpful tips from their experiences.

Be a clinician first.

Physician leaders should never forget the patient. With one exception, each of the women profiled in these pages began their careers as practicing clinicians and although most have given up their day-to-day management of individual patients as they transitioned into more senior leadership positions, it was their work as a physician first that gave them the unique perspective required to be an excellent healthcare executive.

Know yourself.

Before considering a transition from clinical medicine to management, do a thorough self-assessment. Are you running from something or purposefully going somewhere? Are you just looking for "greener pastures" or do you have a realistic picture of what is ahead? Clarify who you are and who you want to become as a person and as a leader. Examine your values and goals. Determine your strengths and weaknesses as well as what brings you the most satisfaction. Making career choices is highly individual.

Be a lifelong learner.

President John F. Kennedy once said, "Leadership and Learning are indispensable to each other," suggesting that an effective leader should always be open to new information and perspectives. This is particularly true for the healthcare system, which is constantly changing.

Look for ways to polish your skills and use those skills as building blocks to move ahead. The physician manager today must have an understanding of the details of the business of healthcare, including finance, accounting, strategic planning, information systems, organizational behavior, human resources, and relevant legal issues. Although there is an increasing trend toward formal education, one way or another, if you aspire to management, you will need these skills.

And even if you have a formal degree, what really counts is experience. A leader needs to establish a track record of tangible experiences and accomplishments. The ability to "talk the talk" without an objective measurable track record won't last long, especially in this present rapidly changing healthcare environment. So take every opportunity to obtain practical experience within the organization. Become a leader within your sphere of influence. The medical world is full of committees, task forces, etc. that can offer exposure to administration, working with people and systems and problem solving. The Related Reading Section that follows contains recommendations by the contributors to this book.

Know your organization.

To borrow a medical analogy, organizations, like organisms, are organic and have specific structures and functions. The structure of a medical organization would cover such issues as the type of legal entity, the mode of governance, financing, etc. On the other hand, the overall way a specific organization functions is affected by what is often called its "cultural climate." For example: How do professional and nonprofessional staff interact? What is the extent of bureaucracy and hierarchy? how much operational responsibility is given to physician managers? Understanding these aspects of your organization is critical to moving ahead.

Network.

Get to know people both inside and outside your organization whom you can tap for information and support. Young people involved in team activities tend to develop this critical skill earlier than those focused on more individual, competitive endeavors. If you are not already a member, consider joining the American Association for Physician Leadership. Founded in 1975 as the American College of Physician Executives (ACPE), the nonprofit association has educated thousands of physicians worldwide and has members in 46 countries at varying stages of their careers.

AAPL's stated mission is to help ensure that physicians continually grow as individuals and become successful health care leaders. Hopefully as more women seek leadership roles, they will see the Association as a great resource for attaining their goals.

Take the initiative.

Don't expect handouts. In the corporate world, upper management promotes people who find and seize opportunities. Actively seek projects to take on. If you see something that needs changing, develop a plan and present it to senior management. Whenever possible, take on projects that give you visibility within the organization.

Be a risk taker.

Be willing to grab opportunities where and when you find them. The most reward comes from a big challenge, so if you want to move ahead in management, you need to learn to take and manage risks. That means understanding that failure goes hand in hand with success. Expect some failures and learn from them.

Whenever you read profiles of people who have had high-level management positions in and out of medicine, you find that they generally got where they are by taking on new assignments. For women, having supportive spouses and families is critical. Creativity helps, too. For example, if you want to participate on a committee and accommodate family needs, suggest doing some of the work through conference calls (including video) and e-mail.

Reassess goals as you go.

Goals developed when you first begin your medical career will likely need adjustment as your personal life circumstances as well as the business/healthcare environment changes. Some people suggest reassessing goals at least every five years. The time increment is less important than having the discipline to do it. Everyone agreed that the higher they moved in their organizations, the broader their vision had to become and the longer view into the future they needed to take. That vision for the organization should inspire, they say. It should impart to all employees the belief that they can do great things.

Learn to negotiate.

If you're not convinced of the importance of honing negotiating skills, consider that you negotiate every day, whether you're resolving conflicts between you and your spouse or children, working out vacation schedules with other physicians or staff, or discussing treatment plans with patients and their families. In terms of moving up the management ladder, men historically have been better at asking for things they need in order to be more productive to get ahead. Refining your negotiating skills and learning to achieve win-win solutions will maximize your leverage as a manager.

Select the right subordinates.

If you're in middle management, the personnel you select will determine how well suited you are for a senior position, because senior managers are generally judged not by how well they do, but rather by how well their staffs do. Senior managers must have a clear vision of the future of their organization. They need to be leaders for change.

Find a mentor and/or role model.

Virtually all the women in the book benefited from mentors. This is not always easy, but it can make all the difference in becoming a successful manager. Find someone you'd like to emulate and ask directly for his or her help. More often than not, that individual will be delighted to share their wisdom. They may be other executives (physicians or not), friends, a coach, family members, each helping in a different way. But the most impactful mentors are the ones who will tell you what you don't want to hear. As you move up in management roles, become a mentor yourself (that means building relationships at every level).

Take time for yourself. Learn to set boundaries.

At a personal level, while many admitted they didn't always do this, all the women recommended carving out time to enjoy family, vacations, and long-lasting friendships. Taking care of yourself physically helps to reenergize and stay healthy. Realistically assessing time needs for various business and personal tasks is critical they said, since they learned that their entire to-do lists will probably never be completed and that's ok. Knowing when to say no, and avoiding personal and work related over-commitment helps.

Summing up

It has been 26 years since the publication of the original monograph *Women in Medical Management: A Mentoring Guide* and women physicians are still under-represented in leadership roles across the healthcare system. So how can we reduce the institutional barriers and promote more female physician leaders in healthcare?

First,we need to showcase our successes as I have done in this latest update: *Lessons Learned: Stories from Women Physician Leaders.* Let our daughters see what women can achieve. Show how we "lean in."

Second, we need to support reversals of traditional domestic roles by encouraging our workplaces to offer paid parental leave for fathers as well as mothers.

Kathleen McCartney, president of Smith College and former dean of Harvard Graduate School of Education, wrote: "I have spent much of my 31-year career as a scholar arguing for family-friendly policies like quality child care, parental leave, and flexible work hours. But if we view these policy changes as supporting maternal —- rather than parental — employment, then roadblocks for women will remain. We understand sexism when it's explicit — unequal pay for equal work -- but we haven't acknowledged gendered cultural biases surrounding parenthood. Our implicit biases limit the aspirations of men and women alike. The solution lies in recognizing the problem. Only then will we change our culture."

Third, we need to eliminate those double standards that penalize women for traits and behaviors rewarded in men such as assertiveness, daring, risk taking, and bravery. If you paid any attention to the 2016 presidential election, you saw that the same media that allowed male candidates the privilege of what I call "political passion" often labeled women candidates with similar characteristics "strident and shrill."

These last two (reversing traditional domestic roles and eliminating double standards) require a paradigm shift that I call a PUSH BACK: a new way of thinking about work and leadership.

That paradigm shift is not seeing women as the problem, but the solution. That shift is in acknowledging that the playing field is still not level. We need to work a lot harder to ensure that the efforts of talented women are fully recognized, valued and rewarded. As Kathleen McCartney wrote in a 2016 *New York Times* op ed "For Women, Glass Ceilings, and Glass Walls, Too," "It's time to take a sledgehammer to the glass walls. The best way to stop coercion is to make the invisible visible by sharing our stories. When we can better name what's happening, we can begin to change the narrative."

So yes we need to **lean in** and we also need to **push back**.

With the increasing complexity of today's ever-evolving US healthcare system, there is no doubt that real leaders are needed to manage the changes required to improve the delivery of care. I am among those who believe that physician executives articulate in the language of health care policy and business are in a unique position to lead the needed reforms.

Women now make up more than half of medical school classes and have moved into clinical areas traditionally off limits to women. The challenge for the future is for talented women physicians to also move into top management roles. While barriers remain, they can be overcome more easily than in the past — especially if we walk through those doors together.

CHAPTER THIRTY-SIX

Related Reading

Babcock, Linda and Laschever, Sara. *Ask for It: How Women Can use the Power of Negotiation to Get What They Really Want.* New York: Bantam; 2009.

Babcock, Linda and Laschever, Sara. *Women Don't Ask: The High Cost of Avoiding Negotiation — and Positive Strategies for Change.* New York: Bantam; 2007.

Barsh, Joanna and Cranston, Susie; and Lewis, Geoffrey. *How Remarkable Women Lead: The Breakthrough Model for Work and Life.* New York: Crown Business; 2009.

Collins, Jim and Hansen, Morten. *Great by Choice: Uncertainty, Chaos and Luck — Why Some Thrive Despite Them All.* Boston: Harvard Business Review Press; 2011.

De Pree, Max. *Leadership Is an Art.* New York: Currency; 2004.

Drucker, Peter. *The Effective Executive: The Definitive Guide to Getting the Right Things Done.* New York: Harper Business: 2006.

Duckworth, Angela. *Grit: The Power of Passion and Perseverance.* New York: Scribner; 2016.

Evans, Gail. *Play Like a Man, Win Like a Woman: What Men Know About Success that Women Need to Learn.* New York: Crown Business; 2001.

Evans, Gail. *She Wins, You Win: The Most Important Rule Every Businesswoman Needs to Know.* New York: Gotham Books; 2003.

Frankel, Lois. *Nice Girls Don't Get the Corner Office: Unconscious Mistakes Women Make That Sabotage Their Careers.* New York: Business Plus; 2014.

Gabow, Patricia A. *TIME'S NOW for Women Healthcare Leaders: A Guide for the Journey.* New York: Productivity Press/Routledge; 2020.

Godin, Seth. *Tribes: We Need You to Lead Us.* New York: Portfolio; 2008.

Goleman, Daniel and Boyatzis, Richard. *Primal Leadership: Learning to Lead with Emotional Intelligence*. Boston: Harvard Business Review Press; 2004.

Grenny, Joseph; Patterson, Kerry; Maxfield, David; et al. *Influencer: The New Science of Leading Change*. New York: McGraw-Hill Education; 2013.

Heifetz, Ronald A; Linsky, Marty; and Grashow, Alexander. *The Practice of Adaptive Leadership: Tools and Tactics for Changing Your Organization and the World*. Boston: Harvard Business Review Press; 2009.

Heim, Pat; Hughes, Tammy; and Golant, Susan. *Hardball for Women: Winning at the Game of Business*. New York: Penguin Publishing Group; 2015.

Helgesen, Sally and Goldsmith, Marshall. *How Women Rise: Break the 12 Habits Holding You Back from Your Next Raise, Promotion, or Job*. Paris:Hachette Books; 2018.

Hunter, James. *The Servant: A Simple Story About the True Essence of Leadership*. New York: Crown Business; 2012.

Jahnke, Christine. *The Well-Spoken Woman: Your Guide to Looking and Sounding Your Best*. New York: Prometheus Books; 2011.

Joiner, Bill, and Josephs, Stephen. *Leadership Agility: Five Levels of Mastery for Anticipating and Initiating Change*. San Francisco: Jossey-Bass; 2006.

Linceoni, Patrick. *Five Dysfunctions of a Team: A Leadership Fable*. San Francisco: Jossey-Bass; 2002.

Lombardo, Michael and Eichinger, Robert. *Eighty-Eight Assignments for Development in Place*. Greensboro, NC: Center for Creative Leadership Press; 1989.

Luntz, Frank. *Win: The Key Principles to Take Your Business from Ordinary to Extraordinary*. New York: Hyperion; 2011.

Marquardt, Michael. *Leading with Questions: How Leaders Find the Right Solutions by Knowing What to Ask*. San Francisco: Jossey-Bass; 2005.

Maxwell, John. *The 21 Indispensable Qualities of a Leader: Becoming the Person Others Will Want to Follow*. New York: Thomas Nelson Publishing; 2012.

Olson, Randy. *Don't Be SUCH a Scientist: Talking Substance in an Age of Style*. Washington, DC: Island Press; 2009.

Patterson, Kerry; Grenny, Joseph; McMillan, Ron; and Switzler, Al *Crucial Conversations: Tools For Talking When Stakes Are High*, Second Edition. New York: McGraw-Hill Education; 2011.

Pfeffer, Jeffrey. *7 Rules of Power: Surprising — But True — Advice on How to Get Things Done and Advance Your Career*. Dallas, TX: Matt Holt; 2022.

Pfeffer, Jeffrey. *Leadership BS: Fixing Workplaces and Careers one Truth at a Time*. New York: Harper Business; 2015.

Pfeffer, Jeffrey. *Power: Why Some People Have it and Others Don't*. New York: Harper Business; 2010.

Scott, Kim. *Radical Candor: How to be a Kick-Ass Boss Without Losing Your Humanity*. New York: St, Martin's Press; 2019.

Scott, Susan. *Fierce Conversations: Achieving Success in Work and in Life, One Conversation at a Time*. London: Platkus Books; 2011.

Sipe, James and Frick, Don. *Seven Pillars of Servant Leadership: Practicing the Wisdom of Leading by Serving*. Mahwah, NJ: Paulist Press; 2009.

Terrell, Grace E. and Bobbitt, Julian, Jr. *Value-Based Healthcare and Payment Models: Including Frontline Strategies for 20 Clinical Subspecialties*. Tampa, FL: AAPL Publications; 2019.

Terrell, Grace, and Bohn, J.M. *MD 2.0: Physician Leadership for the Information Age*. Tampa, FL: ACPE Publications; 2012.

CONTRIBUTORS

Elaine Batchlor, MD, MPH
Chief Executive Officer of MLK Community Healthcare and MLK
Community Hospital

Selma Harrison Calmes, MD
Retired Clinical Professor of Anesthesiology, UCLA School of Medicine,
Los Angeles, CA

Margaret Cary, MD, MBA, MPH, PCC
Founder and CEO, The Cary Group Global

Eliza Lo Chin, MD, MPH, MACP, FAMWA
Executive Director, American Medical Women's Association

Laura Esserman, MD, MBA
Director, UCSF Breast Care Center

Patricia A. Gabow, MD, MACP
Professor Emerita, University of Colorado School of Medicine

Elizabeth I. O. Garner, MD, MPH
Women's Health Physician and C-suite Pharmaceutical Executive

Janelis Gonzalez, MD
Chief Resident, University of Florida, College of Medicine,
Department of Medicine

Kathleen Goonan, MD
Partner, Guidehouse

Deborah E. Hammond, MD
Executive Medical Director, Healthfirst, New York, New York

Mona Hanna-Attisha, MD MPH FAAP (she/her)
C.S. Mott Endowed Professor of Public Health, Associate Professor,
Department of Pediatrics and Human Development
Michigan State University College of Human Medicine

Florence Haseltine, PhD, MD
Presidential Distinguished Professor,
Medical Director – North Texas Genome Center, University of Texas,
Arlington

Eugenie Komives, MD, FAAFP
Chief Medical Officer

Barbara LeTourneau, MD, MBA, FACEP
Physician Executive and Healthcare Consultant — retired

Kathy E. Magliato, MD, MBA, FACS
Cardiothoracic Surgeon, St. John's Health Center, Santa Monica, CA
Founder, CEO, CMO Cordex Systems, Inc.

Jayne McCormick, MD, MBA
Chief Medical Officer, Presbyterian Healthcare Services — retired

Ana Pujols McKee, MD
Equity and Inclusion Officer, The Joint Commission
Executive Vice President and Chief Medical Officer, Chief Diversity

Kathleen Maletic Neuzil, MD, MPH
Myron M. Levine MD, DTPH Professor in Vaccinology
Professor, Medicine and Pediatrics
Director, Center for Vaccine Development and Global Health,
  University of Maryland School of Medicine

Asha Padmanabhan, MD, FASA
Medical Director, Anesthesia, Bethesda West Hospital
Owner, Leadership Rx Coaching

Donna L. Parker, MD
Professor of Medicine
Senior Associate Dean for Undergraduate Medical Education,
  University of Maryland School of Medicine

Ora Hirsch Pescovitz, MD
President, Oakland University

Christine A. Petersen, MD, MBA
Principal, The Petersen Group — retired

Theresa Rohr-Kirchgraber, MD, FACP, FAMWA
President 2022-2023, American Medical Women's Association
Professor of Medicine, AU/UGA Medical Partnership

Eneida O. Roldan, MD, MPH, MBA
Chief Executive Officer, FIU Health Care Network
Associate Dean, International Affairs

Kelly Z. Sennholz, MD
CEO, RealSenn

Deborah M. Shlian, MD, MBA
CEO, Shlian & Associates, Inc. (executive/physician search and medical
  management consulting)
Author of fiction (shlianbooks.com) and nonfiction

Daniela Sosa, MD
University of Michigan School of Medicine combined Internal Medicine/
  Pediatrics Resident

Susan Ford Stark, MD, MBA, CPE
Chief Medical Officer and Medical Director, various organizations
  — retired

Ellen Strahlman, MD, MHSc
Partner, The Reillen Group, LLC

Grace E. Terrell, MD, MMM, CPE, FACP, FACPE
Executive in Residence, Duke Master of Management in Clinical
  Informatics Program
Practicing Physician in Atrium Health
Senior Advisor for IKS Health and Oliver Wyman

Traci Thompson, MD, MBA, CPE
CEO, Dr. Traci's House Inc.
Regional Vice President, Humana Healthy Horizons Florida

Kathleen L. Yaremchuk, MD, MSA
Chair, Department of Otolaryngology
Head & Neck Surgery
Professor, Wayne State University School of Medicine
Henry Ford Hospital

Josephine Young, MD, MPH, MBA, FAAP
Medical Director, Commercial Markets, Premera Blue Cross

CPSIA information can be obtained
at www.ICGtesting.com
Printed in the USA
BVHW060532190222
629513BV00004B/5

9 780996 663250